FAITH EXAMINED

Faith Examined

New Arguments for Persistent Questions

Essays in Honor of Dr. Frank Turek

EDITED BY
CLARK R. BATES

FOREWORD BY
Sean McDowell

INTRODUCTION BY
Jorge Gil Calderon & Clark R. Bates

WIPF & STOCK · Eugene, Oregon

FAITH EXAMINED
New Arguments for Persistent Questions, Essays in Honor of Dr. Frank Turek

Wipf & Stock
An Imprint of Wipf and Stock Publishers
199 W. 8th Ave., Suite 3
Eugene, OR 97401

www.wipfandstock.com

PAPERBACK ISBN: 978-1-6667-4929-8
HARDCOVER ISBN: 978-1-6667-4930-4
EBOOK ISBN: 978-1-6667-4931-1

To Frank—a mentor to more people than he could possibly know

Contents

Foreword

Sean McDowell

More than two decades ago I distinctly remember seeing Frank speak for the first time. Immediately, I realized several things about him that are obvious to the thousands of people who have heard him speak since. First, Frank is smart. If you have ever heard him lecture, read his books, or seen him debate, it cannot be denied that he is a first-rate intellectual. Second, Frank is funny. This might not seem that important in a field like apologetics that deals with evidence and reason, but knowledge of these issues is effective only if it can be relatable to an audience, and a sense of humor goes a long way toward achieving this end. Needless to say, Frank has an excellent sense of humor. I have seen him engage audiences comprised of both Christians and skeptics, making them all laugh through his wit and charm. If you spend any time with Frank at all, it becomes clear that he has very strong convictions and takes his stand firmly on those beliefs, but also that he does not take himself too seriously. Third, he is fearless. In 2 Tim 1:7 Paul encourages his disciple Timothy, writing that God did not give us a spirit of fear, and Frank demonstrates the ethos of this sentiment in the topics that he engages with publicly, the leading skeptics he engages in debate, and his willingness to regularly hold live question and answer sessions with his audiences on college campuses.

As I have gotten to know Frank over the years, both in ministry and off stage, my respect for him and his ministry has only grown. His relationship with his wife and children is an inspiration to me. Even recently he wrote a book analyzing the cultural fascination with superheroes and its relationship to the Christian faith with his son Zach. Because Frank hails from New Jersey and never minces words about what he believes, it can be easy for some to miss that he has a big heart and caring spirit. As my friendship with Frank has grown, this, more than anything else, has become increasingly clear to me. A natural extension of his care for others, and a commendable trait of his, is Frank's team spirit. Frank is, at his core, a kingdom-minded Christian who is not in apologetics ministry for himself, or to defend his "brand." On numerous occasions, I have witnessed Frank act as a cheerleader for other apologists and elevate their voices, including my own, even at the expense of his own platform. This book serves as a testimony to that fact, because each of the contributors has been encouraged and equipped and, in a sense, "cheerleaded" by Frank.

There is one final thing about Frank that needs to be said: *he has been faithful in both his character and message.* It has become all too easy to take a public figure's personal life testimony for granted, but with the increasing number of stories about ministers who have abused their power and platform, we cannot afford to do so any longer. Frank's personal life serves as an undeniable apologetic for his Christian faith, and in a world where we are also seeing more and more public voices compromise on fundamental Christian teachings, Frank's steadfastness in doctrine and biblical fidelity are a model for all of us in an age of compromise. On behalf of the contributors of this volume, I want to thank Frank for being faithful in both his life and his ministry for decades.

You will find the contributors to this book to be exceptional in their message and faith, all of which have benefited directly from Frank and his ministry. Each chapter serves as their way of honoring him, and this is seen in the topics presented, most of which are issues Frank himself engages with regularly. These topics include the existence of God and the historical Jesus, but also some fresh issues that have become specialties of individual contributors. Regardless of whether the material is something you have read or heard before, I have no doubt that the content will encourage you, challenge you, and enrich your faith.

I would like to end this foreword with a note to Frank, which expresses the heart of those who have participated in this volume and many more. *Frank, this book is for you, my friend. Thank you for boldly speaking the truth. Thank you for being a selfless cheerleader for others and for being a team player. We love you, brother, and are grateful for you and your ministry. We hope you see these essays as one way in which we want to honor you and your work for the kingdom.*

Take a moment and enjoy.

List of Contributors

Clark R. Bates is professor of New Testament at Forge Theological Seminary and a PhD candidate with the University of Birmingham, UK, researching the earliest known commentaries on the book of Ephesians. He was the first fellow of the Text and Canon Institute at Phoenix Seminary, working alongside Old and New Testament scholars Drs. John Meade and Peter Gurry to research the textual transmission of the New Testament and the historical development of the biblical canon. He holds graduate degrees in pastoral ministry from Liberty University and theology from Phoenix Seminary, as well as a certificate in Greek paleography from Lincoln College at Oxford University. Clark has been published in scholarly journals such as *The Byzantine Review*, *The Expository Times*, and *Diogenes*, and is the coeditor of the book *That Nothing May Be Lost: The New Testament Text and Its Transmission as Observed in Fragments*. Prior to his PhD studies, Clark wrote an apologetics blog for several years, the backlog of which is viewable at http://exejesushermeneutics.blogspot.com/.

Jorge Gil Calderon is an international speaker frequently traveling to Latin America and the Caribbean to present the case for Christianity. He also conducts apologetics and social media training in the United States and abroad to equip the body of Christ to defend their faith and effectively communicate their message through technology. Jorge holds certificates in biblical and theological studies as well as systematic theology from Western Seminary and has been trained in apologetics ministry by Ravi Zacharias International Ministries and CrossExamined. He specializes in philosophy and religious studies with a concentration in apologetics with Southern Evangelical Seminary and is one of the founders of the *Sociedad de Apologistas Latinos* while also serving as an adjunct professor at BANAH de Cristo School of Theology.

Eric Chabot is the director of Ratio Christi, a national apologetics ministry at The Ohio State and Columbus State Community College. He holds an MA from Southern Evangelical Seminary and is the CJF Ministries Midwest representative in Columbus, Ohio, where he lives with his wife Lucy and two children, Elise and Jack. Eric has spoken and taught at multiple churches and conferences including the SES National Apologetics Conference. He is author of *The Resurrection of the Jewish Messiah*, coauthor of *Does God Exist: Why It Matters*, and *Is Jesus the Jewish Messiah?* He blogs at ThinkApologetics.com.

Alisa Childers is a wife, mom, author, blogger, podcaster, speaker, and worship leader. She was a member of the award-winning CCM recording group ZOEgirl and is a popular speaker at apologetics and Christian worldview conferences, including Stand to Reason's Reality Conference and Summit Ministries. She has been published at *The Gospel Coalition*, *Crosswalk*, *The Stream*, *For Every Mom*, *Decision Magazine*, and *The Christian Post*. She is the author of two books with Tyndale House Publishers, *Another Gospel: A Lifelong Christian Seeks Truth in Response to Progressive Christianity* and *Live Your Truth (and Other Lies): Exposing Popular Deceptions That Make Us Anxious, Exhausted, and Self-Obsessed* and regularly hosts the Alisa Childers Podcast. Most recently, she has been speaking alongside Natasha Crain and Dr. Frank Turek on the Unshaken Faith tour. You can connect with Alisa online at www.alisachilders.com.

Natasha Crain is a speaker, blogger, podcaster, and author of four books who equips Christians to think more clearly about holding to a biblical worldview in an increasingly challenging secular world. Her latest book is *Faithfully Different: Regaining Biblical Clarity in a Secular Culture*. She is also the author of three apologetics books for parents: *Keeping Your Kids on God's Side*, *Talking with Your Kids about God*, and *Talking with Your Kids about Jesus*. Natasha is a frequent guest on radio and TV shows across the US and Canada. She has an MBA from UCLA and a certificate in Christian apologetics from Biola University. A former marketing executive and adjunct professor, Natasha lives in Southern California with her husband and three children and is currently appearing alongside Alisa Childers and Dr. Frank Turek in the Unshaken Faith tour. She writes at www.natashacrain.com.

Melissa Dougherty is best known for her creative videos in which she discusses theology, apologetics, and culture. Being a former New Age practitioner herself, a primary focus of her ministry is refuting these practices that have misled many in the church and pointing them back to Christ. Melissa has engaged in counter-cult ministry to Mormons and Jehovah's Witnesses for more than a decade and currently holds degrees in religious studies, liberal arts, and early childhood multicultural education. She is currently working on an MA in Christian apologetics from Southern Evangelical Seminary and is a member of the CrossExamined apologetics team, posting regular content on their website. Her work can be seen at https://www.melissadougherty.co/.

Phil Fernandes is the senior pastor of Trinity Bible Fellowship and the president of the Institute of Biblical Defense. He has a PhD in philosophy of religion from Greenwich University and a DMin in apologetics from Veritas International Seminary. Phil has also earned an MA in religion at Liberty University and a BTh from Columbia Evangelical Seminary and teaches philosophy, apologetics, and world religions at Veritas International University, Northwest University, Shepherds Bible College, and Crosspoint High School. He has publicly debated atheists and other non-Christian thinkers at schools throughout America such as Princeton, Washington State University, the State University of New York, and the University of North Carolina–Chapel Hill. He is the author of books like *No Other Gods* and *The Atheist Delusion*, in addition to coauthoring works on the Christian worldview and historical Jesus studies. Phil is currently the president of the International Society of Christian Apologetics. His work can be found at www.philfernandes.org.

Eric Hernandez is an evangelist and apologist with a heart for proclaiming the gospel and defending his faith on theological and philosophical grounds. He is a licensed minister, certified formation therapist, and the apologetics lead for the Baptist General Convention of Texas. He has spoken and debated on university and college campuses defending the Christian faith against atheist, agnostic, and deistic professors of different worldviews. He holds undergraduate degrees in social science and theology and a certificate in apologetics from Biola University, and is currently enrolled at Dallas Baptist University. He is the founder of Eric Hernandez Ministries, which encompasses speaking engagements, apologetics seminars, training courses, and debates and serves as a contributor to Soteriology 101, the ministry of Dr. Leighton Flowers. His work can be seen at www.youtube.com/EricHernandez.

Alex McElroy is an international speaker, author of *Blueprint for Bible Basics*, and host of the YouTube page Relentless Pursuit of Purpose. He is a founding pastor at Engage Community Church in Chicago and has served in youth and teaching ministries for more than fifteen years, teaching discipleship courses designed for Christians to learn, fellowship, and grow in their faith. Alex has also trained hundreds of teachers and ministers to be well equipped to deliver lessons in proper lifestyle, biblical study, focused preparation, and apologetics in order to maximize their effectiveness in and for the kingdom of God. He is the founder of Proof for the Truth, which provides apologetics workshops as well as an annual apologetics conference in Chicago. Alex has studied apologetics at the CrossExamined Instructor Academy and RZIM. He also holds a master's degree in Christian apologetics from Liberty University. His work can be seen at https://www.proofforthetruth.org/.

William Soo Hoo is an executive director in the biotechnology industry developing immunotherapies for cancer and other debilitating diseases. He has published in peer-reviewed journals on topics such as cancer, infectious diseases, and diagnostic assay development. William received his bachelor's degree in biochemistry and cell biology at the University of California, San Diego, and a PhD studying molecular immunology from the University of Illinois, Urbana. In 2016, William completed his master's degree in Christian apologetics from Biola University and teaches youth and adults in his church on scientific and general apologetic topics and has been an invited speaker at multiple churches and organizations.

Timothy A. Stratton holds a graduate degree in Christian apologetics from Biola University and a PhD in theology from North-West University in Potchefstroom, South Africa. He is a professor at Trinity College of the Bible and Theological Seminary and the author of *Human Freedom, Divine Knowledge, and Mere Molinism: A Biblical, Historical, Theological, and Philosophical Analysis*. Dr. Stratton is also a contributor of written articles and videos to CrossExamined and their affiliated YouTube channel, in addition to producing media content and podcasting through his own ministry. His apologetic specialty is metaphysics, epistemology, and the theological philosophy known as Molinism. More of his work can be seen at http://freethinkingministries.com/.

Introduction

By Jorge Gil Calderon and Clark R. Bates

It may be a foregone conclusion that many who pick up this book will already be familiar with its honoree, Dr. Frank Turek. However, since the book is expansive in its content, some readers may be approaching this work for what it contains more than to whom it is in referent. What is more, even those who may be familiar with Dr. Turek's work and writings may know him only at the level of apologist, and this book seeks to honor Frank as more than an apologist, but also as a mentor and friend—to more people than he even knows. For this reason, the authors and editor of this book wanted to bring others into the world of Dr. Frank Turek, beyond what they see in media, in the hopes that our desire to thank him for his tireless ministry into our lives is understandable to the readers. The best way to do this is to give you the insights from one who knows him best, Jorge Gil Calderon, former social media director to Frank's CrossExamined ministry; leader of its outreach to Latin America; speaker at the annual CrossExamined Instructor Academy (CIA); and close, personal friend.

DR. FRANK TUREK, THE APOLOGIST

Anyone who does an internet search will find that Frank was born in 1961, is married with three grown sons, and is head of CrossExamined ministries. They will also know that Frank is most well known for his book *I Don't Have Enough Faith to Be an Atheist* (Crossway, 2004), coauthored with the late Dr. Norman Geisler. This book has since spawned a student curriculum and further publications. Frank is also the author of *Stealing from God: Why Atheists Need God to Make Their Case* (NavPress, 2015) and *Correct, Not Politically Correct: How Same-Sex Marriage Hurts Everyone* (CrossExamined,

2017), and contributor to several edited volumes. While knowing this can certainly engender respect for Frank and his ministry, my (Jorge's) experience with Frank is more personal, and that is what I would like to share with you.

I met Dr. Frank Turek in 2013, during the National Conference on Christian Apologetics in Charlotte, North Carolina. I remember I was rushing to a session, and he was walking down the sidewalk on the way to moderate a panel discussion. He was kind enough to stop in the middle of his rushed walk and take a picture with me. I told him that I would do anything to talk to him later, if possible, and he just told me to look for him. I saw him again during that conference, but it was my first national conference, and I was trying to use my time to meet with as many people as possible, so I was not able to speak with him like I had hoped.

Shortly after that experience, in 2014, I learned about the CrossExamined Instructor Academy, a weekend-long conference developed by Frank through his CrossExamined ministry to train Christians to be apologists. There were multiple speakers, including Frank, and I desperately wanted to go, but, at the time, I was going through a very difficult period and could not afford it. I spoke with my local pastor, and he agreed to pay for half of the fees. A friend from my church, who now works for CrossExamined as their motion graphics animator, agreed to pay the other half. My late aunt even agreed to pay for a hotel during my stay. This is how I ended up at my first CIA and was finally able to sit and talk with Frank.

During that CIA I developed a relationship with him and with two other speakers, J. Warner Wallace and Dr. Richard Howe. I kept in contact with the three of them from that time on. The year 2014 brought many struggles for me emotionally and spiritually. During that year I dealt with the tragic loss of family members, the breakdown of my marriage, and taking sole custody of my two children. After receiving the call from the authorities to notify me that my aunt and uncle had died tragically, I collapsed in tears and reached out to the first person who came to mind, Jim Wallace. Aware that Jim was a former police officer, I knew he had experience with the kind of events that took my aunt and uncle and thought he could help in some way. During our call he was able to comfort and encourage me, and shortly afterwards, I received a call from Frank. Even though I had known him for only one month, this world-famous apologist cared enough to call and check on me. He offered to help with anything I might need.

Frank was always open and kind, and even gave me his direct phone number and email to contact him at any time. Approximately five or six months later, I had begun a local ministry with what I had learned through CIA, and I was presenting the *I Don't Have Enough Faith to Be an Atheist* curriculum—something all graduates of the CIA are permitted to do—in North Carolina. I had been posting the materials on my social media platforms along with some of my own material, and one day, I received an email from Gil Gatch who was, at that time, the administrative assistant for Frank's CrossExamined ministry. He asked if I would like to volunteer to help with their social media platforms. I quickly agreed and started creating graphics for their posts and streamlining their social media content.

Within about one week Frank called and told me there was an opening for a social media director and that I should apply. So, I compiled my resume, gathered letters of recommendation, and applied. I was terrified. I had been in the same job for twelve years. This job would not require me to relocate, and with my parenting needs it would be like a dream come true. But I was also very hesitant about my own personal abilities. I prayed and fasted and meditated on a lot of Scripture. Convinced that this was the right decision, I sent in my application. Roughly one week later, I received a call asking to meet with me before doing an official interview. This took the form of a three-way phone call.

After speaking with Frank and Jim Wallace on the phone, we arranged an in-person interview. I traveled to Charlotte about two weeks later and met with Frank in the conference room of the old Southern Evangelical Seminary conference building. The interview was very straightforward, but I was also allowed to make any requests known, so I asked, as part of the arrangement, for Frank to train and mentor me to become a public speaker. My goal was to become an apologist for the Spanish-speaking community and Latin America as a whole. Frank agreed. By the next week I was offered the job.

Within two years the Lord had blessed everything that we were doing, especially on social media. We grew so quickly that we needed more help, and Frank instructed me to find somebody who could help and become a possible replacement—because he wanted to give me the opportunity to branch out into my own speaking career. Shortly after, we hired several new employees, and I began traveling to Latin America to conduct apologetics training, starting in the Dominican Republic, then Honduras, Mexico, and Costa Rica. I went from being a man struggling to keep his life together to having a new chance at life, and it is all because of Frank. He once told me that in spite of my past (I had a criminal record as a teen), if I had repented and allowed God to transform me, then I deserved a second chance because God is the God of second chances. That has stayed with me all these years and reinforced my work ethic. But more than that, through everything, I can say that Frank is not only a mentor, but a friend.

During my time with CrossExamined I witnessed Frank do many things. He is an exemplary leader, always praying for his staff and letting them use their God-given talents. He refuses to micromanage his team, and he is always ready and willing to help others. He has an awareness of things that most people do not and always asks questions about the well-being of others. When someone is hurting or in trouble, the first thing Frank asks is "How can I or my family or the ministry help?" He is a leader who cares about his people.

Most people who know of Frank think only of his public personality. They think of his New Jersey-style approach to apologetics, and oftentimes get the wrong impression. I have heard people criticize his directness and boldness, and even cast doubt on his sincerity, but what they do not see is that Frank has a relentless desire to see souls come to Christ. I do not think I have ever seen anyone who travels as much he does. He takes advantage of every opportunity he has to share Jesus with others. If he is not traveling, he is developing curriculum, recording an online course or television show, or being a guest on a podcast or radio program. He is constantly working to spread the gospel. I have seen Frank continue to travel and work when he is feeling low, or sick, or hurting. Nothing interferes with his mission.

Frank is the type of person who was created to do the work that he does. When it comes to engaging with skeptics or being placed in situations that would infuriate most, he expresses patience and temperance. Even when circumstances do not go the way he expects, or mistakes are made, he is always willing to have a one-on-one conversation and treat people with love. In my decade of knowing him, I have seen him become frustrated only twice, and neither involved the ministry.

In our time together, Frank always encouraged me to consider new things. He opened certain doors for me to walk through and never pushed me in an uncomfortable way. He always had a whisper or wise word when I was unsure. Looking back, I have probably asked him for advice on everything from my career to my personal life, marital life, and parenting life, and he is always willing to give it. I trust Frank because I have seen in him a consistency of character. Frank is a person who is always the same person, on stage or at home, with old friends or when he meets new people. He does not change, and I believe he is an example to follow.

DR. FRANK TUREK, THE PERSON

In the years that I have known Frank, I have spent months on the road with him, stayed in his home, and experienced every aspect of life by his side. In the world of apologetics, it can be too easy to separate one's devotional and spiritual life from the mental or intellectual life. Apologetics can become so intellectual that it leaves little room for the spiritual, but for Frank there has never been a separation between the two. I have witnessed him in daily prayer and devotion. I have seen him practicing the spiritual disciplines of the Christian life on stage and in private, seeking the empowering of the Holy Spirit in all areas of his life. His ministry was born out of his devotion to our Lord. Whether it involved the planning and growth of the CrossExamined Instructor Academy or choosing where to speak, Frank has always sought, first and foremost, to see God lead.

More than being a minister and public speaker, Frank is a husband, father, and grandfather. The hospitality he extends to those who enter his ministerial orbit is only amplified in his family life. His wife, Stephanie, is the center of his life. His love for her resonates throughout any room where both are present, and that love has influenced his children for the Lord in many ways. Historically it has been the curse of evangelists to become absent from their families while serving in ministry, but Frank has never spent time away from his wife and children without speaking to them and praying for them daily. As an employer and instructor, seeing this part of his life only reinforces in me the importance of family and the needed balance for all in Christian ministry. As a father, Frank sought to raise his children in the nurture and admonition of the Lord, but also with a clear understanding of why they should believe in Christianity and what the outside world would think of their beliefs. In 2022, Frank even coauthored an apologetics book with his son Zach titled *Hollywood Heroes: How Your Favorite Movies Reveal God* (NavPress).

Having studied under the late Norman Geisler, Frank is also a man of the mind. His appetite for learning and reading is seen in his publications and his personal library. It is very rare to see Frank without a book in his hand, or seeking out scientists, philosophers, and theologians to help him better understand a topic. He has been influenced by men like Dr. Timothy Keller and Dr. Michael Heiser, encouraging the CrossExamined team and his global audience to be in constant prayer for both men as they endured their cancer diagnoses. The same memory with which God has gifted Frank with concerning his friends and their needs extends to his learning. I have witnessed Frank call to mind numerous amounts of information and details, from memory, during his talks and in conversation, and like everything, Frank uses this gift in service to the kingdom.

As a man of faith, I have never seen him waiver. He has a strength of conviction that resounds in everything he does. That is not to say that he has never grieved. I was with him when he lost his father, shortly after when his dear friend Dr. Mike Adams passed away, and even recently at the passing of Dr. Heiser. In those moments I saw my friend grieve deeply. The loss of a family member and those friends who are as close as family is difficult for anyone to bear. Even Jesus wept at the loss of his friend. But Frank never grieved as one who did not have hope. That strength of faith that he carries on stage held him up through those dark times. It held us all up. Frank could grieve authentically without losing faith because he is certain how the story will end. Frank knows that he will see his father and friends again, and he knows that until that day, he has a mission in this life. A mission he is intent on finishing well.

I have said it several times already, but Frank cares for others. He knows that his mission does not end with him, and so he is fully invested in passing on the faith to the next generation. He is intentional in bringing godly people into his ministry and fanning the flame of faith in their lives. He is passionate about ensuring that the truth prevails, and that the next generation has an opportunity to hear it in a way that is convincing and compelling. To me, Frank is more than a mentor or an employer; he is my friend, and I am blessed to be able to say that. My decade working alongside him has been the most formative years of my life, and I look forward to walking with him for many more years to come. May God continue to grant him increase.

THE HISTORY OF THE CIA

The CrossExamined Instructor Academy (CIA) started in 2008, led by Frank Turek, Greg Koukl, Richard Howe, Brett Kunkle, and other professors from Southern Evangelical Seminary. Frank's ultimate goal was to train Christians to be able to take apologetic curriculums like *I Don't Have Enough Faith to Be an Atheist*, *Tactics*, and other materials to the local church. He was not looking to create the next million-dollar apologist, but rather millions of one-dollar apologists who could reach their communities.[1] The CIA was begun to equip local leaders to become dynamic communicators of the truth.

Since its inception, the CIA has graduated roughly eight hundred Christian lay people. It has met consecutively for sixteen years and taught

1. This phrase was popularized by J. Warner Wallace and means that Christians should not be striving for apologetic platforms that reach thousands of people, like the ones they may see in the media, but rather strive to be apologists to their local communities. This approach is considered far more effective in spreading the gospel than the former.

hundreds to share the truth of the gospel in creative and dynamic ways. Students are given lectures by multiple speakers on various topics in Christian apologetics, then expected to present their own topics in the presence of the instructors. At the end of the weekend all students have been given feedback from top-level apologists on their individual presentations and resources to grow in presentation skills and deeper apologetic learning. By 2014, it was clear that the growth of CIA would require expanding its reach. In 2016, Jorge Gil Calderon was added to the teaching roster with the specific goal of training attendees on effective uses of social media. Jorge's expertise with expanding the social media presence of CrossExamined enabled him to teach students about the most important platforms, best recording software and equipment, programs that enabled a user to post regularly across all social media profiles with minimal work from the user, and how to produce quality audio and video content.

In the early years of CIA, meetings were held in the conference room of Southern Evangelical Seminary in Charlotte, North Carolina. The courses did not earn a profit for CrossExamined and were exclusively a service to the church. After 2016, attendance grew to approximately sixty registrants per year, and Dr. Turek decided that, despite the costs, the conference should be moved to different states on a rotating basis. Moving the conference in this way enabled more people to attend who could not afford to travel to the East Coast. Any costs that exceeded the registration fees were absorbed by the ministry.

Another feature instituted in later conferences was the CIA scholarship program. Because the heart of the CIA was to serve the church, the program began to offer all-inclusive scholarships for those interested in attending but, for any reason, were unable to afford the costs. Despite these costs to the ministry, Dr. Turek maintained, and still maintains, a reduced speaking fee and offers to speak without a fee, if necessary.

As the CIA began to travel, new requests were made, specifically regarding the dates of the conference. Originally, the academy was held annually in August, but due to the standard school year beginning around the same time, many people interested in attending, who either had children or worked within the education system, were unable. In response, the CIA was moved to the month of July to accommodate these needs. A central tenet of CrossExamined has always been to serve, and Dr. Turek seeks to live out this tenet in every aspect of his work. The multiple changes to the academy are a direct reflection of this ethos.

In recent years, the CIA has continued to expand its list of instructors, bringing on former graduates and accomplished apologists—and contributors to this volume—Alisa Childers and Natasha Crain, as well as adding a virtual option. Rather than continuing to increase the number of apologists on the dais, the CIA now offers a rotating list of speakers, demonstrating a varying array of apologetic ministries, each bringing their own, unique skill sets and experiences. With the growing interest in Christian apologetics within women's and parenting ministries, CIA has also witnessed a shift from 90 percent male and 10 percent female attendees in 2008 to 60 percent male and 40 percent female attendees in 2022.

With the growing interest, the instructors also began to see past attendees returning to refresh their training. Their return brought with it an added interest from graduates to pursue a more intensive level of training that built upon what they had learned in their first CIA. This gave birth to the Advanced CIA. The perquisite for this course was to have attended at least one basic academy prior and have an interest in pursuing speaking and apologetics ministry on a larger scale. Students of the Advanced CIA are offered an increased exposure to the mechanics of building interactive and engaging presentations, effective communication skills, advanced philosophical and theological thought, and more critical reviews of their existing practices. The students who have graduated from both courses have repeatedly expressed the positive impact this course has had on their abilities and ministries. Within sixteen years God has grown what began as a simple idea to help spread apologetics to the local church into a platform that has trained hundreds of Christians nationally and begun several, nationally renowned apologists and authors.

CONTENTS OF THE PRESENT VOLUME

The chapters of this volume serve not only as a testament to the impact of Dr. Frank Turek on the lives and ministries of each author, but also as an introduction to new voices and new approaches to various apologetic issues. The novice reader, just beginning their journey into Christian apologetics, will be introduced to various approaches to Christianity from science, philosophy, and the Bible that will stretch them intellectually and strengthen them spiritually. The seasoned reader, already immersed in the variety of Christian apologetics materials already in circulation, will find original approaches to age-old questions, and likely be introduced to arguments or challenges to the faith that they have, thus far, not seen. Be they pastor, seminarian, or layperson, this volume seeks to provide all believers, regardless of their knowledge, a reasoned answer to those who ask about the hope that rests within them, and to do so with gentleness and love.

The chapters themselves have been separated into thematic sections, to aid in referencing specific fields of study, all of which are themes employed by Dr. Turek in his various presentations. The first section, "Science," begins with a masterful treatment of the Darwinian evolutionary cornerstone, abiogenesis, from a senior director in the biotechnology industry, **Dr. William Soo Hoo**. William's experience and training in molecular immunology provides an inside look into the world of biological development at a level rarely found in Christian literature. The chapter's combination of detailed, scientific inquiry and relatable illustrations challenge all readers to consider, or reconsider, the fundamental claim that macroevolutionary development is both possible and even probable, given the 4.5-billion-year time span from the moment of the big bang to the existence of life on planet Earth.

Immediately following this is a chapter devoted to the famed cosmological argument. Far from being a restating of the Kalam cosmological argument (KCA), made famous by Christian apologists like Dr. William Lane Craig, pastor, apologist, and author **Dr. Phil Fernandes** draws readers into the history and details of three variations on the cosmological argument preferred by Thomas Aquinas, Bonaventure, and Gottfried Wilhelm Leibniz. His discussion and differences with the KCA provide readers with alternative approaches to the age-old question of origins inherent in the presence of an event horizon like the big bang.

The second section, "Philosophy," begins with a tour de force introduction to Christian philosophy and its impact on our daily lives, by **Alex McElroy**. Alex draws from his years of ministry training and working with Chicago youths to find their purpose in life and pairs this with the need for logical, rational, and above all, truthful philosophical presuppositions. For the reader who might be new to Christian philosophy, this chapter prepares them for the more technical philosophical approaches that follow; and for the more knowledgeable reader, Alex's union of Christian apologetics with Christian living is a needed encouragement for a field that often overlooks spiritual formation for intellectual acquisition.

Christian apologist **Eric Hernandez** brings his unique case against physicalism in his treatment defending the existence of the soul. For those who have been pressed by the naturalist's claims that all that can exist is material, or that one cannot prove one has a soul, Hernandez's clear mastery of the subject matter will equip them for future discussion. The author's defense of substance dualism, the belief that the mind and the body are two distinct substances, stands in direct opposition to the "mere physicalism" of naturalists like Daniel Dennett, Paul Churchland, and Alex Rosenberg.

Dr. Timothy Stratton rounds out the philosophical discussions by carrying the work of the preceding chapters into the realm of theology and divine knowledge. Exercising his expertise on the thought of sixteenth-century Spanish theologian Luis de Molina, Dr. Stratton defines and defends his support for Molinism—the belief that God possesses "middle knowledge." This chapter deftly argues that Molina's theology offers the best apologetic available for Christians against the problem of evil and that Christians of all theological backgrounds should make use of it when engaging with nonbelievers.

The third section of this work presents readers with three discussions related to Christianity and the Bible. These begin with **Alisa Childers** employing her years of research into progressive Christianity to caution readers against the increasingly popular hermeneutic of Richard Rohr, dubbed the "Jesus Hermeneutic." Using Rohr's own words, Alisa analyzes the various Gospel passages by which Rohr defends his hermeneutic. She examines each text and offers a biblical refutation, demonstrating that Rohr's hermeneutic is far from that used by the Jesus of Scripture.

Moving more directly into the Bible itself, Ratio Christi's **Eric Chabot** introduces a problem many Christians have failed to examine for themselves, namely how Jesus's resurrection proves his messiahship. The New Testament authors repeatedly assert that the Lord's resurrection proves that he is the long-awaited Messiah of Israel, yet, as Eric points out, there are no prophetic passages in the Hebrew Bible that speak explicitly about a resurrection of the Messiah. When engaging with Jewish believers, this is a contentious issue and one that many are not prepared to answer. Eric's research into Hebrew texts and engagement with leading Jewish scholars, provides an excellent foundation for following in the apostles' footsteps, and defending the claim that the Jewish Messiah was meant to die and rise again on the third day.

Lastly, **Clark R. Bates** engages in an expedition into the defense of the Bible's reliability, ultimately arguing that questions about reliability reveal a deeper need within the human psyche. In this chapter, Clark offers brief responses to challenges of the historical reliability of both the Old and New Testament, followed by an in-depth discussion on the textual reliability of the Bible and, finally, what he calls its "epistemic reliability," or the ability for the Scriptures to be a trustworthy guide for life.

In the last section, devoted to matters within the church, **Melissa Dougherty** addresses the ecclesiastical creep toward supernatural experiences. Melissa writes from her personal journey through experience-driven movements and argues against the teachings of current church leaders who defend the adoption of New Age practices into church worship. This chapter serves as a clarion call for the church to seek biblical discernment and oppose that which God calls evil. It is followed by **Natasha Crain**'s exhortation to parents, promoting the training of children in apologetics. With years of experience both as a parent and speaker to parents, Natasha exposes the cultural moves against the Christian faith that children will inevitably face. She then encourages parents to put aside their reservations against apologetic instruction and see that it is neither daunting nor impossible to make this education a part of their daily lives. Natasha closes by providing parents with several steps for taking this journey with their kids, closing this book in the way it began, uniting the practice and discipline of apologetics with daily Christian life.

This volume began as an idea, roughly four years ago, born from a felt need to share with the world the impact Dr. Frank Turek has had on a new generation of apologists. The authors involved in this project were chosen because they all attended Dr. Turek's CrossExamined Instructor Academy and went on to engage in apologetics ministry, either full-time or alongside their professional disciplines.[2] However, as it developed, it became clear that this project represents more than just what Dr. Turek has done for other apologists; it represents the power of the Christian message across all walks of life. The authors in this book cross cultural, theological, gender, and racial lines. They serve as ministers, scientists, youth workers, and academics. They work in the inner city, the college campus, the laboratory, and the home. Despite these differences, the authors are united in their love and respect for Dr. Turek, but even more so in their shared conviction that the gospel of Jesus Christ is the only message of salvation to a dying world. In a world increasingly divided, this book demonstrates how the gospel unites, and this is what Dr. Turek would rejoice in more than anything else.

2. https://crossexamined.org/what-is-cia/.

Science

To say that a scientist can disprove the existence of God is like saying a mechanic can disprove the existence of Henry Ford. It doesn't follow.

—Frank Turek, *Stealing from God*

Abiogenesis: No Time, No Chance—No Way!

William Soo Hoo[1]

Four and a half billion years—a very long time indeed. That is the accepted age of the Earth based on multiple lines of scientific evidence.[2] It is so huge an expanse of time that no human being can truly appreciate the true meaning of it, because there are almost no comparisons to help us comprehend it. So, it is not surprising that people would find it reasonable to believe that evolution—an unguided process of biological change, supposedly responsible for the origin and diversity of life on Earth—would require such a huge expanse of time. Not surprisingly, arguments in favor of evolution also benefit from such a large timescale. Evolution is broadly predicated on the need for large amounts of time for descent with modification and natural selection to achieve its purposeless goals, and, not inconsequentially, evolution has long been the fundamental rationale for denying the existence of God. If the emergence and biodiversity of living things can be explained from a naturalistic standpoint, then there is no need for God. Biologist Richard Dawkins reflects the importance of evolution in atheistic thought, writing, "Darwin made it possible to be an intellectually fulfilled atheist."[3] But what if it is shown that evolution couldn't even get off the ground? What if attempts to establish prebiological evolution, or *chemical* evolution, show that life could not originate on its own, without the input of

1. Thanks to Dr. Turek and his ministry, I have learned a great deal from Dr. Turek's deftly handled question and answer sessions through the years and had the privilege of conversing with him at the 2017 CIA Instructor Training. His advice and encouraging words have helped me greatly in my own apologetics ministry.

2. Dalrymple, "Age of the Earth."

3. Dawkins, *Blind Watchmaker*, 6.

design and information from an intelligent source? If the scientific evidence pointed away from a naturalistic origin of life, what then?

Biological evolution requires a living system separate from its environment, which can maintain its own biochemical equilibrium. The system must be physically separate from its surroundings and able to exchange energy with its environment through a system of chemical reactions that allows the living system to maintain itself, grow, and replicate. Prior to this "biotic" phase, molecules had to have developed through a gradual process of unguided change in a sort of chemical evolution, producing "prebiotic" molecules as precursors to the first living system we know as a single cell. As with all processes, the gradual evolution of life on Earth had to have a set of primary biochemical properties that ultimately led to the Last Universal Common Ancestor (LUCA).[4] There are still several competing ideas as to the nature and characteristics of LUCA, but one concept persists: LUCA possessed many, if not all, of the biochemical mechanisms that modern cells have today (e.g., a genetic code, a mechanism to translate that code to make proteins, metabolic pathways to exchange a transmute energy, etc.). One thing is certain, LUCA conceptually represents the successful transition from *chemistry* to *biology*. This is the starting point of biological evolution that neo-Darwinian thought claims is ultimately responsible for the biodiversity observed on Earth.

Defenders of naturalism have been critical of attempts to refute evolution via challenges to the origin of life. Proponents of naturalistic evolution say that the origin of life is a completely separate problem for science and any problems with origins of life theories have little to no bearing on evolution as a whole. I find this rejoinder difficult to accept when there is an entire body of scientific literature that refers to chemical evolution, prebiotic evolution, molecular evolution, and the evolution of biospheres. It would seem perfectly reasonable to refer to these fields of research to see that the origin of life is part and parcel of the entire evolutionary project. The language of evolution, in fact, permeates origin-of-life science literature. One finds phrases describing "chemical evolution" and "natural selection" of biochemical pathways frequenting the origins of life writings. That said, it is justifiable to present a challenge to the naturalistic origin of life as also being a challenge to evolution. In this chapter, I will challenge the naturalistic origin of life, also known as *abiogenesis*, from three aspects: time, chance, and mechanism. In each aspect, the naturalistic, physicochemical processes needed are insufficient to bring about abiogenesis. Plainly stated, there is no time, no chance, and overall, no way.

4. Forterre, "Displacement of Cellular Proteins."

NO TIME

To some, four and a half billion years might be a reasonable time frame to diversify into today's collection of about five million extant species (not counting the millions of species that have gone extinct).[5] However, what about the time necessary to go from chemicals, to biomolecules, to macromolecules (i.e., chains of similar molecules chemically linked, such as proteins, carbohydrates, RNA, DNA), subcellular systems, and finally, to the first self-replicating living cell (LUCA)?

To answer this question, we will use a time frame based on the standard cosmological model, also known as the Lambda cold dark matter model or the big bang. Virtually without exception, modern scientists accept this model as fact because of the tremendous amount of empirical data by which it is supported. According to the data from both the European Space Agency and NASA, the age of the universe is estimated to be 13.8 billion years old—give or take a few hundred million years. This is all the time, *ever*, that we have to work with. But a closer examination of the events taking place during this time is necessary to answer the question of whether this is enough time to go from lifeless, preorganic molecules to the first living cell.

At the moment of the big bang, the initial conditions were such that there were no atoms present, nor subatomic particles. In the first 10^{-43} seconds (Planck time), matter as we know it was not yet formed. It was not until this point in time that the separation of the four fundamental forces of nature occurred (gravity, electromagnetism, strong and weak nuclear forces), allowing for the formation of subatomic particles such as protons, neutrons, and electrons within the first seconds. Subsequently, atoms formed in this early stage of the universe, which lasted some 200- to 300,000 years after the initial big bang when the earliest stars formed, collected into galaxies after roughly 400,000 years, then gradually formed the modern galaxies we see today, for 1 to 10 billion years and beyond. Data from the James Webb Space Telescope, launched in 2021, is even now supplying us with more accurate data, but for the majority of the 13.8 billion years, there was no opportunity or conditions for life to begin—let alone exist.

Where should we place our demarcations when we are talking about the origins of life on Earth? A commonsense definition of this range of time would be the time between the earliest point that the Earth could have sustained life and the earliest known evidence for the existence of life. First, we need to know when the Earth appears on the cosmological time line. Figure 1 illustrates the entire time span of the universe from its beginning 13.8

5. Costello et al., "Can We Name."

billion years ago (far left: *Ga* for *giga* [billion] and *annum* [year]) to the far right end labeled "Present Day."

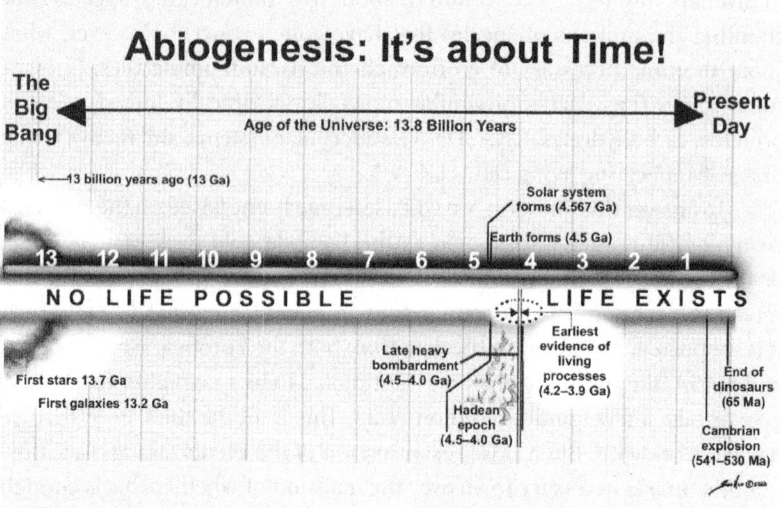

Figure 1. A time line of the universe. From 13.8 to ~4.5 billion years (Giga-annum) ago, no life was possible. The Hadean epoch and late heavy bombardment kept the Earth in a sterile state. The first appearance of life may be as early as 4.1 Ga ago. The sliver of time for the development of the first living cell is extremely narrow.

At the 4.567 and 4.5 Ga mark is when the solar system and the Earth formed, respectively. Now that the Earth has formed on our time line, we have a *place* for the origin of life. By knowing more of the cosmological events surrounding the formation of the Earth, you can establish the left-side timeframe, which would denote the earliest time point at which the Earth could sustain life. As the Earth formed 4.5 billion years ago, it needed time to cool down. Temperatures of the Earth during the beginning of its formation, marked by the collision event producing the moon, were estimated to be over 3600°F[6]. Compare that to the temperature of lava erupting from Mount Kilauea, 2100°F[7]. This time period was known as the Hadean eon, the time range of which has been estimated using impact rocks found on the moon by Apollo Missions Fourteen, Fifteen, and Sixteen. The dating of these lunar samples were correlated with similar events on the Earth at the time. In addition, the lunar data reveals cosmic collisions with

6. Sleep, "Hadean-Archean Environment," 3.

7. "Lava," para 5.

space-bound asteroids constantly bombarding the nascent Earth, causing it to be in a continually superheated state (i.e., sterile).

The thermodynamics of rocky bodies indicates that the Hadean eon extended well beyond the time expected to cool the Earth. Taken together, the evidence suggests that these cosmic, bolide (missile-like) collisions, dubbed the late heavy bombardment (LHB) era of the Earth, occurred near the end of the Hadean eon, creating a sterilizing effect. Over the last ten years, reports have called into question the exact dates of the end of the LHB, or even its existence. However, in a 2017 scientific review of the topic, it was concluded that the findings, with all the pros and cons and caveats, suggest that the most likely possibility is that some form of hybrid model occurred. Over the early period of Earth's history, bombardments certainly took place, albeit in discrete periods throughout the Hadean eon.[8] Looking at the entire time line then, to the left of the LHB, *no life was possible.* And most estimates place the time that the Earth was cool enough to sustain life at nearly 4.1 to 3.8 Ga ago.

Now, let us turn our attention to the right side of the time line to determine the point at which the earliest evidence of life is observable. Anything to the right of that point cannot be considered for our discussion about the development of life because after this point, *life already exists.* So, when is the earliest evidence of cellular life on Earth? By most estimates the earliest forms of cellular life appeared from 3.45 to 3.85 Ga ago. Depending on the type of evidence you use, it breaks up into three phases. The later date (3.5 Ga) is based on microfossil formations called stromatolites found in Western Australia thought to have been made by photosynthetic bacteria. Earlier than this, it is difficult—if not impossible—to obtain fossil evidence because of the highly metamorphosed rock (rocks that changed because of melting heat) at this level. Withdrawing further back in time, scientists must now look for indirect evidence, such as chemical compounds, that a living organism would have left behind—a sort of *biosignature.*

Once this type of biochemical trail was discovered, the origin of cellular life was pushed back to 3.8 Ga. However, in a 2015 report in the *Proceedings of the National Academy of Sciences*, radiometric data was the telltale clue for life in deposits of carbon isotopes in ancient crystals of zircon.[9] It is known that living organisms use a preferred isotope of carbon. Of the two isotopic forms of carbon relevant to this discussion, one is carbon 12 (written as ^{12}C), meaning that it has the usual six protons and six neutrons in its atomic nucleus, and the other is ^{13}C, which has six protons and seven neutrons. As

8. Bottke and Norman, "Late Heavy Bombardment."

9. Bell et al., "Potentially Biogenic Carbon Preserved."

it happens, living organisms use the ^{12}C isotope in their biological processes. What all this means is that, if there is an unusually high proportion of ^{12}C to ^{13}C present, then it is highly likely that a living organism is responsible for this. These deposits of ^{12}C were found to be as old as 3.85 Ga. In more recent findings, isotopically light carbon traces have been found in the remains of hydrothermal vents in the Nuvvuagittuq Belt in Canada dating from 3.8 to 4.3 Ga ago.[10] Let us say then that the earliest signs of biological life appear at approximately 4.0 Ga.

Because of differences in estimations, these two time ranges—the end of the LHB (4.1 to 3.8 Ga) and the earliest evidence of life (4.3 to 3.8)—overlap. Therefore, the time frame between the two events is extremely small. Depending on the estimates, scientists have tried to place the time range between 10 to 100 million years, which is a mere "wink of an eye" on the cosmic time line. This makes it acceptable to propose that the time period available for the origin of life is somewhat less than 100 million years.

What Needs to Get Done?

When your boss asks you to do something, there are at least two important questions to ask. One is "*What* do I need to do?," and the other is "*How much time* do I have in order to do it?" For the origin of the first living cell, we now have a time frame. In answering the first question, "What do I need to do?," origin-of-life scientists generally agree that there are a set of conceptually distinct stages necessary to successfully construct a living cell. First, the proper chemical reactions must occur in a prebiotic (i.e., "before life") environment, resulting in organic monomers—building blocks to more complex molecules. Second, these monomers must have sufficient stability to accumulate into a critical concentration that allows further reactions that result in larger, more complex chains of chemically linked macromolecules. These macromolecules must then polymerize—connect themselves together in a fashion similar to beads of pearl or LEGO bricks. As early as the nineteenth century a large number of simple organic molecules were being synthesized under non-biological conditions, suggesting that the building blocks of life could have developed in the early Earth. However, it is not enough *that* the parts form. An insanely complex coordination of *all* the parts would be necessary for the development of a "simple" cell.

The basic components of a cell include four macromolecules—lipids, carbohydrates, proteins, and nucleic acids. In a general sense, the first three

10. Dodd et al., "Evidence for Early Life."

of these macromolecules have more to do with structure and function of the cell, while nucleic acids harbor the information that makes upon the cell (fig. 2). With the exception of lipids, the other molecules are in their most functionally relevant state as linkages of monomers, much like railroad cars are linked to form a train. Lipids themselves represent a large class of fatty acid molecules similar in general structure but highly nuanced regarding specific chemical groups. Some of the groups that allow them to serve as barriers are: membranes, which segregate the contents of the cell from the outer environment; energy carriers; raw material for the cell to manufacture hormones; and other biomolecules. These molecules consist of long chains of carbon atoms and have two different ends to them—a hydrophilic (loves to be exposed to water) and a hydrophobic (avoids water). These properties enable lipids to spontaneously form enclosures (much like soap bubbles) that protect the first cell from the outside primordial world.

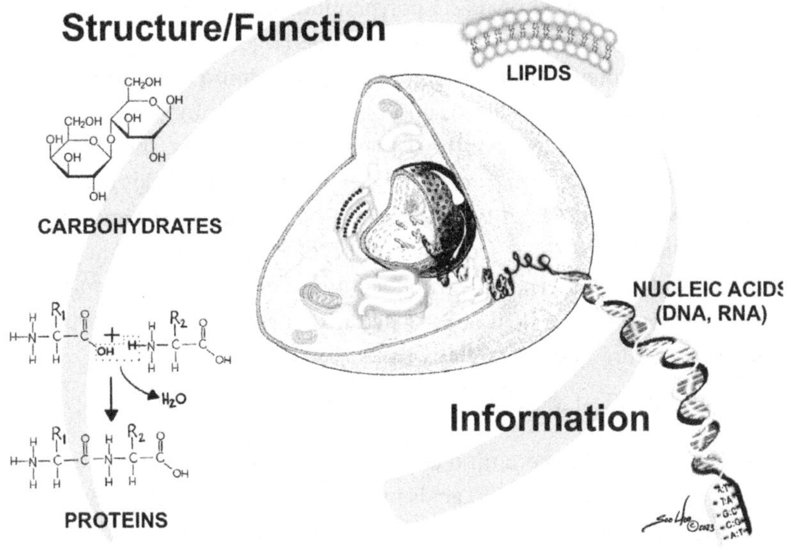

Figure 2. A typical mammalian cell. Lipids form membranes, which serve as boundaries between cellular compartments. Carbohydrates form chains of sugars, which can modify proteins or take part in energy transfers. Proteins act as structural and functional molecules. Finally, nucleic acids (DNA, RNA) contain the genetic information necessary to reproduce the cell.

Carbohydrates can form complex, often large-branched structures composed of monomers (referred to as glycosides) and different simple sugars. They can link to lipids or proteins to modify membranes, enzymes, and other proteins. Proteins that have large-branched networks of carbohydrates connected to them are said to be glycosylated, and this modification can serve the purpose of increasing a protein's half-life in the bloodstream or allow it to be recognized more efficiently by other protein receptors on other cells. Carbohydrates can often "fine-tune" proteins for highly nuanced functions within the cell.

Proteins are sometimes known as the cell's molecular workhorses because they are used for so many different functions. These polypeptide molecules represent a collection of nearly 100,000 different proteins possessing differing functions ranging from cellular structure and scaffolding, to immune protection (antibodies), to catalyzing biochemical reactions (enzymes). Proteins are generally composed of a single chain (i.e., no branching) of monomers called amino acids. Twenty different biologically relevant amino acids are possible in all proteins, and a given length of linked amino acids is also generally known as a polypeptide. Smaller polypeptide chains can range from 50 to 100 amino acids, while larger ones can number up to the largest protein, Titin, coming in at 27,000 amino acids. The median length of most human proteins is approximately 430 amino acids.

Key to protein function is the sequence of amino acids. The sequence is known as the *primary structure.* Each of the twenty amino acids has unique chemical properties. These twenty amino acids are the "working pool" of protein building blocks. Depending on the protein, the sequence may use all or some, and in a pattern that is unique for that protein. For example, each of the twenty amino acids is abbreviated with a single letter, and a protein primary structure might look like this:

F-V-N-Q-H-L-C-G-S-H-L-V-E-A-L . . .

These are the first fifteen amino acids of the B chain of human insulin. In a given sequence, these amino acids interact with their neighboring amino acids much like magnets are repelled or attracted. This causes the amino acids to fold into a *secondary structure.* Sequences then interact with other sequences in the same chain but farther downstream, giving the protein yet another level of structure known as the *tertiary structure.*

Many proteins are also conglomerates of multiple chains, a classic example of which is the antibody molecule made up of four long polypeptides. The association with other chains is called the *quaternary structure.* It is this three-dimensional shape that gives proteins their functionality. Change the sequence, and function ceases. For example, hemoglobin is comprised of two pairs of polypeptide chains, 141 amino acids (two alpha chains), and

146 amino acids (two beta chains) in length and essential for oxygen transport. A single amino acid change in the beta chain at position 6, from glutamic acid to valine, results in a conformational change, reducing its ability to bind oxygen, resulting in sickle cell anemia.

Nucleic acids are the "information-bearing" biomolecules known as deoxyribonucleic acid (DNA) and ribonucleic acid (RNA). DNA is a single linear chain composed of a sequence of monomers called nucleotide bases. There are four bases, named adenine (A), cytosine (C), guanine (G), and thymine (T). RNA uses the same three bases A, C, G, and a fourth base, uracil (U), in place of thymine. The genetic code has been aptly compared to the machine language of computers, because, just as computer code contains information, so too does the genetic code within a strand of DNA.

The two macromolecules, nucleic acids and proteins, play a critical role in the transmission and use of specific biological information in a distinct and directional manner. In what is known as the central dogma, DNA is transcribed to RNA, which is then translated into protein. The order of base sequences in DNA makes up a gene. A particular gene is a unique sequence of DNA. It is the *sequence* that dictates what the protein will be, what it will look like, and most importantly, what it will do: one gene, one protein product. DNA, being the precious blueprint for all the cell's proteins, stays safe within the confines of the cell nucleus. However, protein synthesis takes place in the outskirts of the cytoplasm. Enter *messenger* RNA (mRNA), which is created in the nucleus, using the DNA gene as the template. The mRNA is quite literally the messenger RNA "copy" of the DNA gene, which leaves the nucleus to be "translated" by the ribosomal complex (a two-subunit structure made of different sequences of RNA). The entire process takes place through a highly orchestrated and intricately timed, intimate dance between proteins and nucleic acid strings. The mRNA enters the ribosomal complex like the paper roll of a player piano, having the instructions from the gene. The code specifies which amino acids link together in the same order specified by the original DNA code. The resulting protein then folds into a specific three-dimensional shape dictated by the primary sequence of amino acids.

As we have seen, the amount of time available for chemical evolution is exceedingly small. Furthermore, conditions on the early Earth also do not make it easy for many of these macromolecules to form spontaneously. Molecules are very sensitive to ultraviolet radiation like that coming from the sun. The light energy here would have caused many of these molecules to degrade before they had a chance to form into something even close to a set of functional compounds.

Carl Sagan, the astrophysicist noted for his *Cosmos* television series, went so far as to say, "The apparatus for the transcription of the genetic code must itself have evolved slowly, through billions of years of evolution."[11] Dr. Sagan was referring to subcellular molecular machines, thousands of them, which reside inside of a single cell. Each machine is an assembly of protein and ribonucleic sequences that form a structure that produces proteins that are originally encoded by a gene sequence in the DNA (fig. 3).

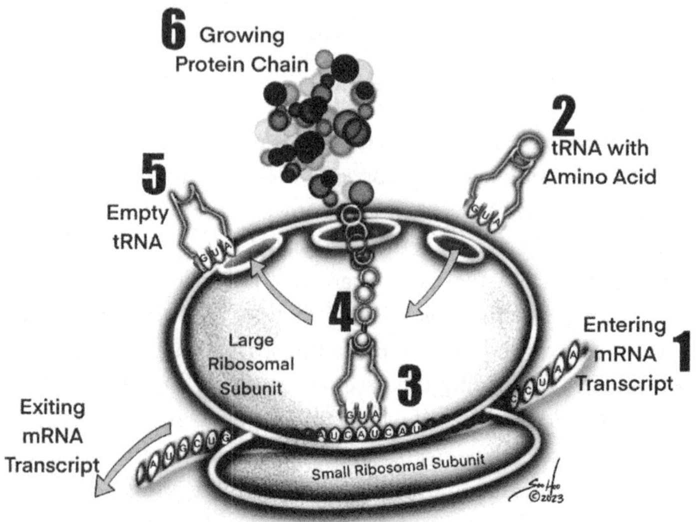

Figure 3. The ribosome complex. Proteins are made using these molecular machines which "read" the genetic code in messenger RNA, which threads through the ribosome (1). The triplet code is "matched" by free-floating tRNA linked with corresponding amino acids (2), which find the matching RNA triplet code (3). The amino acid is then chemically bonded (4) to the previous amino acid, and the "empty" tRNA leaves the ribosome (5), resulting in an emerging chain of amino acids, and the emerging protein (6) then folds into a specific three-dimensional shape dictated by the sequence of amino acids.

In the context of a single cell, this is a minuscule component among a panoply of subcellular machines within the vast complexity of the cell (fig. 4). By that line of reasoning, if what Sagan says is true, or even a close approximation, then it suggests that the remaining subcellular machines and systems, which are just as complex or more, must also have taken billions of years to have developed. The geologic evidence says there is not enough time.

11. Shklovskii and Sagan, *Intelligent Life in Universe*, 237.

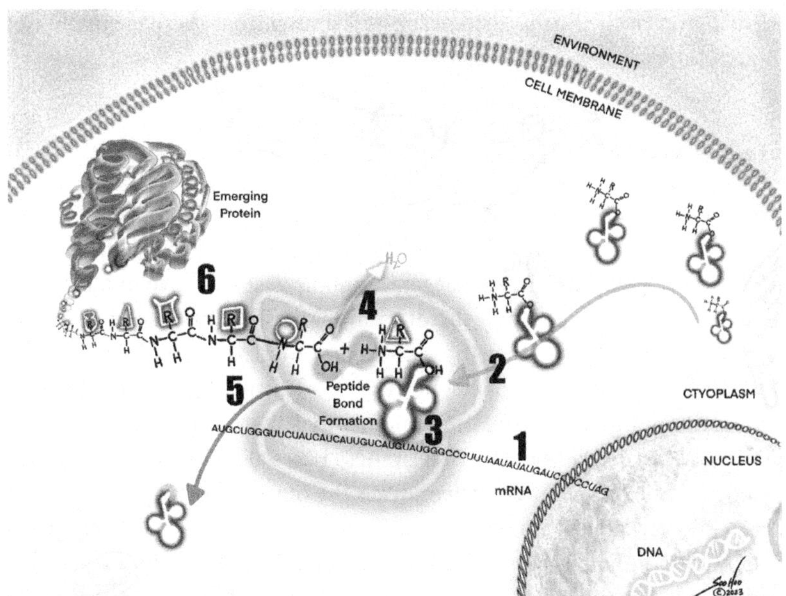

Figure 4. Protein synthesis in the context of the cell. Beginning with the DNA code, mRNA is transcribed to match the DNA code (1). The mRNA transcript then leaves the nucleus and encounters the ribosome complex (2), where the mRNA transcript is translated (3), a peptide bond is formed, and a molecule of water is expelled (4); and the chain of amino acids (5) folds into a polypeptide chain as the final product (6).

This stunningly narrow time frame has not gone without notice and remains one of the more obvious challenges in origin-of-life science. Richard E. Dickerson of the National Academy of Sciences and professor of biochemistry at UCLA wrote in a *Scientific American* article, "Perhaps the most striking aspect of the evolution of life on the Earth is that it happened so fast."[12] Origin-of-life scientist Leslie Orgel wrote, "We do not understand how a self-replicating system originated on the primitive earth, so it is impossible, on the basis of chemical arguments, to set upper or lower limits on the time that would be required."[13] However, based on the criteria discussed above, I would think that it is reasonable to attempt some kind of time range—one that would be independent of any knowledge of mechanisms for the start of life but that uses the observations of the evidence found in the geologic environment and biologic emergence. Given the cosmological time line of events, it seems evident, considering the tremendous amounts of molecular

12. Dickerson, "Chemical Evolution and Origin," 70.

13. Orgel, "Origin of Life," 95.

organization needed in precise order and timing, that there is simply not enough time for abiogenesis to occur.

NO CHANCE

In his book *Signature in the Cell*, philosopher of science Stephen C. Meyer relates his experience in a lecture on the structure of the DNA double helix—a realization that was as elegantly simple as it was tremendously significant.[14] As he looked upon the diagrammatic structure of the molecule of life, he suddenly saw that there were no differential bonding affinities between the four different nucleotide bases, adenine (A), thymine (T), cytosine (C), and guanine (G). This implied that there was no constraining physical law to determine the order of these bases along the DNA molecule strand. Yet, the order of the nucleotides is the most important aspect of the DNA code. Granted, physicochemical laws would govern the formation of certain prebiotic molecules, even the formation of building blocks such as amino acids and nucleotide bases. Figure 5 illustrates a similar situation in the structure of proteins. Although protein shapes are determined by known chemical laws, the *order* of the amino acid sequence is not determined by the sequence of coding DNA, which is also not determined by any physical or chemical laws.

Dean Kenyon and Gary Steinman promoted the notion that life was virtually predestined to arise because of the biochemical properties and physicochemical laws governing them.[15] Interestingly, Kenyon later abandoned this view after coming to the realization that protein sequences of amino acids could not have developed without the information encoded in DNA. Kenyon later became a fellow at the Center for Science and Culture, an intelligent design organization.[16] If there is no physical law, no chemical affinity, and/or no type of constraining guidance that would produce the specific order of DNA, RNA, or proteins, then the only option to create a meaningful sequence without the aid of an intelligent source is random, stochastic processes—pure chance.

14. Meyer, *Signature in the Cell*, 241–51.

15. Kenyon and Steinman, *Biochemical Predestination*, 80–119.

16. See https://www.discovery.org/p/kenyon/ for biographical sketch.

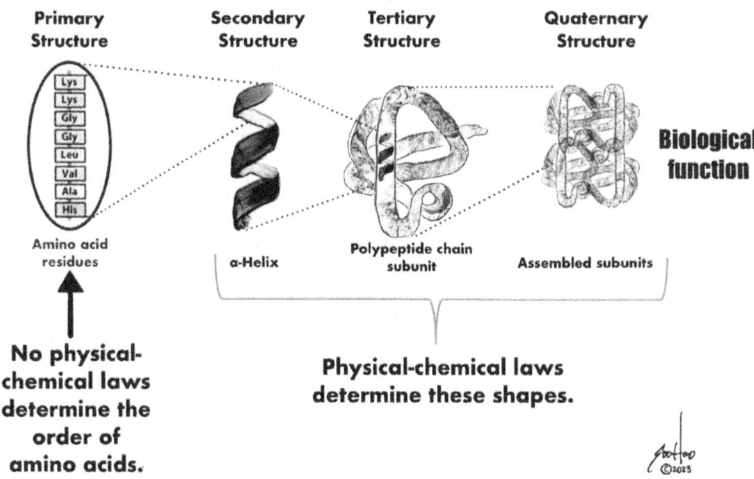

Figure 5. The levels of protein structure. From left to right: Proteins are composed of a chain of linked amino acids whose sequence is called the primary structure. Different amino acids have various electrochemical properties causing them to repel/attract and fold upon one another, resulting in a localized secondary structure. Distant interactions cause the chain to fold, which becomes the tertiary structure. Finally, several chains may interact with one another to form a quaternary structure. Physical properties account for the secondary, tertiary, and quaternary structures, but no laws govern the primary structure.

The DNA code is the fundamental source for all proteins made by the cell. DNA resides safely in the nucleus and is transcribed by a set of specific catalytic enzymes into mRNA. RNA is a nucleic acid intermediary that mimics the DNA sequence. The sequence of DNA coding for a protein is called a gene. As a cell expresses its genes, it is safer for the original DNA to stay within the cell nucleus while an mRNA "copy" of those DNA sequences is made and sent out from the nucleus into the cell to code for the final chain of amino acids, forming the final protein. The ribosome complex translates the mRNA sequence into the sequence of amino acids that makes up the final protein product, which then performs its function. Without the cell's molecular machinery, each of these three macromolecules (DNA, RNA, and proteins) has the same problem: there are no physicochemical laws to bring about the specified sequence; therefore we are left with random chance.

Several explanations using statistical calculations have shown that a random process to derive a given sequence is utterly untenable. Briefly, a simple statistical formulation would be that the probability P of a given specified sequence would be expressed as one chance out of the number of possible outcomes. For example, when you flip a coin, there are two potential outcomes: heads or tails. The probability *P* of one outcome (e.g., heads) is one chance out of two outcomes or half (50 percent). If we want to know the probability of a specific sequence of events, say the chances of getting heads in two consecutive flips (we shall call this H:H), then the probability is the product of these two probabilities, ½ x ½ = ¼. If we want to calculate the probability of getting two heads and one tails (H:H:T), we would multiply the probability of heads with the probability of heads with the probability of tails, and mathematically it would look like this: $(\frac{1}{2}_{\text{heads}})(\frac{1}{2}_{\text{heads}})(\frac{1}{2}_{\text{tails}}) = 1/8$. Notice that the number of outcomes (two) is multiplied against itself each time you increase the number of sequences. In the last example, two is multiplied by itself three times, which then can be expressed as 2^3. You can generalize this calculation by saying the probability *P* of any specified sequence of coin-toss results equals one over the number of possible outcomes (two, heads or tails) raised to the power of the number of consecutive coin flips or sequences (in this last case, raised to the power of three). As the specified sequence grows in length, you can see how the probability gets smaller and smaller, because the result is one over a denominator that grows quickly with each addition to the sequence.

Applying this principle to DNA, which has four possible nucleotide outcomes (ATCG), to randomly create a nine-nucleotide sequence of ATGCCCGCG, the probability would be one over four (the number of possible nucleotides) raised to the ninth power (the number of nucleotides in the sequence). This calculates to a chance of 1 in 4^9 or 1 in 262,144. This does not sound so bad, but genes are not that short. For example, for a length of DNA of 501 nucleotides, the probability of randomly producing the exact sequence would be given as $P = 1/4^{501}$, which calculates to 1 chance in 4.3×10^{301}. The chances are similarly abysmal for RNA. In the case of RNA, one could ask whether the chances of producing a smaller-sized functional string of RNA could be more reasonable. Take, for example, a self-catalytic RNA molecule of approximately 52 nucleotides developed by Robertson et al.[17] The same number of possible nucleotides applies in the case of RNA (i.e., AUCG). In order to create this primitive molecule, the chances would be 1 in 4^{52} or one chance in 2.0×10^{31}. Again, not very encouraging odds. In fact, the Robertson lab had to synthetically create this RNA sequence using lab techniques and special instrumentation to directly synthesize this specific sequence. To make matters worse, in water, RNA does not polymerize at all and is extremely unstable. Both DNA and RNA have little chance to develop in complexity.

17. Robertson and Joyce, "Highly Efficient Self-Replicating RNA."

Protein sequences of amino acids link together by a peptide bond. The sequence of amino acids is coded by the DNA of the gene for that particular protein. Again, there are no physical or chemical laws that influence the order of the amino acid sequence. We know that this sequence is determined by the gene. But what if there were no genes at the time before the first cell? What would be the chances of a 100-amino acid protein of a particular sequence forming from the primordial soup randomly? The calculation would be one chance in twenty (the number of possible amino acids) to the exponent of one hundred (the number of amino acids in the sequence) or $20^{100} = 1.3 \text{ x } 10^{130}$.

The probability becomes even more dismal when one factors in other, highly relevant, probabilities, as Doug Axe of the Biologic Institute aptly describes in a segment of a video on the origins of life.[18] In this segment, Axe points out that the protein problem has more complexity than merely the primary sequence of amino acids. There is the chirality problem, or the fact that the formation of amino acids evenly produces two different forms of each amino acid—a "left-handed" form and a "right-handed" form. Living cells exclusively use the left-handed form. Any incorporation of the right-handed form results in a nonfunctional protein. For a sequence of one hundred amino acids, you have a fifty-fifty chance of incorporating the correct form in the case of *each amino acid in the sequence.* And that is assuming you have equal numbers of left- and right-handed amino acids in the same mixture. That would be two outcomes to the power of one hundred or $P_{chirality} = (1/2)100$. Another probability to factor in is the chemical formation of the peptide bond that links all the amino acids together. Either a bond forms in solution or it does not, thus giving a probability calculation for ninety-nine bonds as $P_{peptide\ bond} = (1/2)99$. In fact, the peptide bond formation in water is extremely unfavorable thermodynamically—it simply does not happen—so saying that the probability is ½ for a single bond is ridiculously generous. Normally, the bond never forms in solution without the aid of a catalyst. Formation of the peptide bond in some water-air interface, in laboratory conditions of a very special nature, have produced peptide bonds, but it has yet to be demonstrated in a scenario comparable to that of the early Earth.[19] Factoring all these probabilities yields an overall probability as a product of each in individual probability calculus:

$$P_{protein} = (P_{100\ amino\ acids})(P_{chirality})(P_{peptide\ bond})$$
$$= 1/(20^{100} \text{ x } 2^{100} \text{ x } 2^{99})$$
$$= 1/[(1.3 \text{ x } 10^{130})(1.3 \text{ x} 10^{30})(6.3 \text{ x } 10^{29})]$$

18. Wintery Knight, "Doug Axe Explains Chance," para. 8.
19. Griffith and Vaida, "In Situ Observation."

$= 1/ 1 \times 10^{190}$

One chance in 10^{190}—that's one followed by 190 zeros, or
1,000,000,000,000,000,000,000,000,000,000,000,000,000,000,
000,000,000,000,000,000,000,000,000,000,000,000,000,000,000,
000,000,000,000,000,000,000,000,000,000,000,000,000,000,000,
000,000,000,000,000,000,000,000,000,000,000,000,000,000,000,
000,000,000,000

There have been rejoinders to these types of probability calculations on atheist websites, but they either mistakenly depend on a biochemical predestination type of approach (i.e., physical chemical laws are sufficient to direct protein sequence and tremendously increase the probability) or posit some type of step-by-step scenario that has few or no empirical facts to support it. One other critical challenge against these probability calculations is that the possibility of simultaneous trials is ignored. This argument states that in the vast oceans of primordial soup, simultaneous "trials" are occurring and therefore one is bound to create a protein in a random process.

This last objection is a fair point. So, let us explore that objection using the following thought experiment. Suppose we could take all the oceans of the primordial Earth and seed them with a maximum concentration of all twenty amino acids. To increase the chances that the peptide bond forms at water-air interfaces, we shall create aerosol droplets with a diameter of 10μm (ten millionths of a meter). We can calculate the number of aerosol droplets if the entire ocean volume was aerosolized, and each droplet becomes a separate "droplet chamber" for reactions.[20] The number of droplet chambers turns out to be 3.8×10^{33} droplets. If each droplet has the maximum concentration of amino acids (1.3 molar is the average solubility of amino acids), then the number of amino acids in a single droplet is 400×10^9 (~four hundred billion). The experimentally determined rate of protein synthesis in the bacteria *E. coli* is fifteen amino acids per second.[21] For the following example, let us be generous and increase that speed to an even twenty amino acids per second. This means that a single one-hundred-amino-acid polypeptide can be generated in five seconds. It works out that each droplet could conduct four billion trials in five seconds. Multiply that by the total number of droplets on Earth and you have (4×10^9 trials/drop) (3.8×10^{33} drops) = 1.5×10^{43} trials in five seconds. Pretty impressive, eh?

We theoretically need to do 10^{190} trials, so at the same rate we have:

1.8×10^{44} simultaneous trials in one minute
1.1×10^{46} simultaneous trials in one hour

20. 2×10^{21} liters. Dong et al., "Constraining the Volume."

21. Talkad et al., "Evidence for Variable Rates," 299.

2.6×10^{47} simultaneous trials in one day
9.5×10^{49} simultaneous trials in one year
9.5×10^{55} simultaneous trials in one million years
9.5×10^{57} simultaneous trials in one hundred million years—we are nowhere even close to 10^{190}, and already one hundred million years have passed
9.5×10^{58} simultaneous trials in *one billion years*
1.2×10^{60} simultaneous trials in thirteen billion years (the age of the universe)

This is still 130 orders of magnitude away from the 10^{190} trials needed, and this is for just *one protein*! The minimum number of proteins estimated for the simplest cell is approximately 470 proteins of various lengths.[22]

Andreas Wagner, who happens to be an evolutionary biologist, presents a similar scenario using the sum total of bacterial cells on the Earth as individual "reaction chambers." In this thought experiment, Wagner concludes that for the creation of the correct metabolic sequence out of a possible 10^{1500} sequences, working to make one sequence every second, all the bacteria in the world (5×10^{30} bacteria) working on the problem simultaneously could not get the job even close to being done, even given four billion years (the length of time bacteria have been around)![23]

It seems obvious that any random process is inadequate to generate a specific, one-hundred-amino acid sequence in even the most generous framework of time. Moreover, any appeal to natural selection as the guiding force leading to complexity misses the idea that natural selection requires *something to select*. If you cannot achieve something that has a function that is selectable, then these molecules will simply succumb to the ravages of degradation by their environment. If you are working with a random process, there's *no chance*.

NO WAY!

In the business of real estate, the adage is, "Location! Location!! Location!!!" Similarly in science, the adage should be, "Mechanism! Mechanism!! Mechanism!!!" Anyone can propose an explanation for a phenomenon, but the critical aspect is proposing a plausible pathway of just *how* the phenomenon could come about. As early as the 1920s, Alexander Oparin and John B. S. Haldane independently wrote about what might be required for the so-called "primordial soup." They speculated on the types of chemical reactions

22. Fraser et al., "Minimal Gene Complement," 397, 400.
23. Wagner, *Arrival of the Fittest*, 92–93.

necessary to produce the basic building blocks of life. From that beginning, each scenario had huge caveats and insurmountable problems, both chemically and geologically, that were firmly based on scientific principles and the evidence at hand. What follows are the four leading scenarios, speculating on the necessary conditions for the origin of life.

The Prebiotic Formation of Amino Acids and the Primordial Soup

In what may have been the kick-starter for modern origin-of-life research, the famous Miller-Urey paper, "A Production of Amino Acids under Possible Primitive Earth Conditions," demonstrated an abiotic process resulting in the formation of amino acids. At the same time, Stanley Miller, a graduate student in the laboratory of his mentor Harold Urey, speculated that his approximation of early Earth's atmospheric and chemical conditions seemed compatible with the primordial soup theory in which organic molecules could be made, gradually collect, and form complex molecules leading to the first cell. In the following decade however, geologists concluded that the atmospheric conditions outlined by Miller were completely different, and under these revised conditions, no amino acids were observed.

Although there has been a great deal of well-justified criticism about the experiment and its relevance to the origin of life from the composition of the early atmosphere to the implications of the work, Miller deserves recognition for bringing the speculative theory of chemical evolution into the realm of empirical investigation.[24] His approach is widely accepted as groundbreaking. The Miller experiment was viewed by many as having solved the mystery of the origin of life. In a 2012 *Scientific American* article commemorating the discovery, science journalist John Horgan wrote that "Miller's results seem to provide stunning evidence that life could arise out of . . . the primordial soup."[25] This popular notion was also promoted in textbooks for decades as strong evidence that life began spontaneously from prebiotic chemicals.

However, the reality is far from this popular characterization. To think that the observation of the abiotic production of amino acids is even close to solving the origin of life with all its interwoven complexity is likened to seeing concrete solidify and hailing this as the discovery of the origin of the Empire State Building. The amino acids produced in Miller's system (1)

24. Bruce Watson, quoted in News Staff, "Early Earth's Atmosphere," para. 3; Dimroth and Kimberley, "Precambrian Atmospheric Oxygen"; Luskin, "Top Ten Scientific Problems," paras. 6–12.

25. Horgan, "Stanley Miller and Quest," para. 3.

cannot associate into any ordered amino acid sequence necessary to make up a protein, (2) cannot form the peptide bond link necessary to form the actual protein, (3) cannot overcome the problem of chemical "handedness" (i.e., chirality), (4) do not address the formation of lipid membranes to encapsulate any potential biological contents, and (5) have no mechanism for self-replication. Moreover, in an analysis of the Miller-Urey experiment, one group concluded that Miller's results were due to contaminants from the borosilicate glassware that contained the reactions. Criado-Reyes et al. showed that when the Miller experiment was replicated in Teflon vessels, amino acids were not produced unless particles of borosilicate (the glass component) was introduced into the vessels, thus acting as a catalyst for the generation of the amino acids.[26] This revelation would suggest that the conditions for a successful Miller-Urey experiment were even further removed from the actual environment of the early Earth. Therefore, this classic example of the origin of life is so far from its public perception that it bears little to no relevance for the problem of the origin of life.

The RNA World

At the time of the Miller-Urey experiment, the "protein-first" or "DNA-first" conundrum was hotly debated. It became clear that DNA housed the genetic code by which proteins were made. However, it was also quite clear that proteins were needed for DNA to replicate itself. The question of which macromolecule came first in the early development of life on Earth presented few clues to the solution. Enter the RNA molecule. In the 1960s, research on the nature and function of RNA showed it to be a molecule capable of storing information in a fashion similar to DNA and able to perform enzymatic functions similar to protein enzymes. The RNA world theory was proposed as the "missing link" that enabled life to form. The Achilles heel to this theory is the inherent instability of RNA. Even in tightly constrained laboratory conditions, RNA is known for its labile nature. RNA is extremely sensitive to low (acidic) and high (alkaline) pH conditions. Since it is normally single stranded, it is also vulnerable to environmental conditions, unlike double-stranded DNA. The half-life (the longevity of a molecule) is considerably short, leading Miller to conclude that RNA would not have been a very strong candidate leading to the origin of life. In fact, in a 1998 study conducted by Miller on the half-lives of all five nucleic acid bases (ACGTU), he found that none of them had sufficient half-lives

26. Criado-Reyes et al., "Role of Borosilicate Glass."

to accumulate enough to take part in formation of either DNA or RNA.[27] Robert Shapiro notes that, among all the nucleotide bases, cytosine (C) was the most problematic base to form, and the synthesis of cytosine is fraught with a number of unproductive side reactions. Shapiro concludes, "On the basis of this evidence, it appears quite unlikely that cytosine played a role in the origin of life."[28] It seems that, although the RNA world hypothesis is still greatly favored by many scientists, the inherent physical and chemical nature of RNA itself disqualifies it as a plausible path to life.

"No Soup for You!" or Does Clay Set the Stage for Life?

The trope of the "primordial soup" has been used in origin-of-life writings since the time of Darwin. However, the evidence for a concentrated ocean of prebiotic molecules is sorely lacking. Geochemists Brooks and Shaw reasoned that Precambrian deposits would have left evidence of nitrogenous compounds, but none were observed.[29] An additional problem with the primordial soup concept is the unfavorable thermodynamic conditions for monomers to form the all-important biopolymers such as proteins and nucleic acids.

With the primordial soup off the table, so to speak, scientists proposed that a certain special clay material, montmorillonite, could serve as a prebiotic scaffold to facilitate the joining of amino acids via the formation of the peptide bond. Indeed, peptide bond formation can be observed under very exacting laboratory conditions using particular clay materials. Investigators have also proposed this as the mechanism by which RNA strands were produced. However, there are also a considerable number of unwanted, occurring reactions that detract from the desired products, and there is no way to concentrate or compartmentalize these desirable products to protect them from chemical degradation. Furthermore, in both the primordial soup and clay models, there is no way to produce any ordered sequence necessary for a functional molecule. We are left with random sequences at best, and yet, to depend on a random process to generate sequences that convey a function of any kind is highly unlikely, to put it in the most charitable terms.

27. Levy and Miller, "Stability of RNA Bases."

28. Shapiro, "Prebiotic Cytosine Synthesis," 4396.

29. Brooks, *Origins of Life*, 118.

Hydrothermal Vents

In 1979, the robotic deep-sea submersible *Alvin* discovered the first deep-sea biosphere near undersea volcanic "hydrothermal vents." Here it is said that the high temperatures could provide the necessary energy to drive chemical reactions, and the basic compounds found in these areas could cause nearby molecules of iron, sulfur, and carbon to combine into primitive prebiotic components necessary for the life. Although this notion is still quite popular today, it has some serious problems. First, the extreme temperatures make it difficult for newly formed molecules to last. As noted earlier, many of these biological molecules have very short half-lives, and energetic environments such as thermal vents would only make things worse for their stability. Again, we are in a watery environment, making any dehydration reaction virtually impossible for the polymerization of monomers. Early observations of life in these extreme biospheres have noted living organisms (e.g., giant tube worms), especially bacteria (e.g., *Thermus aquaticus*) that thrive in these elevated temperatures.[30] However, these organisms have highly specialized adaptations that allow them to live in these environments. Their DNA is protected by specialized proteins that have unique sequences that allow the proteins to maintain their three-dimensional shape and function at high temperatures. Rather than observing simple organisms, we are met with even more complexity. After assessing these popular ideas of how the origin of life could have occurred, there is simply no pathway, no mechanism—*no way* life could have evolved chemically.

WHAT MY ARGUMENT IS NOT

Many scientists admit that we may never know how the naturalistic origin of life occurred. At the end of the Symposium Origin of Life (SYOL) at UCSD in 2011, it was concluded that, "in spite of huge scientific progress and increased interdisciplinary culture, self-replicating chemical systems remain difficult to grasp. The spontaneous emergence of the biological molecular code remains mysteriously hidden."[31] My argument is certainly not a "god of the gaps" argument. I am not appealing to ignorance. I do not invoke a creator to say that "we do not know, therefore God did it." Cosmological and geological time lines reveal a very small fraction of time for the origin of

30. *Thermus aquaticus* is where we get the enzyme that makes the polymerase chain reaction (PCR) work, so we can thank this hydrothermal vent denizen for making paternity tests, Ancestry.com, COVID tests, and CSI possible.

31. Jacobs et al., "Symposium Origin of Life," introduction.

life to occur. There are a huge number of chemical and molecular tasks to be successfully accomplished within this time, and the conditions that satisfy them are often mutually exclusive. In a laboratory, scientists can separate conditions and purify products, but not in nature. Complex polymeric biomolecules cannot self-assemble randomly into sequences having a biological function, and even so, the same forces that would allow their formation also destroy them just as easily. This argument against the naturalistic origin of life is not based on ignorance but rather solidly based on what we know about the physical, chemical, and molecular properties and behaviors of what is necessary to assemble a living cell. These are intractable problems no matter which naturalistic theory you consider.

PERHAPS, ONE WAY?

Molecular biologist and codiscoverer of the structure of DNA Francis Crick is often quoted in apologetics writings, saying, "An honest man, armed with all the knowledge available to us now, could only state that in some sense, the origin of life appears at the moment to be almost a miracle, so many are the conditions which would have had to have been satisfied to get it going." When this quotation is cited by many apologists, the apologists usually stop there. To be fair, the rest of Crick's thought needs to be heard (here comes the "but"):

> But this is not to be taken to imply that there are good reasons to believe that it could not have started on the earth by a perfectly reasonable sequence of fairly ordinary chemical reactions. The plain fact is that the time available was too long, the many microenvironments on the earth's surface too diverse, the various chemical possibilities too numerous and our own knowledge and imagination too feeble to allow us to be able to unravel exactly how it might or might not have happened such a long time ago, especially as we have no experimental evidence from that era to check our ideas against.[32]

It is evident that Crick was no fan of miracles. He quickly steers away from that notion by appealing to a host of unknown factors such as "fairly ordinary chemical reactions" (which he does not specify); "diverse," unspecified microenvironments; "too numerous" chemical possibilities; and finally the limitations of our own knowledge and imagination. My question is, who is appealing to ignorance now? Is this not a "*science* of the gaps" argument?

32. Crick, *Life Itself*, 88.

The origin of the genetic code, a key feature to the origin of life, remains unsolved. William Dembski writes that no natural causes give rise to what he calls complex specified information, of which the genetic code is an example.[33] Given that life arose so quickly, and that there is no law, physical or otherwise, nor random process to generate the amount of information embedded in DNA, the inference to a mind as the origin and design of life seems reasonable and, in light of all the physical and chemical caveats, even plausible. It seems perfectly reasonable to believe that an intelligent creator would be responsible for the origin of life, and conversely therefore, the origin of life points to the existence of a creator.

If there were an ideological armada defending naturalism, evolution would certainly be its flagship vessel. At the higher levels of academia, mechanisms of evolution are hotly debated; nevertheless, in popular culture, evolution itself is vigorously taught as an unassailable fact. This chapter challenges this notion by defining the actual amount of time available for a specific aspect of evolution, and knowing the properties and behaviors of the molecular components and events required for the origin of life and subsequent evolution to take place, we can reasonably conclude that it is extremely unlikely—nearly impossible—for life to have originated unaided, randomly, and without design. If the time for these events is shown to be prohibitive, and the currently proposed mechanisms of abiogenesis are fraught with untenable problems, then the flagship of naturalism sinks even before its launch.

33. Dembski, "Intelligent Design," para. 43.

Bibliography

Bell, Elizabeth A., et al. "Potentially Biogenic Carbon Preserved in a 4.1-Billion-Year-Old Zircon." *PNAS* 112 (Oct. 2015) 14518–21.

Bottke, William F., and Marc D. Norman. "The Late Heavy Bombardment." *Annual Review of Earth and Planetary Sciences* 45 (Aug. 2017) 619–47.

Brooks, J. *Origins of Life*. Kidderminster, UK: Lion, 1985.

Costello, Mark J., et al. "Can We Name Earth's Species before They Go Extinct?" *Science* 339 (Jan. 2013) 413–16.

Criado-Reyes, Joaquín, et al. "The Role of Borosilicate Glass in Miller-Urey Experiment." *Scientific Reports* 11 (Oct. 2021). https://www.nature.com/articles/s41598-021-00235-4.

Crick, Francis. *Life Itself: Its Origin and Nature*. London: Touchstone, 1982.

Dalrymple, G. Brent. "The Age of the Earth in the Twentieth Century: A Problem (Mostly) Solved." *Geological Society London Special Publications* 190 (Jan. 2001) 205–21.

Dawkins, Richard. *The Blind Watchmaker: Why the Evidence of Evolution Reveals a Universe without Design*. London: Norton and Co., 2015.

Dembski, William. "Intelligent Design as a Theory of Information." Access Research Network, 1998. www.ARN.org/docs/dembski/wd_idtheory.htm.

Dickerson, Richard E. "Chemical Evolution and the Origin of Life." *Scientific American* 239 (Sept. 1978) 70–87. https://www.scientificamerican.com/article/chemical-evolution-and-the-origin-o/.

Dimroth, Eric, and Michael M. Kimberley. "Precambrian Atmospheric Oxygen: Evidence in the Sedimentary Distributions of Carbon, Sulfur, Uranium, and Iron." *Canadian Journal of Earth Sciences* 13 (Sept. 1976) 1161–85.

Dodd, Matthew S., et al. "Evidence for Early Life in Earth's Oldest Hydrothermal Vent Precipitates." *Nature* 543 (Mar. 2017) 60–64. https://www.nature.com/articles/nature21377.

Dong, Junjie, et al. "Constraining the Volume of Earth's Early Oceans with a Temperature-Dependent Mantle Water Storage Capacity Model." *AGU Advances* 2 (Mar. 2021). https://agupubs.onlinelibrary.wiley.com/doi/pdfdirect/10.1029/2020AV000323.

Forterre, Patrick. "Displacement of Cellular Proteins by Functional Analogues from Plasmids or Viruses Could Explain Puzzling Phylogenies of Many DNA Informational Proteins." *Molecular Microbiology* 33 (Aug. 1999) 457–65.

Fraser, C. M., et al. "The Minimal Gene Complement of *Mycoplasma Genitalium*." *Science* 270 (Oct. 1995) 397–403.

Griffith, Elizabeth C., and Veronica Vaida. "In Situ Observation of Peptide Bond Formation at the Water-Air Interface." *PNAS* 109 (Aug. 2012) 15697–701. https://www.pnas.org/doi/10.1073/pnas.1210029109.

Horgan, John. "Stanley Miller and the Quest to Understand Life's Beginning." *Scientific American*, July 2012. https://blogs.scientificamerican.com/cross-check/stanley-miller-and-the-quest-to-understand-lifes-beginning/.

Jacobs, Karin, et al. "Symposium Origin of Life (SYOL): Overview." Deutschen Physikalischen Gesellschaft, 2012. https://www.dpg-verhandlungen.de/year/2012/conference/berlin/static/syol.pdf.

Kenyon, Dean, and Gary Steinman. *Biochemical Predestination*. Chicago: McGraw-Hill, 1969.

"Lava." National Park Service, last updated May 5, 2021. https://www.nps.gov/havo/learn/nature/lava.htm.

Levy, M., and S. L. Miller. "The Stability of RNA Bases: Implications for the Origin of Life." *PNAS* 95 (July 1998) 7933–38. https://www.pnas.org/doi/full/10.1073/pnas.95.14.7933.

Luskin, Casey. "The Top Ten Scientific Problems with Biological and Chemical Evolution." Discovery Institute, Feb. 2015). https://www.discovery.org/a/24041/.

Meyer, Stephen C. *Signature in the Cell: DNA and the Evidence for Intelligent Design.* New York: HarperOne, 2009.

Miller, Stanley L. "A Production of Amino Acids under Possible Primitive Earth Conditions." *Science* 117 (May 1953) 528–29. https://www.science.org/doi/10.1126/science.117.3046.528.

News Staff. "Early Earth's Atmosphere Was Similar to Present—Day One." *Science News*, Nov. 2011. https://www.sci.news/geology/early-earth%E2%80%99s-atmosphere-was-similar-to-present-day-one.html.

Orgel, Leslie E. "The Origin of Life—How Long Did It Take?" *Origins of Life and the Evolution of the Biosphere* 28 (1998) 91–96.

Robertson, Michael P., and Gerald F. Joyce. "Highly Efficient Self-Replicating RNA Enzymes." *Chemistry & Biology* 21 (Feb. 2014) 238–45. https://www.sciencedirect.com/science/article/pii/S1074552113004262?via%3Dihub.

Shapiro, Robert. "Prebiotic Cytosine Synthesis: A Critical Analysis and Implications for the Origin of Life" *PNAS* 96 (Apr. 1999) 4396–401. https://www.pnas.org/doi/10.1073/pnas.96.8.4396.

Shklovskii, I. J., and Carl Sagan. *Intelligent Life in the Universe*. San Francisco: Holden-Day, 1966.

Sleep, Norman H. "The Hadean-Archean Environment." *CSH Perspectives* 2 (June 2010) 1–14.

Talkad, Venugopal, et al. "Evidence for Variable Rates of Ribosome Movement in *Escherichia Coli*." *Journal of Molecular Biology* 104 (June 1976) 299–303.

Wagner, Andreas. *Arrival of the Fittest: Solving Evolution' Greatest Puzzle*. London: Oneworld, 2015.

Wintery Knight. "Doug Axe Explains the Chance of Getting a Functional Protein by Chance." Wintery Knight, Aug. 5, 2012. https://winteryknight.com/2012/08/05/doug-axe-explains-the-chances-of-getting-a-functional-protein-by-chance-2/.

Three Types of Cosmological Arguments

PHIL FERNANDES[1]

IN 2004, MY "NEW Jersey buddy" Frank Turek and my former professor, the late Norman Geisler, coauthored their influential book *I Don't Have Enough Faith to Be an Atheist*. This book continues to be one of the finest introductions to Christian apologetics (i.e., the defense of the Christian faith) in print. Since then, Frank Turek has established himself as one of the nation's leading apologists for the Christian faith, and that book has sold more than 300,000 copies. Frank has lectured on apologetic issues throughout the world and trained multitudes of Christian apologists in the past few decades.

In Geisler and Turek's book, the authors present a robust defense of the Christian faith, arguing for the existence of truth and man's ability to know it, the existence of the theistic God (i.e., the personal, infinite, eternal Creator God), the possibility of miracles, the historical reliability of the New Testament, the reality of Jesus's resurrection and deity, and the inspiration and inerrancy of the Bible.[2] They argue from objective moral laws to the existence of a supreme moral Lawgiver.[3] They offer their readers two separate forms of teleological arguments—the argument for God from design. The first argues from the design in the universe to God as the intelligent Designer.[4] The second argues from the complexity and order found in simple and

1. Though Frank Turek and I both grew up in New Jersey, we met each other in North Carolina near Southern Evangelical Seminary. I consider him a dear friend and a brother in the Lord. I am eternally thankful for him and all the work he does.

2. Geisler and Turek, *I Don't Have Enough*, 33.

3. Geisler and Turek, *I Don't Have Enough*, 169–73.

4. Geisler and Turek, *I Don't Have Enough*, 95–112.

complex life forms to the existence of God as the Designer of life.[5] Geisler and Turek also utilize the cosmological argument, primarily the Kalam cosmological argument, which argues that the fact that the universe had a beginning means it must have a cause.[6] In this chapter, I will discuss the Kalam cosmological argument used by Geisler and Turek alongside two additional types of cosmological arguments. In doing so, this chapter offers readers with a variety of defenses from cosmology in favor of the existence of God.

At its core, the cosmological argument for the existence of God reasons for the existence of God from the existence of the universe or some being in the universe.[7] This argument begins with the facts of experience and concludes that there must be a cause or reason to explain these facts. There are three distinct types of cosmological arguments. Thomas Aquinas (1225–1274) based his form of the argument on the principle of existential causality (all limited, dependent existence needs an unlimited, necessary cause for its continuing existence).[8] Bonaventure (1221–1274) employed the Kalam cosmological argument (everything that has a beginning needs a cause).[9] Gottfried Wilhelm Leibniz (1646–1716), in his formulation of the cosmological argument, adopted the principle of sufficient reason (everything that exists must have an adequate explanation for why it exists).[10]

AQUINAS AND EXISTENTIAL CAUSALITY

Thomas Aquinas is most widely known for his five ways to prove God's existence.[11] In his first way, he argued from the observable movement or change in the universe to the existence of an unmoved Mover, writing:

> The first and more manifest way is the argument from motion. It is certain, and evident to our senses, that in the world some things are in motion. Now whatever is in motion is put in motion by another, for nothing can be in motion except it is in potentiality to that towards which it is in motion; whereas a thing moves inasmuch as it is in act. For motion is nothing else than the reduction of something from potentiality to actuality. But

5. Geisler and Turek, *I Don't Have Enough*, 113–69.

6. Geisler and Turek, *I Don't Have Enough*, 73–94.

7. Craig, *Apologetics*, 62.

8. Aquinas, *Summa Theologica*, 1.2.3; Craig, *Apologetics*, 63.

9. Bonaventure, *Commentary on Ecclesiastes*, 89–90; Moreland, *Scaling the Secular City*, 18.

10. Leibniz, *Monadology*, paras. 31–32; Craig, *Apologetics*, 65.

11. Aquinas, *Summa Theologica*, 1.3.1.

> nothing can be reduced from potentiality to actuality, except by something in a state of actuality. Thus that which is actually hot, as fire, makes wood, which is potentially hot, to be actually hot, and thereby moves and changes it. Now it is not possible that the same thing should be at once in actuality and potentiality in the same respect, but only in different respects. For what is actually hot cannot simultaneously be potentially hot; but it is simultaneously potentially cold. It is therefore impossible that in the same respect and in the same way a thing should be both mover and moved, i.e. that it should move itself. Therefore, whatever is in motion must be put in motion by another. If that by which it is put in motion be itself put in motion, then this also must needs be put in motion by another, and that by another again. But this cannot go on to infinity, because then there would be no first mover, and, consequently, no other mover; seeing that subsequent movers move only inasmuch as they are put in motion by the first mover; as the staff moves only because it is put in motion by the hand. Therefore it is necessary to arrive at a first mover, put in motion by no other; and this everyone understands to be God.[12]

Aquinas's second way reasons that the causality found in the universe demands the existence of a first, uncaused Cause. He writes:

> The second way is from the nature of the efficient cause. In the world of sense we find there is an order of efficient causes. There is no case known (neither is it, indeed, possible) in which a thing is found to be the efficient cause of itself; for so it would be prior to itself, which is impossible. Now in efficient causes it is not possible to go on to infinity, because in all efficient causes following in order, the first is the cause of the intermediate cause, and the intermediate is the cause of the ultimate cause, whether the intermediate cause be several, or only one. Now to take away the cause is to take away the effect. Therefore, if there be no first cause among efficient causes, there will be no ultimate, nor any intermediate cause. But if in efficient causes it is possible to go on to infinity, there will be no first efficient cause, neither will there be an ultimate effect, nor any intermediate efficient causes; all of which is plainly false. Therefore it is necessary to admit a first efficient cause, to which everyone gives the name of God.[13]

12. Aquinas, *Summa Theologica*, 1.3.1.

13. Aquinas, *Summa Theologica*, 1.3.1.

His third way concludes that the existence of an independent Being must be the cause for the continuing existence of all dependent beings:

> The third way is taken from possibility and necessity, and runs thus. We find in nature things that are possible to be and not to be, since they are found to be generated, and to corrupt, and consequently, they are possible to be and not to be. But it is impossible for these always to exist, for that which is possible not to be at some time is not. Therefore, if everything is possible not to be, then at one time there could have been nothing in existence. Now if this were true, even now there would be nothing in existence, because that which does not exist only begins to exist by something already existing. Therefore, if at one time nothing was in existence, it would have been impossible for anything to have begun to exist; and thus even now nothing would be in existence—which is absurd. Therefore, not all beings are merely possible, but there must exist something the existence of which is necessary. But every necessary thing either has its necessity caused by another, or not. Now it is impossible to go on to infinity in necessary things which have their necessity caused by another, as has been already proved in regard to efficient causes. Therefore we cannot but postulate the existence of some being having of itself its own necessity, and not receiving it from another, but rather causing in others their necessity. This all men speak of as God.[14]

The first three ways utilized by Aquinas to prove the existence of God are fundamentally cosmological arguments, and each exercises the principle of existential causality, which states that all possible, contingent existence needs a necessary, noncontingent cause for its continued existence. Unlike the first three, Aquinas's fourth and fifth ways to prove God's existence are not cosmological arguments. The fourth way—the limited perfections in other beings must be caused by the existence of a most perfect Being—could be classified as a moral argument, whereas his fifth way—mindless nature's movement toward specific goals implies the need for an intelligent Mind to guide these natural processes—is a teleological argument.[15]

The thrust of these first three arguments is as follows: experience demonstrates to humanity that limited, dependent beings exist. These limited, dependent beings need other beings to sustain their continued existence. For example, humans and animals depend on air, water, and food to sustain their existence. If any one of these things were removed from their lives,

14. Aquinas, *Summa Theologica*, 1.3.1.

15. Aquinas, *Summa Theologica*, 1.3.1.

both animals and humans would cease to exist. They are therefore *dependent* beings. Furthermore, Aquinas argues that adding limited, dependent beings together will never produce an unlimited and independent whole. Therefore, the sum total of limited, dependent beings (i.e., the universe) is itself limited and dependent. Hence, concludes Aquinas, the ultimate cause of the continuing existence of all limited, dependent beings must itself be unlimited and independent.

An alternative way to state this argument is that if everything that exists has the possibility of not existing, then, given enough time, nothing will exist in the future. This is because, given enough time, every possibility for nonexistence will eventually be actualized. But, this also means that if we were to go backwards in time we would eventually reach a point in which the same situation would have been obtained (i.e., the moment "before" the big bang). At both points, nothing would exist. But, since from nothing, nothing comes, something must have always existed without any possibility of nonexistence, in order to ground the continued existence of all beings that have the possibility of nonexistence. The Christian believes the biblical depiction of God identifies him as this necessary Being, a being with no possibility of nonexistence. This necessary Being is by definition unlimited and totally independent. It is a Being that cannot not exist—it must exist.

Aquinas further argues that there cannot be two or more unlimited and independent beings, since if there were, they would limit one another's existence; but then they would not be unlimited. Therefore, there can be only one unlimited and independent Being. Also, for two beings to differ, one of the beings must possess something the other being lacks or lack something the other being has. Like the first objection, this demonstrates that there cannot be two or more unlimited beings. For a Being to be unlimited, it must have every possible perfection and must have each of these perfections to an unlimited degree. But, for another being to differ from this unlimited Being, it would have to lack at least one of the perfections or have at least one of the perfections to a less than unlimited degree. If this being differs from the unlimited Being in any way, it would not itself be unlimited. Again, only one unlimited Being can exist—there cannot be two or more unlimited Beings.

Additionally, this unlimited Being must have all its attributes in an unlimited way. Otherwise, it would not be an unlimited Being. This Being must be all-powerful, for it would be the source of all the power in the universe. No other power can limit it. It must be eternal, for it is not limited by time. It must be everywhere present, since it is not limited by space. It must be immaterial, since it is not limited by matter. This Being must be all-good, since it is not limited by evil.[16] It must also be all-knowing, since it is not limited by ignorance.[17]

If we add Aquinas's teleological argument at this point, it serves to refine his cosmological defense even further. Since mindless nature works towards goals (such as acorns always becoming oak trees and not something else), there must be an intelligent Designer overseeing the natural processes. Without intelligent design, nature's processes would be left to chance, and orderly patterns, describable as natural laws, would not be observed. Therefore, this infinite and independent Being, upon whom all finite and dependent beings depend for their continued existence, must be an intelligent Being.[18] Christian philosopher Norman Geisler was a modern proponent of Aquinas's cosmological argument and the use of the principle of existential causality.[19] Winfried Corduan, another contemporary Christian philosopher, also employs this type of cosmological argumentation in his writings, both finding this classical approach to be thoroughly convincing.[20]

BONAVENTURE AND THE KALAM COSMOLOGICAL ARGUMENT

Saint Bonaventure utilized the Kalam cosmological argument for God's existence, arguing that whatever began to exist must have a cause.[21] He believed that it could be proven that the universe had a beginning, and therefore concluded that the universe must have a cause.[22] Both Bonaventure and Aquinas believed that the universe had a beginning, and being theologians rather than scientists, they accepted this because it was taught in the Bible. However, they differed in that while Aquinas did not believe this could be proven philosophically, Bonaventure did. While Aquinas argued in favor of a sustaining cause of the universe (existential causality), Bonaventure argued in favor of a cause for the beginning of the universe (i.e., the Kalam cosmological argument).[23]

16. The concept of evil as a privation of good can be found in the Greek church as well, in the writings of Origen, Basil the Great, Athanasius, and Gregory of Nyssa. Hick, *Evil and the God*, 47.

17. Geisler, *Thomas Aquinas*, 103–35; Geisler, *Christian Apologetics*, 237–59.

18. Aquinas, *Summa Theologica*, 1.2.3.

19. Geisler, *Christian Apologetics*, 237–59.

20. Corduan, *Reasonable Faith*, 102–21.

21. Moreland, *Scaling the Secular City*, 18.

22. Copleston, *Medieval Philosophy*, 251–52.

23. Copleston, *Medieval Philosophy*, 262–65.

Bonaventure contended that if the universe had no beginning, then there would exist an actual infinite set of events in time. However, he reasoned that an actual infinite set is impossible. If an actual infinite set were possible, then contradictions would be generated, and contradictory situations cannot be true. For example, let's say that there are two sets of numbers. Set A contains all possible even numbers, making it infinite. Set B contains all possible even *and* odd numbers. Set B would then contain twice as many members as Set A; still, Set A and Set B are equal because they are both infinite. Thus, the contradiction is evident. Bonaventure did not deny *potential* infinite sets, but he did deny infinite sets of *actual* things, such as actual events in time.[24]

Bonaventure also concluded that since it is impossible to traverse an actual infinite set, then the universe could not be eternal. It had to have a beginning. If the universe were eternal, consisting of an infinite regress of moments, one could never reach the present moment. For no matter how many moments one passes, one will never pass an infinite set of moments. But, if the universe were eternal, then there are an infinite set of moments in the past, and one would not be able to reach the present moment. However, since mankind has reached the present moment, it is proof that the universe had a beginning.[25]

LEIBNIZ AND SUFFICIENT REASON

Gottfried Wilhelm Leibniz articulated and promoted what is known as the principle of sufficient reason to argue for the existence of God. This principle states that there must be a sufficient reason or explanation for everything that exists. Many beings exist that do not contain in themselves the reason for their existence. For instance, a man depends on his parents for his birth, and he needs air and food for his continuing existence. Leibniz argued that there cannot be an infinite regress of explanations, because then there would be no explanation why anything exists at all. Therefore, reasoned Leibniz, something must exist that contains within itself the reason for its own existence. This Being explains not only its own existence but the existence of all else as well.[26] Leibniz was not claiming that God is self-caused, but that God is self-explained. God is the explanation for his own existence precisely because he is an uncaused Being.[27]

24. Copleston, *Medieval Philosophy*, 263.

25. Copleston, *Medieval Philosophy*, 264.

26. Copleston, *Modern Philosophy*, 324–25.

27. I disagree with Geisler and Corduan on this point. They consider only the

FOLLOW THE SCIENCE

In addition to this philosophical evidence, we now have strong scientific evidence for the beginning of the universe as well. Though not available in the days of Aquinas, Bonaventure, or even Leibniz, it can be used by contemporary apologists to strengthen or confirm cosmological arguments. Scientific evidence for the beginning of the universe includes the second law of thermodynamics (energy deterioration) and the big bang model.[28] The second law of thermodynamics is one of the most firmly established laws of modern science, stating that the amount of usable energy in the universe is running down.[29] This means that at some point in the finite future all available energy in the universe will become useless. In other words, if left to itself, the universe will reach an end. If the universe is going to have an end, it must have had a beginning. At one point in time, in the finite past, all the energy in the universe was usable. This point would mark the beginning of the universe. Additionally, if the universe is "winding down," it must originally have been "wound up." Hence, the universe is not eternal; it had a beginning. Since it had a beginning, it needs a cause. For from nothing, nothing comes.[30]

The big bang model also teaches that the universe had a beginning.[31] In 1929, astronomer Edwin Hubble discovered that the universe is expanding at the same rate in all directions, indicating that as time moves forward, the universe is growing apart.[32] This means that if one were to go back in time, the universe would gradually become increasingly small. Eventually, if one were to retreat far enough into the past, the entire universe would be what scientists call "a point of infinite density." This marks the beginning of the universe, often called the big bang.

In 1984, Christian philosopher William Lane Craig addressed two main attempts by modern scientists to refute the beginning of the universe. The first is the steady state model. This view holds that the universe had no

---

Thomistic cosmological argument using the principle of existential causality as successful. I find the arguments put forth by Geisler and Corduan against both the Kalam cosmological argument and the use of the principle of sufficient reason unconvincing. See Geisler and Corduan, *Philosophy of Religion*, 172–74. Geisler later changed his view concerning the Kalam cosmological argument and used it in *I Don't Have Enough Faith to Be an Atheist*.

28. Craig, *Apologetics*, 81, 88.

29. Geisler and Anderson, *Origin Science*, 117.

30. Moreland, *Scaling the Secular City*, 35–38.

31. Craig, *Apologetics*, 81–82.

32. Peacock, *Brief History of Eternity*, 83–85.

beginning but rather always existed in the same state. This view, which never gained wide acceptance in modern times, was largely discredited as early as 1965 when the background radiation of the universe was discovered. This radiation indicated that the universe was at one time in an extremely hot and dense state, and therefore had not existed throughout all eternity in a steady state.[33]

The second attempt to escape the beginning of the universe is the oscillating model. This model teaches that at some point during the universe's expansion, gravity will halt the expansion and pull everything back together again. From that point there will be another big bang. This process will be repeated over and over again throughout all eternity. Where the oscillating model fails is that there is no known principle of physics that would reverse the collapse of the universe into another big bang. Additionally, current scientific research has shown that the universe is not dense enough for gravity to pull it back together again. Even if it could be proven that several big bangs have occurred, the second law of thermodynamics would still require an initial big bang, which would still require a cause that meets the criteria established above.[34]

But what if the cause of the universe needs a cause? Could not an infinite chain of causes and effects exist, stretching backwards in time throughout all eternity? The answer is no, as it has already been shown that an actual infinite set of regresses is impossible. There had to be a first cause, and this cause must be uncaused. Nor could it be self-caused, because it is absurd to say that a being preexisted its own existence in order to cause its own existence.[35] Therefore, only an eternal, uncaused Cause can be the cause of the universe.

It must be remembered that arguments in favor of the existence of God do not function individually but as a collective. A cosmological argument may be insufficient on its own to provide a convincing case for some, and so, other arguments should be marshaled to strengthen the case. As was said above with Aquinas, the teleological and moral arguments for God's existence can be introduced to fortify the cosmological argument. Since intelligent life is found in the universe, the cause of the universe must be an intelligent Being. It has yet to be shown how intelligence could evolve from mindless nature, and since intelligence cannot come from non-intelligence, there again must be a source.[36]

33. Craig, *Apologetics*, 82–83.

34. Craig, *Apologetics*, 84–90.

35. Geisler, *Christian Apologetics*, 246.

36. Schaeffer, *Frances A. Schaeffer Trilogy*, 283.

Morality also exists in the universe. Without morality, there are no formal ways of speaking in terms of right and wrong. However, the moral judgments people make on a daily basis reveal that they believe in an objective standard of right and wrong. But nature is amoral. No one holds a rock morally responsible for tripping them. Lions are not put on trial for killing zebras. Apart from humans, there are no moral agents in the material world. Since nature is amoral but morality exists in the universe, morality must have a cause. Therefore, the cause of the universe must also be a moral Being.[37]

If morality is relative to the individual, then each person can decide for themselves what qualifies as right and wrong. For a large section of society, this is an attractive, even preferred approach. However, if morality is subject to the determination of the individual, it becomes impossible to objectively condemn the brutal actions of someone like Adolph Hitler. Society cannot serve as the cause or arbiter of moral laws, since societies often pass judgment on one another. One society, when judging another society, has no choice but to appeal to a moral authority that transcends all societies and to which all societies should conform. Only an absolute moral Lawgiver who is qualitatively transcendent to humanity and societies can be the cause of a moral law that transcends both and judges their actions. Therefore, the uncaused cause of the universe must be an intelligent and moral Being.[38]

FINDING COMMON GROUND

The cosmological argument for God's existence in any of its three forms—existential causality, Kalam, sufficient reason—is probably the strongest argument for God's existence. Still, non-Christians often reject that it proves God's existence. Much of this objection surrounds what is meant by "prove" and its use in the sciences. In many instance, something must be "proved" within a mathematical certainty, but the apologist, though drawing on scientific reasoning, is not attempting to prove God's existence in this way. In reality, very little (if anything) can be known by humans with mathematical certainty concerning the real world, and what the apologist is arguing is on the level of probability. While the existence of God is not something that can be demonstrated with mathematical certainty, it can be demonstrated from premises that are beyond reasonable doubt. The denial of these premises is often absurd, forced, or temporary. The premises can be viewed as actually

37. Lewis, *Mere Christianity*, 19, 26–29; Geisler and Anderson, *Origin Science*, 112–13.

38. Geisler, *Christian Apologetics*, 249.

undeniable, since each premise must be affirmed in any attempt to deny it. Therefore, God's existence can be proven with a high degree of probability or with actual undeniability, even if not with logical certainty.[39]

Probability arguments can be extremely convincing. The everyday decisions that one must make are rarely, if ever, based on certainty. They are instead based upon a high degree of probability. When a person drives over a cement bridge extended hundreds of feet above the ground, that person is implicitly trusting that the bridge will support the weight of their vehicle. This is not a blind and irrational faith but one built on observable and repeatable evidence for humanity's ability to build such structures. The person driving across the bridge is basing their faith on this available evidence, even though absolute certainty that the bridge will not crumble eludes them. In like manner, the existence of God can be proven with a high degree of probability. Because humanity is limited in knowledge and vulnerable to errors, their knowledge in many areas is necessarily limited and extends only to the realm of probability or actual undeniability (also known as existential necessity). Therefore, probability is the most anyone can hope for in relation to the certainty of God's existence. It should also be noted that a person may know something to be true with a high degree of probability, though they may not be able to prove it.[40] A suspect of a crime may know they are innocent yet not be capable of proving it. Similarly, many Christians know, with a high degree of probability, that God exists, though they cannot prove that he does.

Having said this, it is now necessary to show that the basic premises of the cosmological argument are beyond reasonable doubt. Once this is shown to be the case, the apologist and the nontheist should share common ground from which the apologist can argue for God's existence. This common ground (which forms the premises for the cosmological argument) consists of four factors: (1) the law of noncontradiction, (2) the law of causality, (3) the principle of analogy, and (4) the basic reliability of sense perception.[41] All people, whether theist or atheist, must live as if these four principles are true—even more, that they are actually undeniable.

39. Geisler and Feinberg, *Introduction to Philosophy*, 129–31; Geisler, *Christian Apologetics*, 239.

40. Moreland, *Scaling the Secular City*, 245.

41. Sproul et al., *Classical Apologetics*, 70–72.

The Law of Noncontradiction

The law of noncontradiction states that something cannot be both true and false at the same time and in the same way. If something is true, then its opposite must be false. If the nontheist attempts to deny the law of noncontradiction, they must first assume it to be true in order to make the denial. Otherwise, the opposite of the denial could also be true. Though a person may deny this law, they must live, speak, and think as though it is true.[42]

The Law of Causality

The law of causality states that everything that has a beginning needs a cause.[43] To deny this law is absurd. If the law of causality is not true, then something could be caused to exist by nothing. However, nothing is, well, nothing. Therefore, nothing can do nothing and can cause nothing. From nothing, nothing comes. If one rejects the law of causality, then there is no basis for modern science. Modern science must assume this law when attempting to discover the relationships that exist between the elements of the universe.[44]

The Principle of Analogy

The principle of analogy declares that two effects that are similar often have similar causes.[45] For instance, a watch shows tremendous design and complexity. So does the universe. In fact, a single-celled animal, which is an infinitesimally small part of the universe, has enough genetic information to fill an entire library.[46] Therefore, it seems reasonable to conclude that since it takes an intelligent being to make a watch, it must also have taken an intelligent being to design the universe. It seems rather unlikely—some would even say statistically impossible—that an entire library's worth of information could have evolved by chance. An intelligent designer is needed.

42. Sproul et al., *Classical Apologetics*, 72–82.

43. Craig, *Apologetics*, 74–75.

44. Sproul et al., *Classical Apologetics*, 82.

45. Geisler and Anderson, *Origin Science*, 69, 124.

46. Geisler and Anderson, *Origin Science*, 162.

The Basic Reliability of Sense Perception

Finally, the basic reliability of sense perception is accepted by theists and nontheists alike.[47] Though people are sometimes mistaken in the conclusions they draw from what their senses perceive, their sense perceptions can generally be trusted. All people live as though their sense perceptions are reliable. They move when rocks are thrown at them. They stand clear of railroad tracks when they hear the whistle of a coming train. Modern science must assume the basic reliability of sense perception in order to examine nature.

Any strong cosmological argument will be built upon these four presuppositions. Though the nontheist might deny these four presuppositions for the sake of argument, they must presuppose them in everyday life. They must live as if they were true. Any philosophy that cannot be lived—such as is the case with a consistent atheistic worldview—should not be believed. Though a person may verbally deny God's existence, they must still live as if the God of the Bible exists.

FIVE FINAL POINTS

First, after examining the theistic arguments, I believe it is evident that the strongest philosophical argument for the existence of God is some type of cosmological argument. However, this does not mean that the other arguments for God's existence have no place in apologetics. As was shown in this chapter, the moral and teleological arguments can be used very successfully to complete the cosmological argument.[48] Premises from the moral and teleological arguments are extremely valuable for unveiling some of the necessary attributes of the uncaused Cause.

Second, when using the Kalam cosmological argument, the Christian apologist should not argue against the existence of an actual infinite set. This is because the Christian believes that God is all-knowing (omniscient). This is usually understood to mean that God knows an actual infinite number of things. Therefore, an actual infinite set does exist, but only in the mind of God. So, the Christian apologist is technically incorrect, or at least inconsistent, when they argue against the existence of an actual infinite set. The Kalam cosmological argument for God's existence does not lose any force by merely arguing for the impossibility of traversing an actual

47. Sproul et al., *Classical Apologetics*, 71–72.

48. Geisler, *Christian Apologetics*, 247–49.

infinite set—something that Zeno's paradox proves.[49] That would be enough to prove that the universe had a beginning and therefore needs a Cause. Conversely, the apologist can simply argue for the impossibility of an actual infinite set existing outside the mind of an infinite God.[50]

Third, when doing apologetics, the Christian should adapt his or her argumentation to meet the personal needs of the listener. For some nontheists, psychological arguments for God's existence will be more persuasive. For others, philosophical arguments are more convincing. The goal of apologetics is to lead people to Christ. Therefore one's apologetics should be tailored to meet the needs of the listener.

Fourth, all defenders of the faith must remember that even if their argumentation is effective, the listener may still choose to suppress the truth. It is not easy for people to admit that a God exists to whom they must answer. The desire for human autonomy is incredibly strong. It is a desire that began in the garden of Eden, after all. Only the inward persuasion of the Holy Spirit, working, in this case, with apologetic argumentation, can convince the human will to accept the existence of the God of the Bible.[51]

Fifth, arguments for God's existence provide strong evidence for the existence of the theistic God. Hence, nontheistic worldviews are proven false through arguments for theism (i.e., belief in a personal, infinite God). Still, historical evidences are needed to show that Christianity is the one

49. Hemming, "Place of Zeno's Paradox," 926–28.

50. I discussed the rejection of this premise ("the impossibility of an actual infinite set") in a Nov. 1994 telephone conversation with Dr. J. P. Moreland, professor of philosophy at the Talbot School of Theology. Moreland used this premise in his book *Scaling the Secular City* and agreed that it is probably best to no longer use this premise in the Kalam cosmological argument, and that the premise of the impossibility of traversing an actual infinite set would be sufficient in establishing the beginning of the universe. Dr. Moreland also related that the premise of the Kalam cosmological argument could be changed to "the impossibility of an actual infinite set in the concrete (outside the mind) realm." This premise could be proven by showing the contradictions that would arise if actual infinite sets existed outside the mind. Some of these contradictions have already been discussed in this chapter. What the Christian should not argue for is the impossibility of an actual infinite set existing in the abstract (inside a mind) realm. For if an actual infinite set cannot exist in a mind, then God cannot know an actual infinite number of things. But, if an actual infinite set exists in a mind, this mind will have to be an infinite mind or omniscient mind. Only an infinite mind can know an infinite number of things. Since it is impossible to traverse an actual infinite set, finite minds will never know everything an infinite mind knows, even if the finite mind continues to learn more and more throughout eternity. Also, the impossibility of traversing an actual infinite set shows that God (the infinite mind) did not attain his knowledge of an infinite number of things by learning them one idea at a time. Instead, God knows an infinite number of things in one eternal glance or thought.

51. Craig, *Apologetics*, 18–27.

true theistic faith, as opposed to the other theistic faiths like Islam and the present-day form of Judaism.[52] This is exactly what Frank Turek has done throughout his decades-long ministry. Not content with merely providing evidence for a personal, infinite God, Turek provides power historical evidence that Jesus is God and Savior, and that the Bible is God's inerrant word. Frank Turek has paved the way for younger apologists by providing a strong case not only for God's existence but also for the truth of biblical Christianity. He has set an example for younger apologists to follow. May God bless his apologetics ministry for decades to come.

Bibliography

Aquinas, Thomas. *Summa Theologica*. Christian Classics Ethereal Library, n.d. https://ccel.org/ccel/aquinas/summa/summa.FP_Q2_A3.html.

Bonaventure. *Commentary on Ecclesiastes*. Translated by Roger J. Karris and Campion Murray. Saint Bonaventure, NY: Franciscan, 2005.

Copleston, Frederick. *Medieval Philosophy—From Augustine to Duns Scotus*. Vol. 2 of *A History of Philosophy*. Chadstone, Aus.: Image, 1993.

———. *Modern Philosophy—From Descartes to Leibniz*. Vol. 4 of *A History of Philosophy*. Chadstone, Aus.: Image, 1993.

Corduan, Winfried. *Reasonable Faith: Basic Christian Apologetics*. Nashville: Broadman and Holman, 1993.

Craig, William Lane. *Apologetics: An Introduction*. Chicago: Moody, 1984.

Geisler, Norman L. *Christian Apologetics*. Grand Rapids: Baker, 1976.

———. *Thomas Aquinas: An Evangelical Appraisal*. Eugene, OR: Wipf & Stock, 2003.

Geisler, Norman L., and J. Kerby Anderson. *Origin Science: A Proposal for the Creation-Evolution Controversy*. Grand Rapids: Baker, 1987.

Geisler, Norman L., and Winfried Corduan. *Philosophy of Religion*. 2nd ed. Eugene, OR: Wipf & Stock, 2003.

Geisler, Norman L., and Paul D. Feinberg. *Introduction to Philosophy: A Christian Perspective*. Grand Rapids: Baker, 1980.

Geisler, Norman L., and Frank Turek. *I Don't Have Enough Faith to Be an Atheist*. Wheaton, IL: Crossway, 2004.

Hemming, Laurence Paul. "The Place of Zeno's Paradox." *Environment and Planning D: Society and Space* 29 (Oct. 2011) 924–37.

Hick, John. *Evil and the God of Love*. 2nd ed. Hampshire, UK: Palgrave Macmillan, 1977.

Leibniz, Gottfried. *The Monadolagy and Other Philosophical Writings*. Translated by Robert Latta. Berkeley, CA: Franklin Classics, 2018.

Lewis, C. S. *Mere Christianity*. Nashville: Harper Collins, 2015.

Moreland, J. P. *Scaling the Secular City: A Defense of Christianity*. Grand Rapids: Baker Academic, 1987.

Peacock, Roy E. *A Brief History of Eternity: A Considered Response to Stephen Hawking's* A Brief History of Time. Wheaton, IL: Crossway, 1990.

52. Geisler, *Christian Apologetics*, 263–65; Geisler and Turek, *I Don't Have Enough*, 221–376.

Schaeffer, Francis. *The Francis A. Schaeffer Trilogy: The Three Essential Books in One Volume*. Wheaton, IL: Crossway, 1990.

Sproul, R. C., et al. *Classical Apologetics: A Rational Defense of the Christian Faith and a Critique of Presuppositional Apologetics*. Grand Rapids: Zondervan, 1984.

Philosophy

Indeed, you can't get away from philosophy. It's like logic. To deny it is to use it.

—Frank Turek, *Stealing from God*

A Life Well Lived: Sustaining Value in a Battle of Worldviews

ALEX MCELROY[1]

IN THE SUMMER OF 2018, I was speaking at the Youth Apologetics Conference (YAC) in Charlotte. Many speakers were included in that week, including Dr. Frank Turek. I knew that these young people had been inundated with evidence and effective methods of communication throughout the week, and as I was the closing speaker, I wanted to offer something else. I didn't want them to walk away from the week only knowing that God exists but wanted to ensure that they understood *why* this evidence matters and *why* God matters. I wanted them to understand that God's existence and his purpose are the only reasons we can live with hope.

1. Attending the CrossExamined Instructor Academy was a pivotal moment in my life. A year prior to attending my first of three trainings with Frank and the CIA team, I had seldom heard the word *apologetics*. As a result of my introduction to apologetics, in large part due to CrossExamined, I now run Proof for the Truth, an apologetics organization with the mission to help people enter into a confirmed, confident, and eternal relationship with the Source of all life and purpose. Through our annual conference, apologetics workshops, and YouTube channel, many people have grown in their ability to evangelize and disciple others. None of this would have been possible without the influence and guidance of Dr. Frank Turek.

Before attending Advanced CIA, I was at a low point financially and though I desperately wanted to participate, I simply could not afford the travel expenses or registration. The organization decided to pour into me and allowed me to attend. One attendee, without even having known me, allowed me to stay at his house with his family. I was later informed that my costs had been covered. I approached Frank, with tears in my eyes and gratitude in my heart, and assured him that I would repay them, but it was done. And Frank had done it. I will be eternally grateful for what I learned, for the generosity shown to me, and for the opportunity to apply all that I have learned to help others.

The Navy SEALs are known to be one of the most elite fighting forces on the planet. Their website details what is expected of potential SEALs and how prospective SEALs train. Concerning running, it reads:

> For running, your 1/4-mile interval pace should initially be about 4 seconds faster than your base pace. For example, if you recently completed a 1.5-mile run in 10:30 with a 1/4-mile base pace of 1:45 then your interval training pace should be about 1:41. For swimming, your 100-yard interval pace should initially be 2 seconds faster than your base. If you completed a 500-yard swim in 10:30 with a 100-yard base pace of 2:06 your intervals should be approximately 2:04.[2]

Additionally, "only up to 25 to 35 percent of those who enter SEAL training make it through the Basic Underwater Demolition training, known as BUD/S, and go on to become full members of the force and get their Trident pin, military sources said."[3]

The process is clearly and intentionally grueling, but there is hope. Hope exists because there is a destination or goal in mind for each potential SEAL who enters the training. Without hope, the percentage of people who could persevere to completion would be reduced even further. Likewise, human experience demonstrates the power of resiliency, perseverance, and hard work in achieving goals, but those characteristics do not ultimately matter without hope. Thankfully, the process of sanctification—becoming more like Christ—, in which God calls us to engage, is nowhere near as *physically* grueling as training to become a Navy SEAL.

That day at the conference, I wanted to show those young people why the evidence does not merely provide hope for eternity but hope in the here and now, born from a life imbued with purpose, and an understanding of our inherent, God-given value. But if true hope is something to be grasped, it must be grounded in something objective. Hope cannot simply be wishful thinking; it must be attached to a real possibility, whereas wishes are attached to only *potential* possibilities.

Meaning and purpose, if they are to be considered objective realities, must be rooted in an ontic referent—a reference point outside of humanity. In this chapter I propose that without inherent value (which can be sustained only in a theistic framework), life has no meaning, and without meaning there is no hope. The fact that Jesus provides a focal point for meaning is the springboard for us to arrive at purpose. By living out our purpose, which

2. See https://navyseals.com/2235/navy-seal-run-training/, lines 34–42.

3. Tahmincioglu, "Want to Be SEAL?," lines 16–19.

cannot be sustained in a naturalistic framework, we glorify and experience God and enjoy a meaningful life in a profound way.

THE SUSTAINING POWER OF TRUTH

Most worldviews would agree, at least in principle, that human beings have a real, inherent value. However, for a worldview to be consistent, it must be able to ground this value with evidence. In fact, without this inherent value of human beings, no discussion of meaning, purpose, or hope can even take place, because meaning and purpose constitute the arena in which human beings contribute to the world and in which Christians contribute to the kingdom of God. A worldview must be able to consistently answer the question of human value, because that foundational truth and meaning are inextricably linked. Without value, there is no meaning and without meaning there is no hope.

The *Oxford English Dictionary* defines hope as the expectation of something desired. An archaic definition, directly associated with its use in Scripture, defines hope as a "feeling of trust or confidence." This is how Paul uses "hope" in Rom 8:24a when he says, speaking of the coming eternal glory, "For in this hope we are saved." Associating hope with trust suggests that *true* hope, whether posited from a biblical, theological, or naturalistic perspective, must be connected to those things for which we can possess a reasonable expectation. Such an end—like Paul looked to—, infused with hope, should spur everyone into actively progressing towards that end.

As early as the nineteenth century, the state of Missouri has been known as the Show-Me State. United States Congressman Willard Duncan Vandiver popularized the sobriquet during a speech at a naval banquet in Philadelphia, saying, "I come from a state that raises corn and cotton and cockleburs and Democrats, and frothy eloquence neither convinces nor satisfies me. I am from Missouri. You have got to show me."[4] The slogan's meaning is clear: do not just tell me what you believe, show me through your actions. This same concept is deeply embedded in Scripture. The apostle James writes, "'But someone will say, 'You have faith, and I have works.' Show me your faith without works, and I will show you faith by my works" (Jas 2:18). True hope, or the feeling of trust or confidence that something expected, should dictate our actions. In Christian circles this is often said as "orthodoxy (right belief) should produce orthopraxy (right actions)." For Christians, the ultimate truth is personified in the incarnation of Jesus Christ (John 14:6). It is his message and his actions that provide the

4. "Why Is Missouri Called," lines 8–10.

template for Christian life. In this way, it is not enough for the Christian to grow in knowledge of propositional truth about Christ (i.e., knowledge of what he said and did) but to live that truth out in an incarnational way (e.g., in their daily lives). This is why I wanted the young people in the audience that day to be spurred to live out the hope they were growing to understand. Once you understand that the same value God gave you has been given to *all* people, that knowledge should be followed by action.

Consider one last analogy. In Chicago, we have a saying that there are two seasons: winter and construction season. Throughout the city, it seems like there is always a new house under development. There are construction vans in the alley behind my house and cranes lifting two-by-fours and drywall. Often, I am rerouted while driving because streets have been blocked off for the various construction projects taking place. Many of the new buildings have different aesthetics because they are constructed by a wide array of companies, but the one thing they all have in common is a strong foundation. Architects know that without a strong foundation, the roof doesn't matter. They could install the most beautiful kitchen fixtures and bathroom amenities, but without a strong foundation those things will come to ruin. If you are constructing a building, the structure is important, but the foundation is the *most* important. If a rock goes through the window, the window can be replaced; if there is a leak in the roof, the roof can be patched; but if there is a crack in the foundation, the building will be condemned.

When one sets about building their life and worldview, the only foundation that will sustain it is the truth. The truth, by its very nature, should be sound, logical, and justifiable. While most people would agree with that, how one determines what is true and the role truth plays in their life is where worldviews often diverge. A guiding principle in properly recognizing truth is the principle of logic, which the *Cambridge Dictionary* indicates is a "way of thinking, especially one that is reasonable and based on good judgment." An illogical foundation in one's life will not align with the truth, and the "building" of one's worldview will become unstable. For this reason, we must examine the ways in which we access and utilize logic in our search for truth.

THE SUSTAINING POWER OF LOGIC

There is a reason that calculus is not taught in the first grade. There is a logical progression of mathematical information, from addition, to subtraction, to algebra, and each step is necessary to grasp the inner workings of calculus. Similarly, there is a progression from learning how to formulate logical conclusions to identifying the necessary components that undergird the use of logic. In fact, the study of logic itself *requires* logic in order for it to function. Logically (no pun intended), one cannot reach logical conclusions regarding human value or where we can place our hope if our worldview cannot sustain our ability to use or understand logic in the first place. The foundational nature of logic is such that there can be only two options to explain its existence: humans were given the means to think and use logic, or we developed the means internally over time. Inherent value, as I said at the outset, can be consistently grounded only in a theistic worldview, like Christianity. This value is spurred on by hope that is informed by the truth of God's word. The foundation of truth is logic; therefore, we must examine which worldview best affirms the existence, use, and focus of logic—naturalism or Christianity.

Internal Structures of Logic

To reach valid conclusions, logic must necessarily be prior to understanding. However, many people assume certain facts that, although they are true, are not logically consistent with the worldview they espouse. To validate conclusions regarding what one knows about God, science, or any metaphysical realities, how those conclusions are reached must be philosophically sound. Unfortunately, most people have never examined the steps necessary to reach their conclusions, and this is where one's worldview stands or falls.

Philosophers J. P. Moreland and William Lane Craig write, "Logic is the study of the rules of reasoning. Although the word is often used colloquially as a synonym for something like 'common sense' logic is, in fact, a highly technical subdiscipline of philosophy akin to mathematics." There are nine rules of logic. An example of two such rules is modus ponens and modus tollens. Modus ponens—Latin for "method of putting by placing"—is a rule of logic that is often misused in conversation due to an ignorance of the formal philosophical language that makes up the rule. The basic premise of the rule is that "from the two premises P → Q and P, we may validly conclude Q."[5] This means that claim P and claim Q are in a relationship such that if P is true, then Q follows. For example:

1. If Grace practices daily, she will learn to ride a bike. (P)
2. Grace practices daily. (Q)

5. Moreland and Craig, *Philosophical Foundations*, 28.

3. Grace will learn to ride a bike. (P→Q)

Modus tollens—Latin for "method of removing by taking away"—works in a similar fashion but with negative statements. "The rule *modus tollens* tells us that from these two premises, we may validly conclude 'Not-P.'"[6] In other words, claim P and claim Q are in a relationship wherein if P is not accomplished, Q will not follow. For example:

1. If Grace practices daily, she will learn to ride a bike. (Not-P)
2. Grace cannot ride a bike. (Not-Q)
3. Grace has not been practicing daily. (Not-P→Not-Q)

One well-known modus ponens argument is the Kalam cosmological argument. This was presented at the YAC and exposed those young people to logical reasons for affirming the existence of God. This allowed them to engage God more sincerely and authentically, so that they could live out the purpose of their Creator. Thinking properly provides more than a defense against unsound arguments; it provides the freedom to live consistently and truthfully—which affirms our inherent value.

Laws of Logic

To sustain human value grounded in something beyond the self, three primary laws of logic are necessary: the law of noncontradiction, the law of identity, and the law of the excluded middle. However, before discussing these laws we must understand two terms and the difference between them: ontology and epistemology.

Ontology focuses on the nature of existence itself, or the general features that are true of all things, and the classifying or grouping of things "that exist in various ways ranging from very specific to very broad types of classification."[7] *Epistemology*, on the other hand, is the study of how we know what we know. "Epistemology is the branch of philosophy that tries to make sense out of knowledge, rationality, and justified or unjustified beliefs. The term epistemology comes from the Greek word ἐπιστήμη (*epistēmē*), which means "knowledge."[8] For example, you most likely are reading this in a book. The book is the ontological reality. How you came to know what a book is stems from epistemology.

6. Moreland and Craig, *Philosophical Foundations*, 28.

7. Moreland and Craig, *Philosophical Foundations*, 161.

8. Moreland and Craig, *Philosophical Foundations*, 61.

Epistemology seeks to determine how one can accurately and objectively arrive at the truth, but for epistemology to exist, truth, in an objective sense, must also exist. Frank Turek writes, "All truths exclude their opposites. . . . Truth is discovered, not invented. It exists independent of anyone's knowledge of it."[9] Therefore, to claim that everything is true is a self-refuting statement in the same way that claiming nothing is true is self-refuting.

This introduces the first law of logic, which is the law of noncontradiction. It states, "P cannot be both true and false at the same time in the same sense."[10] Statements that refute each other cannot be true both at the same time and in the same sense. The statement "I am reading" and the statement "I am not reading" cannot be true simultaneously.

The law of the excluded middle is similar but different in its assertion. It states that P must be either true or false, meaning that when two competing propositions are presented, one of them must be necessarily true.[11] In essence, there is no middle option.

The law of identity, the most basic of the three laws, states, "P is identical to P."[12] It seems obvious, but the law of identity must be stated in order to prevent the logical fallacy of equivocation. Moreland writes, "This is the fallacy of using a word in such a way as to have two meanings. This fallacy is committed in the following argument: 'Socrates is a Greek; Greek is a language; therefore, Socrates is a language.'"[13] It is easy to see how misappropriating terminology can lead to inconsistent and nonsensical conclusions. Now we must see how this directly informs our understanding of human value.

Some years ago, when my eldest daughter was around five years old, she, my wife Kasie, and I were waiting for my father-in-law to come to the car so that we could go on our trip to the zoo. My wife took her phone and placed it near her mouth and began to speak sentences that she was communicating to her dad in the voice-to-text feature of the phone. Kasie said, "Hey. Comma. We are in the parking lot to the left. Period." Upon entering the car, my daughter said to her grandfather, "Hey, Comma!" Once we figured out her confusion at thinking that was some sort of nickname for grandpa, we all died laughing. Although my daughter was familiar with cell phones, she was unfamiliar with the voice-to-text feature. There was a piece of prior knowledge missing for her, which led her to the incorrect

9. Geisler and Turek, *I Don't Have Enough*, 37.

10. Moreland and Craig, *Philosophical Foundations*, 173.

11. Moreland and Craig, *Philosophical Foundations*, 173.

12. Moreland and Craig, *Philosophical Foundations*, 173.

13. Moreland and Craig, *Philosophical Foundations*, 50.

conclusion of calling her grandfather "Comma." She had unknowingly violated the law of identity. This is what happens when prior, foundational knowledge is ignored or unavailable when we attempt to tackle larger questions. One of the largest questions in life is why humans have inherent value, and like my daughter, if we lack the proper foundational knowledge before we attempt to answer that question, we are likely to make serious errors in our conclusion.

Noetic Structure

Noetic structure refers to how one builds upon the beliefs one obtains. For example, one must first believe in color to believe that a banana is yellow. When we examine the noetic structure of what is required to arrive at logic, we find that the reasoning the naturalist uses to arrive at their understanding of logic is epistemologically flawed. To support their worldview, the naturalist must first assume certain immaterial realities such as the mind, genetic information, the laws of logic, and the ability of an evolutionary system to produce these metaphysical elements. Both metaphysical and evolutionary forms of naturalism are self-refuting propositions because they contain a flawed noetic structure. This violates the law of noncontradiction, because to claim that immaterial realities do not exist, while using immaterial realities to prove that only natural realities exist, is inherently contradictory. In other words, naturalism constructs a building that is missing its foundation.

Naturalists operate under the assumption that the natural or material realm is all that exists. From this starting point they believe that they can, in conjunction with the laws of logic, present a thorough case for the origin and function of the universe and humanity. Sam Harris, a notable atheist philosopher and neuroscientist, writes:

> (1) Whatever can be known about maximizing the well-being of conscious creatures—which is, I will argue, the *only* thing we can reasonably value—must at some point translate into facts about brains and their interaction with the world at large; (2) the very idea of "objective" knowledge (i.e., knowledge acquired through honest observation and reasoning) *has values built into it*, as every effort we make to discuss facts depends upon principles that we must first value (e.g., logical consistency, reliance on evidence, parsimony, etc.); (3) beliefs about facts and beliefs about values seem to arise from similar processes at the level of

> the brain: it appears that we have a common system for judging truth and falsity in both domains.[14]

Confident assertions like those of Harris err in several ways. First, the fact that we have "systems for judging truth and falsity in both domains" says nothing about how we acquired that capacity for said judgment. Second, statements 1 and 2 in Harris's list are contradictory. Harris writes both that "every effort we make to discuss facts depends upon principles that we must first value" and that "maximizing the well-being of conscious creatures is . . . the *only* thing we can reasonably value." While we should value his use of logical principles, it is contradictory to say that human well-being is the only reasonable thing to value while also saying you must value logical principles before having the discussion regarding human value. Third, if the basic tenets of naturalism are correct, single-celled organisms originated from nonliving organisms that originated from energy at some point in the distant past.[15] Then, through a process of slow but certain evolutionary advancements, more complex and significant structures began to emerge, culminating in the species known as Homo sapiens, or humans. If this theory is accurate, several propositions follow: The material world is all that exists. Therefore, immaterial realities do not exist. However, logic and knowledge are immaterial realities, so the material world cannot be all that exists. Furthermore, why should one suppose that his or her brain, blindly originating from more simple species and ultimately from energy, is a trustworthy source for engaging in epistemological endeavors? Charles Darwin once wrote, "But then with me the horrid doubt always arises whether the convictions of man's mind, which has been developed from the mind of lower animals, are of any value or at all trustworthy. Would any one trust in the convictions of a monkey's mind, if there are any convictions in such a mind?"[16] Lynn Gardner notes, "Darwin used and trusted his mind in developing his theory of evolution. But when his mind suggested the idea of a Creator, he suddenly could not trust his mind."[17] The glaring issue for naturalism and naturalistic philosophy is not whether naturalism can provide valid answers, *but can such a worldview even justify asking the questions?*

Alvin Plantinga says that in philosophy, "knowledge is warranted true belief, and a belief has warrant for some person, 'if and only if' that belief was formed by cognitive faculties that are functioning properly and in accordance with a good design plan in a cognitive environment appropriate

14. Harris, *Moral Landscape*, 11.

15. Jastrow, *God and the Astronomers*, 14–15.

16. Gardner, *Christianity Stands True*, 129.

17. Gardner, *Christianity Stands True*, 129.

for the way those faculties were designed and when the design plan for our faculties is aimed at obtaining truth."[18] We must ask, then, "Does naturalism profess a 'good design plan' where cognitive faculties can grow?" Moreland responds:

> Now the notion of proper function, understood as functioning the way something ought to function, makes clear sense for artifacts that are designed by an intelligence. Why? Because the claim that something functions the way it ought to, is easily understood in terms of functioning the way it was designed to function. . . . The naturalist owes us an account of what it would mean for humans to have properly functioning cognitive and sensory faculties that can avoid the idea of a designer, and, says Plantinga, those accounts have not been successful.[19]

This would imply that a prerequisite for sound reasoning can be sustained only in a theistic framework, where a designer is present. It is only in this case that the noetic structure does not collapse but leads to the conclusion that humans have the capacity to reason, experience hope, and live with meaning. If humans are not created, humans have no *inherent* value. Our value is reduced to a utilitarian or pragmatic lie unless it is grounded in God.

THE SUSTAINING POWER OF MEANING

Theistic Theories for Logic

With the ground appearing less and less firm, the naturalist may choose to affirm that the laws of logic are merely a human invention, but the laws of logic do not depend upon humans being present. At the beginning of the universe, before there were any dogs on the planet, the statement "there are no dogs on the planet" would still be a true and logically consistent statement. Therefore, the laws of logic are prior to—and independent of—human understanding or recognition of them. The naturalist must presuppose the laws of logic in order to conduct their scientific research, but they do so without acknowledging a transcendent and primary source for those laws. As Frank Turek writes, "Science can't, in principle, discover the origin for the laws of logic because science can't proceed without using the laws of logic! The scientific method can't discover metaphysical principles anyway.

18. Moreland and Craig, *Philosophical Foundations*, 93.

19. Moreland and Craig, *Philosophical Foundations*, 93.

All it can do is use them. . . . The absolute truth is that it's impossible to deny the laws of logic without using them."[20] Alternatively, theistic worldviews in general, and Christianity in particular, are able to ground the existence of the laws of logic. An omniscient, omnipresent, omnipotent, eternal, and omni-benevolent being would have the faculties and desire to create such rules, so that lesser created beings could function with regularity. For theists, this being is God.

DNA and Logic

At the YAC I asked those young people if we had evidence that we were created. I suggested that one need look no further than DNA. Professor and scientist Dr. Stephen Meyer writes, "As [atheist] Richard Dawkins notes, 'The machine code of the genes is uncannily computer-like.' Software developer Bill Gates goes further: 'DNA is like a computer program but far, far more advanced than any software ever created.' . . . Is this striking appearance of design the product of actual design or of a natural process that can mimic the powers of a designing intelligence?"[21] In other words, if DNA—the basic molecule of life—is itself logically and intentionally designed, how could natural processes alone account for that level of intentionality? Alvin Plantinga succinctly states:

> If Dawkins is right that we are the product of mindless unguided natural processes, then he has given us strong reason to doubt the reliability of human cognitive faculties and therefore inevitably to doubt the validity of any belief that they produce—including Dawkins' own science and his atheism. His biology and his belief in naturalism would therefore appear to be at war with each other in a conflict that has nothing at all to do with God.[22]

Charlotte Omoto, a professor of cell biology at Washington State University, writes, "DNA is the genetic material, it contains all the instructions that 'tell' a living cell what it is supposed to do."[23] It is important to understand that DNA is not simply genetic material composed at the molecular level. It is material that communicates specific information. Werner Gitt, an engineer who was head of the Department of Information Technology at the German Federal Institute of Physics and Technology, has studied and

20. Turek, *Stealing from God*, 34.

21. Meyer, *Signature in the Cell*, 12.

22. Horgan, "Can Faith and Science," para. 4.

23. Omoto and Lurquin, *Genes and DNA*, 9.

outlined five levels of information: statistics, syntax, semantics, pragmatics, and apobetics.[24] The most basic level, statistics, could be illustrated with a mixture of random numbers and letters in this way:

K) J J S F J 9 2 A M C N 3 4

It would be very difficult to make sense of what this jumble of numbers and letters is attempting to communicate, but on some level, it is still information. According to Gitt, the fourth and fifth levels are of utmost importance:

> Up to the semantic level, the purpose the sender has with the transmitted information is not considered. Every transmission of information indicates that the sender has some purpose in mind for the recipient. In order to achieve the intended result, the sender describes the actions required of the recipient to bring him to implement the desired purpose. We have now reached an entirely new level of information, called pragmatics (Greek πραγματική [*pragmatikē*] = the art of doing the right thing; taking action).[25]

The fifth level, apobetics, derived from the Greek ἀποβαῖνον (*apobīnon* = result, success, conclusion), goes one step further in that the sender of the information "has some purpose [in mind] for the recipient."[26]

The information within each DNA molecule is at the level of apobetics. That level of communication is always the product of a mind, because natural processes would not be capable of producing such a complex and intentional form of communication. Gitt writes, "The apobetics aspect is thus obvious for anybody to see; this includes the observation that information never originates by chance but is always conceived purposely."[27] God alone is capable of "purposely conceiving" a system of messages that could direct an organism how to think, live, breath, move, and grow—not impersonal, physical forces. This is problematic for the naturalist, as it is precisely this apobetic level of information that is necessary to engage in logical deductions. This epistemic flaw in naturalism breaks the noetic structure that would allow humans to justify their having inherent value. If a mind is necessary to produce the specified complex level of information within, a worldview that originates *mindlessly* cannot account for the presence of such information, even in the most basic evolutionary state of existence.

24. Gitt, *In the Beginning*, 81.
25. Gitt, *In the Beginning*, 74.
26. Gitt, *In the Beginning*, 77.
27. Gitt, *In the Beginning*, 98.

If a worldview cannot explain how an informational system with communicative power could exist without an original communicator, then it cannot later explain how the beings produced by that language can understand that same language. Naturalism cannot account for the information within DNA. Nor can it account for the laws of logic—to say nothing of the difficulties with demonstrating how human beings came to be—or why we alone appear to have such existential and philosophical questions about meaning and hope.

The Mind and Logic

If the laws of logic exist independent of the persons who discover them, one must account for how those laws came to exist. The brain is a collection of matter composed of neurons, but consciousness and memory are immaterial and metaphysical realities for which science cannot account. Likewise, the laws of logic are also immaterial realities. Therefore, some atheists have chosen to negate the idea that humans have either a mind or consciousness. Daniel Dennett, a cognitive scientist and an atheist, "asserts that consciousness is an illusion."[28] But, how could Dennett make that claim if he was not conscious?

Moreland writes, "Naturalism has a view about what is real: physical entities are all there are. The mind is really the brain, free actions are merely happenings caused in the right way by inputs to the organism along with its internal 'hardware' states, and there is no teleology or purpose in the world."[29] Using our minds allows us to see the internal inconsistencies in what many naturalists assert, but this haphazard influx of ideas and concepts is what the naturalist must employ, because cellular information and the laws of logic themselves are components that are not present in the building blocks of naturalism.

It seems apparent that human beings have minds that supersede the composition of brain matter. They motivate us to create, to remember, to invent, and to maintain consciousness. So, what best accounts for the reality of the mind, naturalism or theism? Marilynne Robinson writes, "Whoever controls the definition of the mind controls the definition of humankind itself."[30] Christian apologist and brain imaging specialist from Cambridge University Sharon Dirckx indicates that there are three views on how to understand the brain-mind relationship, writing:

28. Turek, *Stealing from God*, 45.

29. Moreland, *Love Your God*, 36.

30. Robinson, *Absence of Mind*, 32.

> Non-Reductive Physicalism (Neuroscientific): The view that the mind has been generated by the brain. When a number of component parts come together and reach a certain level of complexity, something new (the mind) emerges. The mind is physical but cannot be reduced to physical exercises.
>
> Reductive Physicalism (Neuroscientific): The view that the mind is reducible to physical processes in the brain. Therefore, there is really no such thing as the mind. The mind is the brain.
>
> Substance Dualism (Neuroscientific): The view that two distinct substances characterize the mind-brain relationship: a physical brain and a non-physical mind. The mind can exist without the brain but in humans they interact. The mind is beyond the brain.[31]

Non-reductive physicalism is contradictory when it asserts that "the mind is physical but cannot be reduced to physical exercises," because it straddles the physical and metaphysical fence. If the brain (i.e., the physical reality) was solely present, it could not create or be aware of the mind (i.e., the immaterial reality). Reductive physicalism fails to answer the question if the brain and mind are one and the same, for it does not answer how the brain maintains or recognizes immaterial realities. Substance dualism presents the most acceptable option for explaining what the mind is and how it coordinates with the brain. It also provides a consistent epistemic chain that allows us to ground the reality of the mind, necessary for comprehending the laws of logic.

The Bible and Logic

When Jesus was asked by a lawyer what was the greatest commandment, he responded, "You shall love the Lord your God with all your heart and with all your soul and with all your mind. This is the great and first commandment" (Matt 22:37–38). According to Jesus, one of the most important aspects of loving God is to use our minds. This presumes the existence of the mind. The Bible, and therefore Christianity, repeatedly affirms the metaphysical reality of the mind. The Bible promises the Christian peace when they keep their mind on God (Isa 26:3), that wrestling with sin and righteousness occurs within the mind (Rom 7:23), and that they are to be transformed by the

31. Dirckx, *Am I Just*, 89.

renewing of their mind (Rom 12:2). The mind is acknowledged as the seat of reason and logic.

Every person uses reason and logic. Before examining the validity of any worldview, they must examine what best explains the logic needed to make its claims. However, logic is only the starting point. It is the necessary foundation for reasoning well. Either God has provided this capacity, or it developed naturally with no directive or direction. Moreland defines reason as "the faculties, in isolation or in combination . . . use[d] to gain knowledge and justify my beliefs."[32] Famed theologian Carl Henry believed "that rationality, rooted in God himself and his creation, is built into the fabric of the universe and into human minds so that minds are capable of using reason to understand the universe and even God."[33]

There are many explanations for why the ability to reason well is necessary. Craig Boyd writes, "Reason is the attempt of the human creature to use science and logic to understand reality as given to our senses and our natural capacity to see inferences and relationships."[34] For the Christian, and especially the apologist, reason is needed to push back against a postmodernist mindset that denies absolutes and objective realities. Christian theism is able to support the existence of the mind and a Creator who instituted the laws of logic for the mind to access. It possesses a consistent, noetic structure and epistemic chain from the existence of logic to the conclusions drawn when using it. Theologian Nicolas Wolterstorff points out that, in spite of this consistency, it often goes unacknowledged by naturalists:

> A lecture by Anthony Flew . . . contended that if one scrutinizes how people guard their religious convictions one sees that they treat them as compatible with the happening of anything whatsoever. In other words, these beliefs are not falsifiable. And because they are not falsifiable, they do not constitute genuine assertions. They make no claims on actuality . . . scientists convinced of the truth of some scientific theory behave exactly the way Flew says religious believers do.[35]

The scientist becomes guilty of the same type of blind faith they falsely accuse the Christian of exercising. However, Christian faith is not blind. It is based upon sound logic supported by a source, God—the Creator of logic and Provider of the mental faculties needed for his creatures to ascertain and build from that logical foundation.

32. Moreland, *Love Your God*, 45.

33. Olson, *Journey of Modern Theology*, 624.

34. Wilkens, *Faith and Reason*, 137.

35. Wolterstorff, *Reason within the Bounds*, 24.

Christian theism also affirms the law of identity, noncontradiction, and the excluded middle. Jesus makes an ontologically unique statement not made prior to or after him. Jesus, the living embodiment of the truth, affirmed that all three laws of logic were validated in himself when he said, "I am the way, the truth, and the life. No one comes to the Father except through me" (John 14:6). Every other religion has a leader, prophet, or guru who claims to have special knowledge or access *to* the truth, but none claimed to *be* the truth. Jesus did not merely say that he *knew* more than everyone else. He said that he *is* more than everyone else. He is utterly unique! Even religions that precede Christianity show evidence that they updated their doctrines to include Jesus after the first century.[36] Only in Christianity is truth more than a concept and embodied in a person. This means to know Christ is to know the truest man to ever live! To know the ultimate truth is to know the ultimate person. In declaring that he is the truth, Jesus identified himself as one and the same with that singular concept, thus affirming the law of identity. In professing that he is the way, the truth, and the life, Jesus implicitly stated that anyone other than him claiming to be those things is contradicting him, and is therefore not the way, truth, and life, thus affirming the law of noncontradiction. Finally, Jesus claimed that one can come to the only Father through him, meaning that there are no middle options, thus confirming the law of the excluded middle.

Determining Value

After the conference I enjoyed some free time in the gym with the young men and women who were present. We had an enjoyable time playing dodgeball and basketball. I love to play basketball when I have the time. The shoes that I find work best for me are "Kobes" (named for Kobe Bryant). If I go to the store and they are on sale for $100, I will probably buy them if I am looking for new shoes. However, if they were to tell me that the cost was $1,000, I would decline because that would not be an accurate assessment of their value. Only two people determine the value of an object: the creator and the purchaser. Value can never *objectively* be self-determined. A one-carat diamond can cost anywhere from $2,500 to $18,000, but there is nothing inherent *in* the diamond that makes it valuable. Humans have ascribed value *to* these clumps of compressed carbon. Similarly, the currency in your pocket has no actual value until the government ascribes value to the coin or piece of paper. Nothing gives value to itself. If nothing can objectively

36. Wallace, *Person of Interest*, 241.

give value to itself, then who gave humans the inherent value they claim to have?

According to the Christian worldview—and *only in a Christian worldview*—the Purchaser and the Creator are the same person. We have been redeemed, *or purchased*, by God, our *Creator.* In an atheistic worldview we are the culmination of a random, unguided assortment of molecules. But a random and unguided process cannot ascribe value to anything. However, in a Christian worldview we can objectively discuss concepts such as intrinsic human value and inherent worth.

That day I explained to the students that this understanding of our value is pivotal, because without value there can never be meaning. Value and meaning are not synonymous, but they are intertwined. In other words, if something is of no value, or no *legitimate* worth can be attributed to it, then it becomes a worthless item. So, the fact that humans are *given* value by a Creator and a Purchaser with the ability to impute value to us is of utmost importance. Neither naturalism, materialism, nor atheism can provide us with an answer regarding life's meaning, because they cannot provide the source from which that meaning would emanate. In a Christian worldview, meaning can be *objectively* sustained, because we are eternally connected to the One who gives meaning to *all* things.

THE SUSTAINING POWER OF HOPE

Secularism continues to present a challenge to the church, however, as its current expression produces increased individualism, tribalism, racism, and a hypocritical "cancel culture." In a postmodern society that is increasingly antagonistic towards any metanarrative, the church must be intentional with its methods of engagement in a world that has assumed that it, and thereby Christ, no longer has a message to communicate. In his seminal work, *The Cost of Discipleship*, Dietrich Bonhoeffer wrote:

> Let the Christian remain in the world, not because of the good gifts of creation, nor because of his responsibility for the course of the world, but for the sake of the Church. Let him remain in the world to engage in frontal assault on it and let him live the life of his secular calling in order to show himself as a stranger in the world all the more. But that is only possible if we are visible members of the Church. The antithesis between the world and the Church must be borne out in the world. That was the

> purpose of the incarnation. That is why Christ died among his enemies.[37]

Bonhoeffer understood that Christians need to be present in every aspect of society if they are influence it with the lived reality of a gospel-infused lifestyle. Not every Christian is called to the pastorate, so when they live "the life of [their] secular calling," they are displaying to those around them—at work and within the community—what it means to have the presence and hope of Christ.

Bonhoeffer did not think the solution for the church was to retreat from the modern world or to completely align with it at the expense of Christianity. Rather, when one, through a pious life inculcated with a firm understanding of the incarnation, death, burial, and resurrection of Jesus, engages with modern society, one will present the only alternative to the evils and ills present in modern culture. He writes:

> What matters is not the beyond but this world, how it is created and preserved, is given laws, reconciled, and renewed. What is beyond this world is meant, in the gospel, to be there *for* this world—not in the anthropocentric sense of liberal, mystical, pietistic, ethical theology, but in the biblical sense of the creation and the incarnation, crucifixion, and resurrection of Jesus Christ.[38]

This eschatological component should have a proactive effect on the life of the believer here and now. A Christian believer should be actively encouraged to live and share the truth of the kingdom of God, based on their heavenly hope and the internal motivation of the Holy Spirit. A proper eschatology (understanding of end times) informs both our sociology (understanding of society) and our anthropology (understanding of human behavior). When these secondary disciplines are informed by the primacy of the truth and hope of the gospel, Christians can, have, and will approach the tasks of evangelism and discipleship within the natural rhythms of their lives.

Living with Hope

When you have hope, that hope is extended to others when you share it (1 Pet 3:15). Some may still think that this hope is a pipe dream or unimportant. Some may assume that Christians place their hope in God in the

37. Bonhoeffer, *Cost of Discipleship*, 264.

38. Bonhoeffer, *Letters and Papers*, 286.

"hopes" that he will grant them a spot in heaven, but a desire for entry into heaven is not the primary reason one should trust God or live for him. Our hope is not in heaven but in the Lord of heaven and earth. Some believe that this eschatological hope is at the expense of hope in this present life. Yet it cannot be denied that such hope will inform the ways in which people function in the here and now. Our young people often live bolder and courageous lives for Jesus once they fully embrace the reality of the hope that he offers.

Our eschatological perspective matters. If you believe that this life is all there is, you may get away with many evils of varying degrees or live without meaning and purpose, but you will most likely also live without any hope. Those who believe life is ultimately hopeless operate under the philosophy that "you only live once, so have fun!" Or, as the apostle Paul puts it, "Let us eat, drink, and be merry for tomorrow we die" (1 Cor 15:32). But often what constitutes "fun" or "merriment" for those individuals is neither moral nor beneficial.

Richard Dawkins writes, "Whether irrational or not, it does unfortunately seem plausible that, if somebody sincerely believes God is watching his every move, he might be more likely to be good. I must say I hate the idea. I want to believe that humans are better than that. I'd like to believe I'm honest whether anyone is watching or not."[39] At another time, in an interview with *The Times* at the Cheltenham Festival, he said that "people may feel free to do bad things because they feel God is no longer watching them." If the noetic structure within naturalism has left out the foundational component regarding how we gained the cellular information we possess—which has given us the capacity for moral intuition—then naturalism cannot legitimately import a meaning for life on the back end of their worldview, and Dawkins recognizes this.

Possessing a joyous anticipation for an eternity with the Lord is to be expected of a Christian, but if this "hope of heaven" rests solely on the idea that it's "better than hell," the message of the gospel has been missed entirely. While there is much to anticipate in heaven, it is not our final destination. The message of the Bible is the bringing of the kingdom of heaven to earth. The first mandate given to mankind states, "Then God said, 'Let us make man in our image, after our likeness. And let them have dominion over the fish of the sea and over the birds of the heavens and over the livestock and over all the earth and over every creeping thing that creeps on the earth" (Gen 1:26). We are to have dominion over the earth. The night before his execution, Jesus, while praying for his disciples, said:

39. Dawkins, *Outgrowing God*, 99.

> And I am no longer in the world, but they are in the world, and I come to you. Holy Father, keep them in your name, which you have given me, that they may be one, even as we are one. While I was with them, I kept them in your name, which you have given me. I have guarded them, and not one of them has been lost except the son of destruction, that the Scripture might be fulfilled. But now I am coming to you, and these things I speak in the world, that they may have my joy fulfilled in themselves. I have given them your word, and the world has hated them because they are not of the world, just as I am not of the world. I do not ask that you take them out of the world, but that you keep them from the evil one. They are not of the world, just as I am not of the world. Sanctify them in the truth; your word is truth. As you sent me into the world, so I have sent them into the world. And for their sake I consecrate myself, that they also may be sanctified in truth. (John 17:11–18)

The goal is not to diminish the beauty and glory of heaven, but our assignment, our mandate, is here on earth. Jesus prayed that we would be in the world and work in the world, and this is not merely something to bide time until we go to heaven.

Author Don Stewart writes:

> The glorious promise of God is that this earth will be made new. . . . Although it is new, it will have some connection with the old. As is the case with the resurrected body of the believer, there is some mystery in this process. What is clear is that the present heaven and earth will pass away in the form that they are presently in, and God will make something new for believers to enjoy with Him.[40]

Scripture repeatedly reminds us of this. Revelation 21:1 reads, "Then I saw a new heaven and a new earth, for the first heaven and the first earth had passed away." Isaiah 65:17 reads, "For behold, I create new heavens and a new earth, and the former things shall not be remembered or come into mind." Scripture is conclusive; we are on earth now and will return to earth in the future.

Our objective is to bring heaven to earth. This is what it means to be kingdom minded. To properly understand heaven, we must understand the goal of God and how the incarnation and resurrection illustrate that goal. God had the power to go directly from heaven straight to hell and defeat Satan, but foregoing the earthly realm would invalidate justice, love, sacrifice,

40. Stewart, "What Are New Heavens," paras. 3, 13.

and God's kingdom rule. If God is just, then he cannot violate his own standard, even though he made the rule. Therefore, the punishment and justice required to satisfy the debt of sin must occur in the earthly realm. Either we must suffer that punishment, or God must do it for us. Thankfully, he chose the latter. Jesus's actions on Calvary, and his resurrection, bring hope into reality. The church is God's epistemological tool for helping the world come to know the source of that hope. Our earthly vantage point does not allow us to see what is lost by misunderstanding the resurrection and incarnation of Jesus. N. T. Wright states:

> Our minds are so conditioned, I'm afraid, by Greek philosophy, whether or not we've ever read any of it, that we think of heaven as by definition nonmaterial and earth by definition as non-spiritual or non-heavenly. But that won't do. Part of the central achievement of the incarnation, which is then celebrated in the resurrection and ascension, is that heaven and earth are now joined together with an unbreakable bond and that we too are by rights citizens of both together. We can, if we choose, screen out the heavenly dimension and live as flatlanders, materialists. If we do that, we will be buying in to a system that will go bad, and will wither and die, because earth gets its vital life from heaven.[41]

In other words, for the believer, our sustenance on earth, in heaven, and on the new earth is none other than God himself. We need not wait to get to heaven in order to know him or to experience a life with him. Nor do we trust in Jesus only for the hope of heaven. We trust in Jesus so that, through the church, the hope of heaven can influence the earth.

The Christian worldview properly justifies and sustains the reality of hope, and that hope should compel us to live with purpose. My prayer for the young men and women in the audience that day at YAC was the same as my prayer for those reading this chapter: that the truth of who God is and what Christ has done will compel you to live incarnationally in a world increasingly devoid of truth and hope. Christians who have intellectually and spiritually assented to a relationship with Christ yet are not compelled by that truth to act incarnationally abdicate their most important obligation. The night before his execution, Jesus prayed, "Sanctify them in the truth," and "I do not ask that you take them out of the world. . . . I have sent them *into* the world" (John 17:15–19). Jesus is telling us to take our *orthodoxy* and demonstrate it through our *orthopraxy*, and thereby change the world! For

41. Wright, *Surprised by Hope*, 251.

Jesus, propositional truth was never divorced from practical application. For Jesus, it was *always* both/and, never either/or. C. S. Lewis writes:

> If none of my earthly pleasures satisfy it, that does not prove that the universe is a fraud. Probably earthly pleasures were never meant to satisfy it, but only to arouse it, to suggest the real thing. If that is so, I must take care, on the one hand, never to despise, or be unthankful for, these earthly blessings, and on the other, never to mistake them for the something else of which they are only a kind of copy, or echo, or mirage.[42]

Our hope, rooted in the God of the hereafter, should produce acts laced with hope in the here and now. Perhaps if the church were more intent on *doing* the work, we could, as Gandhi reputedly said, "turn the world upside down and bring peace to a battle-torn planet." God is the focal point and grounding of human value and fills our lives with meaning and hope. The reality that life possesses meaning is the springboard from which we can arrive at our individual purposes. And a life of purpose is the best life to live. It is through doing that our lives—young and old—, infused with meaning and purpose, will climax in the culmination of the hope to which we are called. May we all seek to practice what we preach, so that what we preach is heard, seen, and most importantly, *felt*.

42. Lewis, *Mere Christianity*, 136.

Bibliography

Bonhoeffer, Dietrich. *The Cost of Discipleship*. Translated by R. H. Fuller. London: Touchstone, 1995.

———. *Letters and Papers from Prison*. Translated by R. H. Fuller. London: Touchstone, 1997.

Dawkins, Richard. *Outgrowing God: A Beginner's Guide*. London: Bantam, 2019.

Dirckx, Sharon. *Am I Just My Brain?* Oxford: Good Book Company, 2019.

Gardner, Lynn. *Christianity Stands True: A Common Sense Look at the Evidence*. Joplin, MO: College, 1994.

Geisler, Norman L. and Frank Turek. *I Don't Have Enough Faith to Be an Atheist*. Wheaton, IL: Crossway, 2004.

Gitt, Werner. *In the Beginning Was Information: A Scientist Explains the Incredible Design in Nature*. Green Forest, AR: Master, 2005.

Harris, Sam. *The Moral Landscape: How Science Can Determine Human Values*. New York: Free, 2010.

Horgan, John. "Can Faith and Science Coexist? Mathematician and Christian John Lennox Responds." *Scientific American* 312 (Mar. 2015). https://blogs.scientificamerican.com/cross-check/can-faith-and-science-coexist-/.

Jastrow, Robert. *God and the Astronomers*. New York: Norton and Co., 2001.

Lewis, C. S. *Mere Christianity*. London: Fount, 1977.

Meyer, Stephen C. *Signature in the Cell: DNA and the Evidence for Intelligent Design*. New York: Harper One, 2010.

Moreland, J. P. *Love Your God with All Your Mind: The Role of Reason in Your Heart and Soul*. Colorado Springs: NavPress, 1997.

Moreland, J. P. and William Lane Craig. *Philosophical Foundations for a Christian Worldview*. Downers Grove, IL: InterVarsity, 2003.

Olson, Roger E. *The Journey of Modern Theology: From Reconstruction to Deconstruction*. Downers Grove, IL: IVP Academic, 2013.

Omoto, Charlotte K. and Paul F. Lurquin. *Genes and DNA: A Beginner's Guide to Genetics and Its Applications*. New York: Columbia University Press, 2004.

Robinson, Marilynne. *Absence of Mind: The Dispelling of Inwardness from the Modern Myth of the Self*. New Haven, CT: Yale University Press, 2010.

Stewart, Don. "What Are the New Heavens and the New Earth?" Blue Letter Bible, n.d. https://www.blueletterbible.org/faq/don_stewart/don_stewart_153.cfm.

Tahmincioglu, Eve. "Want to Be a SEAL? Tough Is Just a Start." *NBC News*, May 4, 2011. https://www.nbcnews.com/id/wbna42884153.

Turek, Frank. *Stealing from God: Why Atheists Need God to Make Their Case*. Colorado Springs: NavPress, 2015.

Wallace, J. Warner. *Person of Interest: Why Jesus Still Matters in a World That Rejects the Bible*. Grand Rapids: Zondervan, 2021.

"Why Is Missouri Called the 'Show-Me State'?" Missouri Secretary of State, n.d. From Official Manual of the State of Missouri, *1979–1980*, 1486. https://www.sos.mo.gov/archives/history/slogan.asp.

Wilkens, Steve, ed. *Faith and Reason: Three Views*. Downers Grove, IL: IVP Academic, 2014.

Wolterstorff, Nicholas. *Reason within the Bounds of Religion*. 2nd ed. Grand Rapids: Eerdmans, 1988.

Wright, N. T. *Surprised by Hope: Rethinking Heaven, the Resurrection, and the Mission of the Church*. 1st ed. New York: Harper Paperbacks, 2008.

I Don't Have Enough Faith to Be a Physicalist: A Case for the Soul

Eric Hernandez[1]

It has become increasingly popular to believe that human beings are nothing more than a physical brain and body and that the idea of an immaterial soul is an outdated, religious belief based upon scientific ignorance. But is this truly the case? Is this foundation of atheistic naturalism true? Scripture tells us in 1 Cor 15 that if there is no resurrection, our faith is in vain and Christianity is false. The Bible teaches us that the resurrection of Christ, and subsequently that of all believers, involves body and soul. Therefore, if there is no soul—as atheistic naturalism claims—there can be no resurrection, and thus Christianity is false. For this reason, the question of the soul is central to the truth of Christianity. In this chapter, I will present a case for the existence of the soul by arguing two basic contentions:

1. Consciousness is not physical, and
2. I am more than a brain and body.

These points are, of course, the inverse of the claims made above, and if these two contentions are demonstrably true, human beings are more than

1. Dr. Turek's coauthored book *I Don't Have Enough Faith to Be an Atheist* was probably the first book on apologetics that I read all the way through (technically, heard, given it was an audiobook!). It was inspiring and life changing for me. In fact, when I first met my wife, the first thing I bought her wasn't a bouquet of flowers but Frank's book (she was curious about apologetics)! Never would I have imagined that years later I would have the opportunity to thank him this way. I am deeply grateful for his work and the impact he's made on my life. Frank is a warrior, a friend, and most importantly, a brother in Christ.

purely physical objects. If human beings are more than purely physical objects, then atheistic naturalism is false.

A NATURALIST VIEW OF HUMAN PERSONS

As it concerns the existence and nature of human beings, there are essentially two dominant positions: physicalism and dualism. Both views attempt to answer two questions central to personhood: (1) What is consciousness? (2) What is the "I" or self? In this chapter, I will defend the existence of the soul from a dualist perspective known as *substance dualism*—the view that human beings *are* souls that *have* bodies. The soul, simply put, is an immaterial substance that possesses consciousness and animates the body.[2]

Alternatively, if atheism is true, then naturalistic, Darwinian evolution becomes "the only game in town" to explain our existence.[3] According to a naturalistic worldview, the physical world is all there is, nothing more, nothing less.[4] When applied to human beings, this is known as *physicalism*—the view that human beings are purely physical objects composed of exclusively physical properties and parts.[5] As atheist philosopher Paul M. Churchland observes:

> The important point about the standard evolutionary story is that the human species and all of its features are the wholly physical outcome of a purely physical process. . . . If this is the correct account of our origins, then there seems neither need, nor room, to fit any nonphysical substances or properties into our theoretical account of ourselves. We are creatures of matter. And we should learn to live with that fact.[6]

If this is the case, then it follows that the most logically consistent position for an atheist to take regarding the nature of human beings is physicalism. Put differently, if atheism is true, then—given naturalism—physicalism must be true.

2. Moreland, *Body & Soul*, 202.

3. Plantinga, *Where the Conflict*, 24, 32, 56, 257.

4. This is known as *philosophical naturalism*. Moreland and Craig, *Philosophical Foundations*, 164, 169.

5. This is known as *strict physicalism*. Moreland and Craig, *Philosophical Foundations*, 211.

6. Churchland, *Matter and Consciousness*, 35.

Let's Get Physical

During my first year of college, I intentionally took a class in philosophy from an atheist professor whom all my peers warned me to avoid. We will call him Professor P. This professor was known for being condescendingly hostile towards Christianity, and I was told that if I took his course, I might lose my faith. While much can be said about my time in his class, one day in particular presented a pivotal shift for my life and ministry.

Professor P began class by reaching into his pocket and pulling out a small antidepressant pill. He held it to the light for us to see. After gazing at the pill pinched between his fingers, he began his lecture:

> Religion wants us to believe in some "immaterial soul," and because of this, we can have hope in an afterlife, seeing our friends and family that have gone before us. And according to Christianity, my thoughts, emotions, and sensations—allegedly immaterial as well—all reside within my "non-physical soul." But here's the problem. If I took this antidepressant pill, *which is physical*, it has the power to change my thoughts, emotions, and sensations. But how can this be? How can something tiny and physical affect the immaterial?
>
> Because, every time a neurologist scans the brain, all he sees are neurons firing, and every time a scientist examines the body under a microscope, all he finds are the basic elements of carbon, hydrogen, and oxygen. But no scientist has ever found *anything* even remotely close to something like a soul. How do we explain this? I'll tell you how, and the answer is quite simple. There is no soul. There is no heaven or hell, there is no God, and there is no afterlife. We are *nothing more than* a physical brain and body. A "meat machine" of physics and chemistry, and we must learn to live with this fact, get on with our lives, and stop believing in these fanciful fairy tales.

As a freshman in college, I had never met someone who didn't believe in the soul (I thought everyone did!), and I had never heard an argument against it. What was more troubling to me was that I knew the existence of the soul was no small matter for Christianity.

To paraphrase the words of Paul in 1 Cor 15:13–18, if Christ has not been raised from the dead, then Christianity is false. This means that the truth of Christianity literally hinges on the truth of the resurrection. As Christian philosopher J. P. Moreland explains, "Death and resurrection are regularly spoken of in terms of the departure and return of the soul," and "The resurrection of the dead involves the re-embodiment of the same soul or spirit."[7] But if there is no soul, then there can be no resurrection, and once again, if there is no resurrection, then Christianity cannot be true. Hence, the question of the soul becomes of vital importance.

Empiricism and Reductionism

In his lecture, Professor P argued against the soul by employing two features associated with—if not inherent to—naturalism as a worldview. The first is an epistemology (i.e., a theory of knowledge) known as *empiricism*—the view that knowledge is restricted and limited to the five senses. This is how he defended his conclusion that there is no soul by alluding to *looking* at brains and *examining* bodies. The second is *reductionism*, which is the attempt to explain some entity *y* (in this case, the soul) by reducing it to some entity *x* (the brain and body). This feature can be identified by spotting "nothing but" or "nothing more than" language. For instance, if I said that marriage is *nothing but* signing a piece of paper for the government, then I've reduced the essence of marriage to *nothing more than* a legal document.

As a result, this leads to what we now know to be physicalism. This is sometimes referred to as materialism, or the view that all things are composed of matter—which is essentially a naturalist ontology (i.e., a view of reality and existence) applied to human beings.[8] Under this view, it follows that human beings are reducible to *nothing more than* physical properties and parts—no soul is needed to explain anything.

Let's Get Metaphysical

When it comes to answering the question of the soul's existence, it is my view that empiricism is the wrong tool for the assessment. To illustrate, suppose you overhear two of your neighbors arguing, and—being the benevolent person you are—you stop to see if you can help settle the dispute. After a few minutes of inquiring about the situation, you learn that neighbor 1 (N1) claims there's an invisible man in his house. Skeptical of this, neighbor 2 (N2) offered to investigate this claim for himself. After five hours of searching, N2 accused N1 of lying. Thus, their argument ensued. Trying not to take sides, you ask N2 why he thinks that N1 is lying. He responds:

> This guy claims an invisible man is in his house. Yet, after five hours of searching, I never *saw him* anywhere! And trust me,

7. Moreland, *Body & Soul*, 28, 33.

8. Moreland and Craig, *Philosophical Foundations*, 121.

> I *looked* everywhere. I *looked* in the closet, I *looked* under the beds, and I even *looked* in the bathroom. But not once did I ever *see* this invisible man myself!

With an angry but puzzled look, N1 pulls at his hair and shouts, "Well, of course you didn't *see* him! He's *invisible*!"

Now, whatever the truth of the matter, no one can deny that what N1 has said in his defense is correct. This would not prove that N1 is right, but it would prove that N2's inability to *visibly see* an *invisible* man cannot be used to argue that the invisible man does not exist. After all, being unable to see something invisible would, at the very least, be logically consistent with the claim and therefore cannot be used as an argument against it. In the same way, if the soul exists and is immaterial, then one cannot use empirical means of investigation, such as studying the brain or body under a microscope, to argue against it. Therefore, appealing to empiricism as an objection to the existence of the soul is misguided and fallacious—even if made by a philosophy professor.

Additionally, this involves the assumption of scientism, which is the view that science is the only, or best, way to gain knowledge about reality.[9] This is a category fallacy.[10] Why? Because, if the soul exists, it is, by definition, a nonphysical entity—whereas science, though a wonderful tool for studying the physical world, is a tool that is able to study only the physical world. One cannot demand that a physically limited discipline like science be used to investigate something nonphysical. As Dr. Frank Turek points out, this is like arguing that plastic cannot exist because a metal detector cannot detect it.[11] It is simply the wrong tool for the assessment.

Finally, and most importantly, questions regarding the existence of the soul are philosophical questions about metaphysics, not science. As atheist philosopher of science Dr. Michael Ruse explains, "Science does not ask certain questions, and so it is no surprise that it does not give [certain] answers."[12] Indeed, some of the world's leading neuroscientists, such as Jeffrey Schwartz, Mario Beauregard, and the late Nobel Prize winner John Eccles, are dualists, and one cannot argue that their belief in the soul is due to an ignorance of neuroscience.

Moreover, both physicalism and dualism are empirically equivalent theories, meaning that no amount of scientific or empirical data would lend

9. Moreland, *Scientism and Secularism*, 26.

10. A category fallacy occurs when you "treat something in one category as if it belongs in another category." Turek, *Stealing from God*, 101.

11. Turek, *Stealing from God*, 160.

12. Ruse, "Curate's Egg," para. 14.

weight to one view over the other.[13] Both the physicalist and dualist agree on all the data. Hence, any conclusions drawn from the data are philosophical in nature, not scientific.[14] As a result, any disagreements between the physicalist and dualist are not about the physics but the metaphysics. It follows then that, if we wish to settle the dispute, we must examine the metaphysics.

THE TWO CENTRAL QUESTIONS AND A FOUNDATION FOR EXAMINING THE METAPHYSICS

What Is Consciousness?

Consciousness is best defined ostensively, meaning that we point to instances or examples of it rather than provide a strict definition.[15] There are five states of consciousness: thoughts, beliefs, sensations, desires, and acts of will (i.e., volition).[16] As an analogy, water is a substance that comes in three states: solid, liquid, and gas, and each of these states is characterized by their respective properties: hardness, fluidity, and vaporousness. While the states and properties may change, water—being the substance that grounds these states and properties—remains the same. Similarly, if substance dualism is true, then consciousness is immaterial and grounded by an immaterial substance: the soul. By contrast, if physicalism is true, then consciousness, if it exists, must be *identical* and/or *reducible* to something physical like the brain.

Leibniz's Law: A Test for Identity

In philosophy, when we say that *x* is identical to *y*, we simply mean that *x* is literally the same thing as *y*. For example, suppose I said that Eric Hernandez is identical to the author of this chapter. In that case, I am referring to one person rather than two, because Eric Hernandez and the author of this chapter are the same person. I am using two labels to refer to *one thing*. As a test for identity, this is known as Leibniz's Law of the Indiscernibility of Identicals, but for brevity's sake, we'll simply refer to this as Leibniz's Law.

According to Leibniz's Law, if two things in question are identical—some *x* and *y*—then whatever is true of *x* will necessarily be true of *y*, and

13. Moreland, *Consciousness and the Existence*, 168.

14. Bennett and Hacker, *Philosophical Foundations of Neuroscience*, 1, 462, 467, 498.

15. Moreland and Craig, *Philosophical Foundations*, 213.

16. Moreland, *Body & Soul*, 158.

vice versa. However, if we can find something true of x that is not true of y, or vice versa, then they cannot be the same thing (i.e., they cannot be identical). To illustrate this principle, suppose you walk into a lab and see two bottles of clear fluids. One bottle is labeled "Water," and the other is "Chemical X," but the label for Chemical X is worn out and illegible. Applying Leibniz's Law, you want to know if these are the same substance because they appear to be identical. Both are fluids; both possess the property of being transparent; and thus, may be the same substance. However, when you turn over the bottle of Chemical X, you find a label that reads, "Caution: Flammable." Given that water is not flammable, but Chemical X is, you now conclude that the two cannot be the same substance. Therefore, even if you don't know what Chemical X is, you now know that, given Leibniz's Law of Identity, it cannot be identical to water. This test for identity will be foundational for answering our two central questions.

What is the I or Self?

I is an indexical word, meaning that it is a label used to refer to something—namely, me, the self. But what kind of a thing am I? If substance dualism is true, then the indexical word *I* refers to me, the soul—an immaterial substance that possesses consciousness and animates the body. This would mean that I am identical to my soul. Put differently, I do not *have* a soul, but rather, I *am* a soul that *has* a body, and a body without a soul is merely a corpse. If I am identical to the soul and the soul is immaterial, then it follows that I am immaterial. Put another way, if the brain and body are something physical, then given substance dualism, I cannot be something merely physical, or reducible to a brain and body. Therefore, I am a soul, i.e., an immaterial substance.

Conversely, if physicalism is true, then the indexical word *I* must refer to something physical, like a brain, a body, or a combination of both. If this is the case, then human beings would be what philosophers call a mereological aggregate (hereafter, aggregate), which is a combination of separate parts held together in a certain structure.[17] Things like watches, cars, and LEGO bricks are examples of aggregates—separable parts rearranged into a specific structure giving rise to their existence and identity. To illustrate this point, consider a tricycle. A tricycle is what it is because of its parts and structure. If you remove a wheel from a tricycle, you now have a bicycle. Metaphysically speaking, this would mean that a tricycle has ceased to exist, and instead, a bicycle has come into existence. Hence, for aggregates,

17. Moreland and Craig, *Philosophical Foundations*, 253.

their existence and identity (i.e., what they are) necessarily depend on the existence of their parts and structure.

So, in summation of the metaphysics, if substance dualism is true, then I am identical to an immaterial substance—the soul. However, if physicalism is true, then I am identical and reducible to an aggregate—a purely physical object whose existence and identity depend on the arrangement of its separable parts and structure.

Physicalism vs. Substance Dualism

With this metaphysical foundation in mind, the atheistic naturalist must demonstrate at least two things for physicalism to be true: (1) that consciousness, if it exists, must be either *identical* or *reducible* to something physical like the brain; and (2) that human beings are either *identical* or *reducible* to the brain, body, or both. By contrast, if it can be shown that neither of these two conditions is true, then it would follow that physicalism (and by default, atheism and naturalism) is false. We can then present a case for the existence of the soul by arguing two basic contentions: (1) consciousness is not physical, and (2) I am more than a brain and body.

A CASE FOR THE SOUL

Consciousness Is Not Physical

The argument for physicalism presented by Professor P revolved around the assumption that the mind is nothing more than the brain. If true, this would mean that whatever is true of the mind must be true of the brain. This means that if we can find just one thing true of the mind that is not true of the brain, then given Leibniz's Law of Identity, they cannot be the same thing. So, to address this purported "argument" in favor of physicalism, we can begin by asking, "Does Professor P's argument satisfy Leibniz's Law of Identity?" That is, did he show that the mind and brain are the same thing? He did not, which brings us to our first response via a rebuttal.

Rebuttal: Identity or Mere Correlation?

In defense of physicalism, many naturalists point to the dependency relationship between the mind and brain, meaning that when a mental state occurs (e.g., thought or belief), there will be a correlating brain state (i.e., neurons firing). For some naturalists, this demonstrates that the mind and brain are identical. In cases of brain damage, such as Alzheimer's, certain regions of the brain are directly correlated with certain functions of the mind, like memory. As a result, damage to these regions has a direct effect on one's ability to recall memories. This demonstrates two things:

1. A dependency relationship between the mind and brain
2. A dependency relationship between specified regions of the brain and specified functions of the mind

The naturalist argues that, because of this, the mind and brain must be the same thing. But is this truly the case? Has neuroscience provided the final nail in the coffin of the Christian worldview? Not at all, because dependency does not establish identity.

To illustrate why this popular argument fails, consider the relationship between a musician and his instrument. A guitarist knows that to successfully play a C chord, he must first press down and strum a specific group of correlated strings. Similarly, he knows that if these correlating groups of strings were to break, he could no longer play the chord. In this analogy, there is both a cause-effect and a dependency relationship between the guitarist and his guitar, and between the strings needed to play the chord, but the mere existence of these relationships does not demonstrate that the guitarist is identical to his guitar or that the C chord and the strings are identical to one another. It would follow then that neither a cause-effect nor a dependency relationship between the mind and the brain demonstrates identity.

But nothing important or profound follows from this. Clearly, no one would say that because a guitarist depends on his guitar, he is therefore identical to, or nothing more than, a guitar. Neither would they say that because damage to the strings will "damage" his ability to play the note C, therefore the note is reducible to a set of strings on the guitar. In other words, if establishing a cause-effect, dependency relationship between guitarists, musical notes, and guitars does not establish identity, then how could the same line of reasoning be used in support of physicalism?

Returning to the antidepressant pill that Professor P presented for his argument, the medication can indeed affect the states of my brain, which, in turn, affect the states of my mind; but what follows from this? That my mental states are identical, reducible, or located within the physical regions of my brain? No more than detuning a guitar (which affects the pitch and sound of the music) proves the C chord is identical, reducible, or located within a physical region of the guitar. Granted, this rebuttal doesn't prove that Professor P is wrong and that consciousness is immaterial, but it does prove that such a correlation should not be used to prove that Professor P is right.

The Nonidentity of Mind and Matter

If we can demonstrate the nonidentity of the mind and the brain (i.e., that they are not the same thing), then given Leibniz's Law of Identity, it would follow that physicalism is false and dualism must be true.[18] Using Leibniz's test for identity, three points defending that the mind and brain are not identical may be presented as follows:

1. *A belief is a mental state that can be true or false, but no state or region of my brain can be true or false.* Saying otherwise is simply a category fallacy. It would be nonsensical to say that one group of firing neurons is true, while another group of firing neurons is false. Therefore, if a belief can be true or false, but its correlating neurons cannot, then the mind and brain cannot be the same thing.
2. *My brain can weigh three pounds, but my thought that grass is green has no weight.* While you may have "heavy thoughts" reading this chapter, it will not require a neck brace. Hence, if my brain possesses weight, but my thoughts do not, then they cannot be the same thing.
3. *My brain can measure seven inches long, but the smell of a rose or the taste of a banana (which are states of my mind) has no length.* Again, saying otherwise is a category fallacy because smells and tastes do not have physical properties like weight or length. Therefore, if my brain has a length but my mental states do not, they cannot be the same thing.

If all the states and properties of my brain are physical, but all the states and properties of my mind are not physical, then it follows that if consciousness exists, it is neither reducible nor identical to anything physical like the brain. However, if consciousness exists and cannot be physical, then consequently, physicalism cannot be true. Syllogistically, this argument can be written as follows:

1. If physicalism is true, then consciousness must be physical.
2. Consciousness is not physical.
3. Therefore, physicalism is false.

18. At minimum, property dualism. See Moreland and Craig, *Philosophical Foundations*, 209.

Physicalism: A Price Tag for Naturalism

In philosophy, a price tag is the "intellectual price" one must pay to be logically consistent while maintaining the implications of their worldview. Given what has been demonstrated above, if the naturalist wishes to be logically consistent, he must now pay the price of denying that consciousness exists (otherwise, the existence of consciousness—being nonphysical—would entail that physicalism is false). Some naturalists, like philosophers Daniel Dennett, Paul Churchland, and Alex Rosenberg, have sought to try and preserve the "integrity" of their worldview by paying this "price tag."

In his book *Consciousness Explained*, Dennett argues that consciousness is just an illusion.[19] Yet, consciousness must exist for illusions to be possible! Again, syllogistically, we can demonstrate the self-refuting nature of this position in the following way:

1. If physicalism is true, then consciousness cannot exist.
2. I am consciously aware of this dilemma.
3. Therefore, consciousness exists.
4. Therefore, physicalism cannot be true.
5. Therefore, physicalism is false.

Moreover, consider the fact that if consciousness does not exist, then the states of consciousness (e.g., thoughts or beliefs) cannot exist either. Both Churchland and Rosenberg hold to this view.[20] Yet, if a person denies that consciousness exists, they are essentially making the self-defeating claim that *they believe that beliefs do not exist*! As before, this can be exposed in a syllogism:

1. If physicalism is true, then beliefs do not exist.
2. I believe this.
3. Therefore, beliefs exist.
4. Therefore, physicalism is false.

19. Turek expands on this point here. Turek, *Stealing from God*, 46.

20. Churchland argues that our commonsense conception of consciousness is "radically false" and must be "eliminated." Churchland, *Matter and Consciousness*, 43; Churchland, "Eliminative Materialism," 67. Rosenberg argues that you cannot have thoughts. Rosenberg, *Atheist's Guide to Reality*, 172, 205, 239.

I AM MORE THAN A BRAIN AND BODY (I AM A SOUL)

We have established that if consciousness exists, then it cannot be physical, and there is no doubt that I am conscious. That is to say, I am what *grounds* and *possesses* my mental states and properties. But what sort of thing am I? Recall the metaphysical implications: If substance dualism is true, then I am identical to an immaterial substance—the soul. By contrast, if physicalism is true, then I am identical and reducible to a purely physical object composed of separable parts (i.e., an aggregate). Consider the following three arguments for the existence of the soul in contrast to physicalism:

Identity through Change

Purely physical objects do not "survive over time as the same object if it comes to have different parts."[21] For example, suppose we changed the tires on a car. Is it the same car? Whatever your answer, imagine that over time we replaced every individual piece of the car: the windshield, wheels, bumpers, every nut and bolt, etc. Again, is it the same car? But before answering this question, suppose further that we took all the replaced parts and put them back together. We now have two cars.

At this point, the question becomes "Which of these cars, if any, is the original?" Regardless of your answer, one thing is certain—they both cannot be the original. This is because, as previously mentioned, purely physical objects do not maintain identity through change or part replacement. Now, consider the syllogism from identity through change.

1. I am either a purely physical object (i.e., an aggregate) or a soul (i.e., an immaterial substance).
2. If I am a purely physical object, I do not retain identity through change or part replacement.
3. I *do* maintain identity through change and part replacement.
4. Therefore, I am not a purely physical object.
5. Therefore, I am a soul.

As a thought experiment, suppose I committed a crime roughly ten years ago. Based on modern science, it is now known that we replace virtually every cell in our bodies every seven to ten years.[22] Now, if physicalism is true and I am identical to a body, then it follows that after part replacement

21. Moreland, *Soul*, 132.

22. Spalding et al., "Retrospective Birth Dating," paras. 1–7.

and change, there is a new body (i.e., a new aggregate composed of different parts) and thus a different person.[23] If I am a new person, then I should not, theoretically, be liable for the crime. Obviously, a court of law would not countenance such an argument and I would be convicted of the crime, because human beings retain their identity through change despite part replacement.[24]

Indivisibility of Personhood

Philosophers distinguish between degreed and non-degreed properties. Degreed properties are certain properties, such as loudness, heaviness, or softness, that can be divided and exist in various percentages or degrees. Sounds can be louder, weights can be heavier, and textures softer. Non-degreed properties are certain properties that exist or do not—an "all-or-nothing" property, so to speak. Even numbers like six and two possess the property of being even. Six cannot be more even than two, and two cannot be less even than six. Hence, while degreed properties may be divided and exist in various percentages or degrees, non-degreed properties cannot. The same principle applies to purely physical objects.

If we took a table and cut it in half, it would make sense to say that we have 50 percent of a table. But note that the same cannot be said of a person. Granted, one could sever my limbs and claim that I have 50 percent of a body. However, having 50 percent of a body does not make me 50 percent of a person, because being a person is an all-or-nothing kind of thing—there is no in-between. Therefore, given that my body can be divided and exist in various percentages or degrees, but I (the self) cannot, it follows that I am not a purely physical object: I am a soul. Hence, the argument:

1. I am either a purely physical object (i.e., an aggregate) or a soul (i.e., an immaterial substance).
2. Purely physical objects can be divided and exist in various percentages or degrees.
3. I cannot be divided or exist in various percentages or degrees—I'm an all-or-nothing kind of thing.
4. Therefore, I am not a purely physical object.
5. Therefore, I am a soul.

23. Rea, "Problem of Material Constitution," 529.

24. For a similar argument by an atheist philosopher, see Kim, *Mind in a Physical World*, 40.

At this point, a physicalist may retort that the brain, instead of the body, is what grounds personhood. However, the same problems arise. To illustrate, consider the rare conditions of Dandy-Walker syndrome or anencephalic disease where a person may possess only 55 percent of a brain, either due to a birth defect or operation. As before, one could say that the person has 55 percent of a brain, but it would not follow from this that, therefore, they are only 45 percent of a person. While they may lose functioning, they do not lose "personhood." Thus, given that there are things true of me that are not true of my brain and body (and vice versa), then it follows that I am not a purely physical object: I am a soul.

The Argument from Free Will

At a minimum, free will is the view that one is the *first mover*, or ultimate, originating source of one's will or actions.[25] For instance, if I, as a first mover, lift my arm to vote, then I was the direct cause of my arm going up. However, suppose I am shocked by a taser, and it causes my arm to go up. In that case, the shock from the taser becomes the first mover, reducing me to an intermediate, secondary mover in this causal chain of explanations. Hence, I would not be free and not the first mover but casually determined by a previous event beyond my control.

If physicalism is true, then human freedom becomes impossible, and determinism is the logically consistent consequence. Determinism is the view that all thoughts, beliefs, desires, sensations, and actions of human beings are causally determined by prior, external factors beyond the human beings' control. Therefore, if human beings are reducible to purely physical objects composed of physical properties and parts, then they do not act on their own but are caused to act by external forces determined by the laws of chemistry and physics.[26] For instance, water does not "freely choose" to freeze at thirty-two degrees Fahrenheit; a bullet cannot "choose" to disobey Newton's laws of motion, deciding to swerve left instead of up; and after putting a dollar into a Coke machine, the machine cannot "choose" to sing a song instead of dropping a Coke. Why? Because purely physical objects do not *freely* move or act on their own but rather are *causally determined* to act based on external inputs and outputs. Hence, purely physical objects are not free but determined.

Consider the following syllogism: I am either a purely physical object (i.e., an aggregate) or a soul (i.e., an immaterial substance).

25. Moreland, *Body & Soul*, 127–28.

26. Moreland, *Body & Soul*, 93.

1. If I am a purely physical object, then I do not possess free will.
2. I possess free will.
3. Therefore, I am not a purely physical object.
4. Therefore, I am a soul.

To illustrate, suppose I moved a rock with a staff. In this chain of events, we can say that the movement of the rock is explained by the movement of the staff, the motion of the staff is explained by the movement of my hand, and the next question becomes "But what moved me?"[27]

To answer this question from a physicalist perspective, it must first be understood that if both naturalism and atheism are true, then the law of causal closure must be true.[28] This is the notion that for every physical event, there will necessarily be a prior, physical cause. No immaterial causes can serve as an explanation; but for free will to be possible, one must be the first mover of one's will or actions. Therefore, if the physicalist desires to preserve the possibility of free will, then given causal closure, they must explain the movement of one's hand by pointing to a prior physical event that ends within the person as the first mover of the action. Without meeting this condition, free will is impossible.

Granted, the physicalist can point to the physical event of neurons firing in the brain, but this does not satisfy the requirements for either causal closure or free will (being the first mover). Why not? Because, for the law of causal closure to be satisfied, there must be an explanation for *every* physical event by way of some *prior* physical cause. This leaves the physicalist with only two options, both of which exclude the possibility of free will. For the first option, the physicalist can propose a prior set of neurons firing to explain the initially proposed neuronal firings above. However, this is still a physical event that, given the law of causal closure, necessarily requires a prior physical cause. Still, the physicalist can posit another set of neurons firing to explain the proposed neurons firing to explain the original explanation. But note, this would lead only to an infinite regress, and as a result, the action could never be accomplished. Thus, given that the action was accomplished, this option becomes logically impossible.

For the second option, no matter how many sets of firing neurons the physicalist may wish to posit, they must now explain them by pointing to some external, physical event that was both *prior to and beyond* the person's control. While this option makes the chain of events possible, it requires moving the source of the cause beyond the person, removing them as the

27. Aristotle, *Physics*, §256a.

28. Kim, *Mind in a Physical World*, 40.

first mover and reducing them to merely an intermediate, secondary mover. Hence, although the law of causal closure is satisfied, it still eliminates human freedom.

For this reason, the only explanation that could, in principle, allow for the *ontological possibility* of human freedom is that human beings are immaterial souls *transcendent* to the body with the causal power to act as first movers. Yet, this option is not available to the atheistic naturalist and, by default, a physicalist view of persons. Therefore, if human freedom is at least possible, then it follows that I am not a purely physical object.

The Price Tag of Denying Human Freedom

The physicalist's only option for denying the existence of the soul is to deny the fourth premise: that human freedom exists. If they take this option, both moral responsibility and intellectual integrity are impossible. If external factors beyond one's control causally determine a person's beliefs, behaviors, and decisions, then no one could ever be held morally responsible for their actions. When a gun is used in a murder, the chain of events is such that the gun fired the bullet; the bullet penetrated the victim's heart and caused the person's death. But note, although the bullet was the *direct cause* of death, neither the bullet nor the gun can be held morally responsible for the crime. The bullet or gun, being purely physical objects, did not act on their own but were caused to act by the prior event of the person pulling the trigger.

If human beings are purely physical objects, then much like the gun or bullet, the person becomes nothing more than an intermediate, secondary mover in this causal chain of events. If determinism is true, then the person didn't choose to act on their own but, like the gun or bullet, was causally determined to act by some prior event beyond their control. If we cannot blame the gun or bullet—because they were intermediate, secondary movers—then we cannot blame the person either. All three were purely physical objects, neither of which was the source of their actions, and thus neither can be held morally responsible.

This is the price tag: either determinism is true and human beings are not morally responsible for their actions, or human beings are morally responsible for their actions and determinism is false. In a syllogism, the price tag can be written as follows:

1. If physicalism is true, then determinism is true.
2. If determinism is true, then human beings are not morally responsible for their actions.

3. Human beings *are* morally responsible for their actions.
4. Therefore, determinism is false.
5. Therefore (based on 1 and 4), physicalism is false.

The Price Tag of Intellectual Integrity

By intellectual integrity, I mean the idea that a person has come to believe something based on the evidence in a rationally responsible way—one's beliefs were formed through a process of rigorous research, analyzing the evidence, and then freely coming to one's own logical conclusion. If this is done, then a person can claim a sense of intellectual integrity with respect to their beliefs, be they atheism or theism. However, this notion of intellectual integrity assumes that, in some sense, one was rationally responsible for their beliefs and had the freedom to come to those beliefs in the first place. Yet, given what we've discussed so far, if naturalism cannot allow for the possibility of human freedom, then it cannot allow for the possibility of intellectual integrity via rational responsibility.

Many atheists call themselves "freethinkers," meaning they are "enlightened," unbound, and not "brainwashed" by the shackles of religion. They are "free to think" for themselves. But if the atheist holds to physicalism and acknowledges that free will does not exist, then they must equally acknowledge that none of their thoughts or beliefs were ever free to begin with. However, if none of their thoughts or beliefs were ever free, then ironically, by their own standards, the last thing they could possibly call themselves is a "freethinker." Syllogistically, it looks this way:

1. If atheism is true, then free will does not exist.
2. Because of the evidence, I freely chose to become an atheist.
3. Therefore, free will exists.
4. Therefore, atheism is false.

CONCLUSION

In the beginning of this chapter, we saw that physicalism and dualism were the two dominant positions seeking to explain the nature of human beings by answering two central questions: (1) What is consciousness? (2) What is the "I" or self? At the outset, empiricism and science were shown to be impotent in providing answers to these questions for at least three reasons:

First, given the nature of the soul, these are the wrong tools for the assessment. Second, they are categorically fallacious (e.g., using one's eyes to look for something invisible or using a metal detector to detect plastic). Third, both physicalism and dualism are empirically equivalent theories, meaning that no amount of scientific, empirical data would lend weight to one view over the other. Thus, any conclusions drawn from the data were philosophical in nature, not scientific. Additionally, given that some of the world's leading neuroscientists are dualists, it becomes erroneous to argue that a belief in the soul necessarily stems from scientific ignorance. Hence, settling the dispute became a philosophical question about metaphysics, not science.

After laying a foundation for examining the metaphysics, I presented a case for the existence of the soul from a substance dualist perspective by arguing two basic contentions: (1) consciousness is not physical, and 2) I am more than a brain and body—I am a soul. Leibniz's Law of Identity served as a foundation for assessing these contentions in contrast to physicalism.

In defining consciousness, we saw that if physicalism is true, then consciousness must be identical and/or reducible to something physical like the brain. It was then demonstrated that a cause-effect or dependence relationship between mind and brain cannot suffice for establishing identity. Conversely, using Leibniz's Law of Identity, three points in defense of dualism were provided to show that the mind and brain are not the same thing, given that they possessed different states and properties (i.e., there were things true of one that were not true of the other and vice versa). Consequently, consciousness cannot be identical or reducible to something physical, and thus, physicalism (and, by default, atheism, and naturalism) is false.

In identifying the "I" or the "self," three arguments were presented, demonstrating that human beings are neither identical nor reducible to a physical brain and body. The first argument revolves around the notion of identity through change. Given that purely physical objects do not maintain identity through part replacement or change, but human beings do, the I is not a purely physical object. The second argument involved the distinction between degreed and non-degreed properties. Given that purely physical objects can be divided and exist in various percentages or degrees, but I cannot—I am an all-or-nothing kind of thing—I cannot be a purely physical object.

The final argument emphasized the possibility of human freedom in contrast to determinism. If physicalism is true, human freedom is impossible, but, if human freedom is, at the very least, ontologically possible, then I must be more than (and transcendent to) a brain and body. If one denies free will, two price tags follow—the impossibility of moral responsibility and intellectual integrity. Thus, if (1) human beings are morally responsible for their actions, and if (2) the atheist freely chooses to become an atheist by freely analyzing the evidence, then physicalism and, by default, naturalism, determinism, and atheism cannot be true. For these reasons, the soul must exist, and thus I simply don't have enough faith to be a physicalist.

Bibliography

Aristotle. *Physics: Books I–IV*. Translated by Philip H. Wicksteed and Francis M. Cornford. Loeb Classical Library 228. Cambridge, MA: Harvard University Press, 1957.

Bennett, M. R., and P. M. S. Hacker. *Philosophical Foundations of Neuroscience*. New York: Wiley, 2021.

Churchland, Paul M. "Eliminative Materialism and the Propositional Attitudes." *Journal of Philosophy* 78 (Feb. 1981) 67–90.

———. *Matter and Consciousness*. 3rd ed. Cambridge, MA: MIT Press, 2013.

Kim, Jaegwon. *Mind in a Physical World: An Essay on the Mind-Body Problem and Mental Causation*. Cambridge, MA: MIT Press, 1998.

Moreland, J. P. *Body & Soul: Human Nature the Crisis in Ethics*. 3rd ed. Downers Grove, IL: IVP Academic, 2000.

———. *Consciousness and the Existence of God*. New York: Routledge, 2008.

———. *Scientism and Secularism: Learning to Respond to a Dangerous Ideology*. Wheaton, IL: Crossway, 2018.

———. *The Soul: How We Know It's Real and Why It Matters*. Chicago: Moody, 2014.

Moreland, J. P., and William Lane Craig. *Philosophical Foundations for a Christian Worldview*. Downers Grove, IL: IVP Academic, 2003.

Plantinga, Alvin. *Where the Conflict Really Lies: Science, Religion, and Naturalism*. Oxford: Oxford University Press, 2011.

Rea, Michael C. "The Problem of Material Constitution." *Philosophical Review* 104 (Oct. 1995) 525–52.

Rosenberg, Alex. *The Atheist's Guide to Reality: Enjoying Life without Illusions*. London: Norton and Co., 2011.

Ruse, Michael. "Curate's Egg: Alex Rosenberg and the Meaning of Life." Rationally Speaking, Apr. 21, 2012. https://rationallyspeaking.blogspot.com/2012/04/curates-eggo-alex-rosenberg-and-meaning.html.

Spalding, Kristy L., et al. "Retrospective Birth Dating of Cells in Humans." *Cell* 122 (July 2005) 133–43. https://www.cell.com/action/showPdf?pii=S0092-8674%2805%2900408-3.

Turek, Frank. *Stealing from God: Why Atheists Need God to Make Their Case*. Colorado Springs: NavPress, 2015.

Apologetics and Molinism: The Apologetic Appeal of Molinism (Even for Non-Molinists)

Timothy A. Stratton[1]

A vital part of defending the truth of Christian theism is to possess and advance a careful and precise systematic theology. Formally defined, *systematic theology* operates on the premise of coherence within Christianity and seeks to make sense of Scripture while maintaining a set of logically coherent theological beliefs. For example, if a pastor makes theological claim *p* from the pulpit on Sunday, but then, on the following Sunday makes theological claim *q* contradicting claim *p*, they are, intentionally or unintentionally, introducing incoherence into Christianity, and the message they convey from the pulpit is that Christianity is not true. Possessing a robust systematic theology not only prevents against unintentionally introducing errors into Christian belief but also enables one to defend against errors when they are intentionally introduced.

Truth will never contradict itself. Therefore, if Christianity is true, it cannot possess contradictions within its system of beliefs—it must be

1. A note of thanks is owed to Dr. Frank Turek for his commitment to apologetics and systematic theology. As an unequipped youth pastor suddenly confronted with a "wave of atheism" crashing upon my youth group in 2008, Turek's work was some of the first apologetics material I found on the internet. At the time, I often found the work of Craig and Moreland (for example) to be too difficult for my uninitiated mind to grasp. Frank Turek, however, has a gift for taking the material scholars discuss and translating it—making it accessible for beginners—and prepared me for academia. Indeed, Frank Turek opened the door for me to a larger world in which I eventually earned a PhD in theology. Since those early days of my journey into apologetics, Frank Turek has taken me under his wing and helped me in both my ministry and in my personal life. I am indebted to Frank Turek and his ministry and am thankful for his friendship.

logically consistent. The laws of logic and rules of reason are God-given tools that allow his image-bearers to examine God's inspired word, handle it correctly, and reach true conclusions. If one does not begin with these tools, one could potentially read the Bible and conclude that Jesus was an atheist, or a mushroom, or anything one wanted.[2] As apologists seeking to make a difference in the world, we ought to ensure that our beliefs are logically consistent. Christianity—if true—will be logical, given that truth and logic are inextricably linked. Thus, Christianity, rightly understood, will be logically coherent in such a way that all of one's theological beliefs will fit together like a puzzle.

Within the framework of systematic theology, this chapter explains and defends the apologetic significance of the system of thought known as Molinism. It will do this by explaining the basic tenets of Molinist theology and compare how it approaches a challenge like the problem of evil in contrast to theological determinism. It will then illustrate how Molinism interacts with other apologetic arguments for the existence of God. Indeed, I contend that it is vital for all apologists to grasp the apologetic significance of Molinism, even if one is not a Molinist.

WHAT IS MOLINISM?

Many Christians have never heard the terms *Molinism* or *Molinist*. Conversely, these same Christians have heard the terms *Calvinism* and *Arminianism*, even if they do not fully understand what is entailed or implied by them. Molinism is a view of God's sovereignty and human freedom/responsibility derived from the last name of sixteenth-century Spanish theologian Luis de Molina.[3] Although the concepts of Molinism were around for centuries prior to Molina's birth, Molina was the first to connect all the theological dots and describe a view of God's sovereignty that makes sense of the whole of Scripture in a manner that diverged from the rise of Reformed theology.[4]

I have taken to calling my view "mere Molinism," borrowing from C. S. Lewis's book titled *Mere Christianity*. Mere Molinism consists of two essential ingredients:

1. Prior to God's decision to create the world, God knew everything that *would* happen in any possible scenario he *could* create (this is part

2. This was an actual claim presented to Frank Turek at Ohio State University. A short clip of the exchange is viewable here: https://www.youtube.com/watch?v=7HJOStAbtpY.

3. MacGregor, *Luis de Molina*, 11–30.

4. Jaros, "Molinist Solution."

of God's middle knowledge if God possesses the power to create a libertarian free creature—even if he never does).

2. As beings created in the image of God, humans, like God, possess libertarian freedom.

Middle knowledge is the knowledge God possesses if he possesses knowledge of things that *would* happen in every possible set of circumstances an omnipotent God *could* create. Prior to creation, an omniscient (perfect in knowledge) and omnipotent (perfect in power) God knows all that he could create. This is known as God's natural knowledge. At the moment of creation (and after God creates), an omniscient God knows all that will happen. This is known as divine foreknowledge. But there is more to know than just what *could* happen and what *will* happen. Prior to creation, an omniscient and omnipotent God also knows what *would* happen if he created one way or the other. This includes God's perfect knowledge of what would happen if he created humans (and angels) with libertarian freedom. This is knowledge that a perfect and maximally great God possesses, even if he never creates a world that includes libertarian free creatures.

As I once explained in a debate on this topic, "If perfect power and perfect knowledge are *necessary* attributes of God, then middle knowledge comes along for the ride. This is because God's decree is contingent, but His attributes—omnipotence and omniscience—are necessary."[5] So, if God is necessarily perfect in both power and knowledge, then God possesses natural knowledge, foreknowledge, and middle knowledge, even if no created person actually possesses libertarian freedom.

Libertarian freedom refers to a person's choice, action, evaluation, or judgment that is not *causally determined* by something or someone else. It is more technically defined as the ability to think, act, or choose such that antecedent conditions are *insufficient* to causally determine or necessitate one's thought, action, or choice. This definition of libertarian freedom stands whether or not there are *alternative* possibilities. However, if one possesses the ability to choose between alternative possibilities in the real world, then one is not determined by something or someone else. It is "the opportunity to exercise an ability to choose between at least two options, each of which is compatible with one's nature in a specific circumstance where the antecedent conditions are *insufficient* to causally determine or necessitate the agent's choice."[6] This is a fancy way of saying the "ability to do

5. Freethinking Ministries, "Is Molinism Biblical," 51:13–46.

6. Stratton and Moreland, "Explanation and Defense," 2.

otherwise." Some biblical passages supporting this definition of libertarian freedom are Deut 30:10–20; 1 Cor 10:13–15; and Gal 5:13.[7]

To summarize, this chapter's use of libertarian freedom will refer to an individual's opportunity to exercise the ability to choose between a range of alternative options, each of which is compatible with their nature at a given moment. It will always mean that when one thinks, acts, or chooses, one is not causally determined or necessitated to think, act, or choose by something or someone else. Therefore, the mere Molinist simply—and merely—affirms that humans possess libertarian freedom, and that God possesses middle knowledge of our free thoughts, actions, and choices.[8] Mere Molinism, not being a soteriological system, is compatible with both Arminianism and Calvinism.[9] If one applied these two essential ingredients to soteriology, one could become a soteriological Molinist by adding the third ingredient of God's omni-benevolence.[10]

Soteriological Molinism requires each of these three key ingredients, whereas competing soteriological models deny at least one. For example, open theists deny that God possesses middle knowledge of possible worlds within his power to create.[11] Divine determinists regularly reject the notion of *any* human libertarian freedom, and some dismiss the omni-benevolence of God.[12] I argue that at least one of the three key aspects of the tenets of Molinism is connected with each of the following apologetic arguments and subsequently has logically consistent access to more arguments for the existence of God and offers powerful defenses to objections raised against it—more so than any other view of God's sovereignty. While this does not prove Molinism is true, it does, for this author, make Molinism a preferable view when it comes to apologetics and evangelism.

The problem of evil (PoE) is often seen as the greatest objection raised against the knowledge of God. Indeed, based upon my experience, it seems

7. Stratton, *Human Freedom, Divine Knowledge*, 24–31.

8. God is the paradigmatic example of a being who possesses libertarian freedom. His attribute of omnipotence entails that God has the power to do more than one thing. God created the universe but is powerful enough to have refrained from creation or to have created differently. Thus, God is an unmoved mover and possesses the power of alternative possibilities (commonly referred to as the ability to do otherwise).

9. Stratton, *Human Freedom, Divine Knowledge*, 252–55.

10. God is a maximally great being who loves and desires the best for all people.

11. Beilby and Eddy, *Divine Foreknowledge*, 144–49.

12. Jerry Walls makes a case against Calvinism quoting the Calvinist Arthur Pink. Walls states that Pink "bites the bullet" and admits the Calvinistic view of God entails that God does not love all people, and encourages all Calvinists to come clean and be as honest as Pink: Evangel University, "Jerry Walls," 46:20; see also Pink, *Sovereignty of God*, 16–19.

to be the primary reason given by atheists as to why they do not believe in God. They would say that:

1. God, by definition, is omni-benevolent, omnipotent, and omniscient.
2. If God is omni-benevolent (all good and perfectly loving), he desires to prevent all evil.
3. If God is omnipotent, he has the power to prevent all evil.
4. If God is omniscient, he knows how to prevent all evil.
5. The world is suffused with evil.
6. Therefore, God is either not omni-benevolent, not omnipotent, or not omniscient (or perhaps none of the above).
7. Therefore, God, by definition, does not exist.

Christians, however, have access to what is known as the "free will defense," which defeats this specific objection raised against God's existence.[13] Yet Calvinists, who deny that humanity possesses libertarian freedom and affirm that God determines all things all the time, do not seem to have logically consistent access to this counter. My friend (or as he has described himself, my "frenemy") Guillaume Bignon is not only a Calvinist but an exhaustive divine determinist. This means that he believes that humans do not ever possess libertarian freedom. Nonetheless, to his credit, he keeps the free will defense in his back pocket and offers it to those who seem to need that important question addressed. In the same way, while all readers may not become convinced Molinists at the close of this chapter, keeping Molinism "in their back pocket" is an effective evangelistic tool.

Bignon has noted that views like Molinism that affirm the libertarian freedom of humanity are "better-off than Calvinism to answer the atheist argument from evil against God's existence. I do affirm that . . . the libertarian has a resource against the problem of evil that the compatibilist [theological determinist] cannot use."[14] It is for reasons similar to these that Dr. Frank Turek often appeals to human libertarian freedom, divine middle knowledge, and mere Molinism when he is engaged in question-and-answer sessions with students.[15] While this approach is perfectly reasonable, I argue here that Molinism is to be preferred to Calvinism and other views of God's sovereignty when addressing the problem of evil and demonstrate

13. Plantinga, *God, Freedom, and Evil*, 29–33.

14. Bignon, "Response," 19.

15. See, e.g., CrossExamined, "Does Molinism."

how mere Molinism relates to other apologetic arguments defending the existence of God.

A COLOSSAL WASTE OF TIME?

A pastor once asked me if all my research and writing regarding Molinism was nothing more than a "colossal waste of time." After all, why should an apologist, whose mission is to argue for the truth of Christianity, spend so much time promoting a specific Christian theology when it concerns such a seemingly peripheral and nonessential issue? Christian apologist J. Warner Wallace agreed with this pastor and once warned me that I was going to pigeonhole myself as "the Molinist guy" and divide my potential audience. Both men believed that the majority of my time as a Christian apologist would be better spent arguing against atheism alone.

Frank Turek was in the room with Wallace and me during that conversation. I will never forget Frank's exclamation: "Jim, what are you talking about? Doing apologetics through the lens of Molinism is Tim's *x*.[16] Molinism is what sets him apart from all the rest of us apologists!" Although I am not merely trying to "set myself apart" from the rest of my colleagues (because I sincerely believe that Molinism is true), I responded to Wallace just as I did to the concerned pastor, by explaining that I believe Molinism to be the best defense against the atheist worldview today. In my experience, not only do I find myself defending Molinism from Calvinists, Arminians, and open theists, but I am also amazed to see the vigor in which atheists also oppose the doctrine of middle knowledge—a fundamental tenet of Molinism.[17] Why should the atheist care about a Christian teaching on divine sovereignty and human responsibility any more than a Christian teaching on baptism, spiritual gifts, or eschatology? I believe it is because Molinism destroys (as Paul says in 2 Cor 10:5) their favorite argument against the knowledge of God—the so-called problem of evil.

MOLINISM AND THE PROBLEMS OF EVIL

World-renowned astrophysicist Neil deGrasse Tyson spends much of his time arguing against the existence of God, claiming:

16. J. Warner Wallace is well known for encouraging Christian apologists to find their *x*. By one's *x*, Wallace means that each person needs to find their niche or something that is going to make their ministry unique and different from the next person's.

17. Graham Oppy is a prominent atheist philosopher who has raised objections to Molinism. See Craig, "Arguing Successfully about God."

> Every description of God that I have heard, holds God to be all-powerful and all-good. And then I look around and I see a tsunami that killed a quarter million people in Indonesia—an earthquake that killed a quarter million people in Haiti. And I see earthquakes, tornadoes, and disease, childhood leukemia. And I see all of this and I say I do not see evidence of both of those being true simultaneously. . . . If there is a God, the God is either not all-powerful, or not all good. It can't be both![18]

Alternatively, atheist philosopher Paul Draper argues, "Logical arguments from evil are a dying (dead?) breed . . . even an omnipotent and omniscient being might be forced to allow E[vil] for the sake of obtaining some important good."[19] This "important good," according to Molinism, is that this finite, affliction-filled world allows humans the opportunity to *freely* love for eternity and teaches us not to take a perfect state of affairs for granted. Why did God call this world "very good" (Gen 1:31)? Because God knew it would lead to an "eternal weight of glory beyond all comparison" (2 Cor 4:17). God has the eternal and infinite future in mind, and so should we.[20]

As a deductive argument, Molinism's response to the PoE looks this way:

1. If God is omni-benevolent, then he desires genuine loving intimacy with humans.
2. If God desires genuine loving intimacy with humans, then he would create humans with libertarian freedom (because):

    2.1. *Genuine loving intimacy between God and humans necessarily requires that humans possess libertarian freedom.*

3. If God creates humans with libertarian freedom, then he must allow humans to experience suffering (because):

    3.1. *Suffering results from the choices of libertarian free humans.*

    3.2. *God created a world in which he knew that unless he permitted (all kinds of) evil, some would not freely choose to eternally preserve the suffering-free state of affairs in the new heavens and new earth (2 Cor 4:17).*[21]

18. Handler, "Does Neil deGrasse Tyson," 0:45.

19. Draper, "Skeptical Theist," 176–77.

20. If an omniscient God possessed this counterfactual knowledge prior to the foundations of the world, then, by definition, God possesses middle knowledge.

21. Not only does this apply to moral and natural evil, but it makes sense of gratuitous evil/suffering. The following thought experiment seeks to make the point: Would

4. God is omni-benevolent.

5. Therefore, God allows humans to experience suffering.

This argument makes use of the three essential ingredients of soteriological Molinism. In fact, no other view of God's sovereignty has logical claim to this specific argument, which both emphasizes God's eternal intent and prevents Neil deGrasse Tyson's laying of "moral guilt" (*mens rea*) at the feet of God.[22] When we keep eternity in mind, we see that this world, suffused with pain, evil, affliction, and suffering, is actually the most loving world God could have created. Peter van Inwagen made it clear when he said, "It used to be widely held that evil was incompatible with the existence of God: that no possible world contained both God and evil. So far as I am able to tell, this thesis is no longer defended."[23]

In spite of this, the majority of modern culture is unaware of these scholarly achievements. The so-called "problems of evil" have often been claimed to be the primary reason for atheistic affirmations. This is why it is vital for the church—from pastors to laypeople (including *you*)—to be aware of the apologetic power of Molinism when engaging in evangelism or influencing culture for God's glory.

MOLINISM AND DIVINE HIDDENNESS

In a previous publication, I briefly alluded to one manner of resolving a specific form of the problem of evil known as the problem of divine hiddenness.[24] I have since coauthored a paper with Jacobus Erasmus arguing against John Schellenberg's *divine hiddenness argument* raised against the existence of God.[25] Schellenberg's position can be stated broadly as follows:

1. If God exists, there will never be any nonresistant nonbelievers.

2. There are some nonresistant nonbelievers.

3. Therefore, God does not exist.

---

a person prefer to live in a world free from any and all suffering, where even the lower animals never suffer? If he awoke tomorrow in that world, would he freely choose to "keep the rules" to make sure no being capable of suffering ever suffers again? If so, it seems that Paul was onto something in 2 Cor 4:17. If not, then he simply will not be allowed to hang out with those who have learned to "keep the rules" for the rest of eternity so that suffering of any kind is never experienced again (at least by those who have learned).

22. *Mens rea* refers to the legal philosophy of the "guilty mind" and criminal intent.

23. Van Inwagen, "Problem of Evil," 66.

24. Stratton, *Human Freedom, Divine Knowledge*, 262.

25. Erasmus and Stratton, "Molinist Response."

It depends upon the following principle:

> (A) Necessarily, if God exists, then, if at time (t), a finite person (S) exists who is a nonresistant seeker at (t), God will ensure that, or provide sufficient evidence for belief in God such that, at (t), (S) will believe that God exists.

Erasmus and I argue that Molinism undercuts principle A. If God possesses middle knowledge, then he knows both what a person would freely do in any circumstances they may find themselves and the repercussions of that person's free actions; thus, there are feasible scenarios in which God knows it is better that a nonresistant seeker does not become a believer immediately or, perhaps, even at all. In other words, given the middle knowledge of an omniscient God, it is possible that God would not ensure—or provide sufficient evidence for belief in God such that—certain nonresistant seekers become believers.

In response to Schellenberg, we offer the possibility that God does not ensure that nonresistant seeker (S) becomes a believer at time (t), because he knows that (S) will become a believer at some later time (t*) and it would be better that (S) become a believer at (t*) than at (t). For example, suppose that Jones becomes a nonresistant seeker at time (t). Suppose further that the following two propositions are true and that God, through his middle knowledge, knows them:

1. If Jones becomes a believer at (t), then Jones will get married in his home country of France and remain there for his entire life, leading no one to faith in God.
2. If Jones does not become a believer at (t), then Jones will move to Africa, become a believer in Africa at time (t*), get married in Africa, start a Christian school there, have a tremendously positive impact on the lives of the many students in his school, and lead 305 people to faith in God, which otherwise would not have been the case.

In this scenario, it would be better that Jones does not become a believer at (t). Indeed, it would be unloving and unwise for God to ensure that Jones becomes a believer at (t) and, hence, a perfectly wise and loving God would not do this.

If anyone seems to be a nonresistant nonbeliever today it would be Jordan Peterson. With this in mind, several years ago I spent much time communicating the gospel to my friend Alex who aggressively resisted my attempts to evangelize him. He would not consider any arguments found in books written by Christian apologists, and I eventually gave up and "wiped the dust off of my feet." A year later I ran into Alex, and he had a huge smile on his face. I asked him why he looked so happy, and he told me that he was now a follower of Christ!

Needless to say, I was shocked and overjoyed and asked him how that had happened. He responded by saying that he had read Jordan Peterson's *12 Rules for Life*. I responded by saying, "But Jordan Peterson isn't a Christian!" Alex replied: "I know, but he got me so close to the cross that everything you said in the past now made perfect sense." It seems that Jordan Peterson was Alex's "gateway drug" for Christianity!

Alex then told me that God knew he had to be reached by someone who was not writing from a Christian perspective. Jordan Peterson was that someone. Thus, it is good that God allows Jordan Peterson—at least for a finite period of time—to remain in a state of nonresistant nonbelief, for the sake of those like Alex.[26] The salient point is that in each individual situation regarding nonresistant seekers, God knows whether it would be better for the nonresistant seeker to become a believer at that particular time or not. However, since there are feasible situations in which it would be better for God not to ensure that a nonresistant seeker becomes a believer at a particular time, principle A is false—it is not the case that God will necessarily ensure a nonresistant seeker would believe that he exists.

Of course, we, as human beings limited in knowledge, will not know the actual reasons why God does not ensure that certain nonresistant seekers immediately become believers, but this does not imply that God—given his middle knowledge—lacks good reasons for doing so. Consequently, since there are possible scenarios that are inconsistent with principle A; it follows that A is false, making Schellenberg's argument unsound. We have seen that Molinism can provide a defense against those seeking to defeat the Christian worldview, but we should not merely have a great defense. The Molinist also possesses a consistent and powerful offense.

MOLINISM AND THE FREETHINKING ARGUMENT AGAINST NATURALISM

The theology of Luis de Molina also provides a foundation for powerful arguments against naturalism—the view that reality is exhausted by nature

26. I also have a friend named Jimmy who experienced the exact same thing. Jimmy was an atheist who appeared on a local television show to contrast my views as a Christian apologist. Shortly thereafter, Jimmy became a Christian, and today we are good friends. He informed me that God used Peterson's *12 Rules for Life* as an instrumental factor along the way to his eventual conversion.

or that the natural world is all that exists.[27] It follows that, if nature is all that exists, then all that exists could ultimately be discovered via the study of nature. Thus, if all that exists is scientifically testable and discoverable, then anything supernatural, like God or the human soul, does not exist. I crafted a response to this common form of atheism that I call the freethinking argument against naturalism.[28] A deductive form of this argument is as follows:

1. If naturalism is true, God and the soul do not exist.
2. If God and the soul do not exist, humanity does not possess the libertarian freedom to think.
3. If humanity does not possess the libertarian freedom to think, then humanity is never epistemically responsible.
4. Humanity is occasionally epistemically responsible.
5. Therefore, humanity possesses the libertarian freedom to think.
6. Therefore, God and the soul exist.
7. Therefore, naturalism is false.
8. The best explanation of God, soul, and the libertarian freedom of humanity is the biblical account of reality.

The final conclusion, unlike the previous three deductive conclusions, is an abductive move (and the beginning of a different conversation designed to engage people with God's inspired word).[29] J. P. Moreland explains that "the argument for God's existence from the reality of libertarian freedom seeks to show that, given freedom, a theistic versus a natural-scientific explanation is epistemically and explanatorily superior." He adds:

> Applied to our case, the claim is made that, on a theistic metaphysic, one already has an instance of an unembodied mind in God which exercises robust libertarian freedom. Therefore, it is hardly surprising that embodied or unembodied finite libertarian agents should exist in the world. But on a naturalist view, mental entities are so strange and out of place that their existence (or regular correlation with physical entities) defies adequate explanation. There appear to be two realms operating

27. Plantinga, *Where the Conflict*, 307–19. Plantinga writes: "Naturalism is the idea that there is no such person as God or anything like him; immaterial selves would be too much like God, who, after all, is himself an immaterial self" (319).

28. Stratton and Moreland, "Explanation and Defense," 1.

29. A deductive conclusion follows necessarily from the premises. That is to say, if the premises are true, the conclusion must be true. An abductive conclusion is not as powerful, but still strong in that it seeks to infer the best explanation of the data.

> in causal harmony and theism provides the best explanation of this fact.[30]

While I have made the case elsewhere as to why a biblical view of God is the best explanation of human libertarian freedom and the soul, the goal of this chapter is simply to defend each premise leading to each deductive conclusion. Premise 1 is true by definition—if naturalism is true, nature is all that exist, and things *other* than nature, like God and things like God, would not exist. While Christian physicalists might not like the second step of the argument, premise 2 is tantamount to the following: if all that exists is nature, then everything about humanity—including all our thoughts and beliefs—is determined by the forces of nature (all of which are outside of human control).[31] Influential atheist Sam Harris notes that according to naturalism our "thoughts and intentions . . . are determined by prior causes and we are not responsible for them, or they are the product of chance and we are not responsible for them."[32]

Although I am not a naturalist, I agree with Sam Harris. It stands to reason that if I am a purely physical kind of thing, then everything about me—including my thoughts—would ultimately be determined by the nonrational laws and events of nature. Some might assert that a nonphysical soul or immaterial thinking thing might evolve or *emerge* from purely physical material and then take control of the physical body, but this assertion not only seems ad hoc, it does not constitute what is strictly defined as naturalism, since something like God could exist even if God, in this view, does not.[33] Moreover, it would violate the view advanced by Carl Sagan

30. J. P. Moreland, "Theism, Robust Naturalism, and Robust Libertarian Free Will," in Copan and Taliaferro, *Naturalness of Belief*, 221.

31. Christian physicalists such as Peter van Inwagen, Nancy Murphy, and Chris Date typically reject naturalism because they believe in a supernatural, immaterial, and nonphysical Creator of the physical universe. So, Christian physicalists still have a good reason to affirm the fact that humans are miraculously endowed with the power to think freely in the libertarian sense. Moreover, although they do not think we are like God in the sense of being an immaterial freethinking thing, they can affirm (like Van Inwagen does) that humanity is like God in the sense that we possess libertarian freedom.

32. Harris, *Free Will*, 5.

33. "In my view, 'emergence' is just a name for the problem to be solved (how could simple emergent properties and substances emerge if you start with particles as depicted by physics and just rearrange them over time?). Among other things, this means that without some pretty serious, wildly ad hoc adjustments, the sort of unity possessed by consciousness (and, perhaps, its ground) cannot be located or otherwise explained, given robust or strong naturalism." J. P. Moreland, "Theism, Robust Naturalism, and Robust Libertarian Free Will," in Copan and Taliaferro, *Naturalness of Belief*, 231.

and endorsed by Peter van Inwagen that naturalism is the view that purely physical objects are "all that ever will be."[34]

While many views are, strictly speaking, *possible*, this view seems drastically unlikely, ad hoc, and just plain miraculous (which is the last thing the atheist wants)! At the very least, it is fair to say that if God does not exist, then immaterial, rational, thinking things, with active causal power and libertarian freedom, *probably* do not exist either. All that to say, we have good reason to affirm that premise 2 is *probably* true, which is all one needs for a premise to be acceptable and the argument to move forward.

Premise 3 states that, if all things are causally determined, this includes all thoughts, beliefs, evaluations, and judgments. If all a person's thoughts, beliefs, evaluations, and judgments are always forced upon them—and they have no opportunity to be more careful and choose better thoughts, beliefs, evaluations, or judgments—then they are simply left assuming (as opposed to rationally inferring) that their determined thoughts, beliefs, evaluations, and judgments are good and true. However, this becomes a much bigger problem when one realizes that the deterministic cause of the effect of each of one's thoughts, beliefs, evaluations, and judgements is not a trustworthy cause.

Therefore, one could never rationally affirm that one's beliefs really are the inference to the best explanation. Given all that has been said, this "belief" can only be assumed without warrant or justification. Moreover, this assumption is merely an instance of passivity, as it would be causally determined and forced upon a person by something or someone else. Accordingly, they are not intellectually responsible, given they could not think, believe, or do anything other than assume, and assume exactly as they have been determined to assume.

To be clear, this is not a *justified* belief, rather, it is merely assumed. What is justified, however, is a sense of vertigo. Consider the words of William Lane Craig:

> There is a sort of dizzying, self-defeating character to determinism. For if one comes to believe that determinism is true, one has to believe that the reason he has come to believe it is simply that he was determined to do so. One has not in fact been able to weigh the arguments pro and con and freely make up one's mind on that basis. The difference between the person who weighs the arguments for determinism and rejects them and the person who weighs them and accepts them is wholly that one was determined by causal factors outside himself to believe and the other not to believe. When you come to realize that your decision to

34. Van Inwagen, "C. S. Lewis's Argument," 115.

> believe in determinism was itself determined and that even your present realization of that fact right now is likewise determined, a sort of vertigo sets in, for everything that you think, even this very thought itself, is outside your control. Determinism could be true; but it is very hard to see how it could ever be rationally affirmed, since its affirmation undermines the rationality of its affirmation.[35]

Vertigo is not worth wanting. Justified true beliefs, however, are something we should all endeavor to attain. Thus, premise 4 is something that we must accept as true, because to rationally argue against it assumes it.

The freethinking argument aims to show that if something nonrational or someone who is untrustworthy determines all of our thoughts and beliefs—our entire reasoning process—then we have reason to doubt our inferred, metaphysical, and theological thoughts and beliefs based upon "our" reasoning process. The idea that humans possess the power of libertarian freethinking in order to infer (and affirm) better and true beliefs makes much more sense according to a theistic worldview than a naturalistic one. Moreland writes: "It should be clear that the appearance of libertarian agents and free will is natural in this theistic view but quite odd, unnatural, and not basic in a naturalist worldview. Thus, again, it may very well be ad hoc and question-begging for someone to claim that a view of libertarian free will is 'at home,' 'consistent with,' or 'not ruled out by' naturalism."[36] Moreland is skeptical that some minimalist versions of both naturalism and libertarian freedom are compossible. He adds:

> The proper question is not, "Can a minimalist version of naturalism and libertarianism be shown to be logically consistent?" Rather, it is "Given the most reasonable form of naturalism and theism as a rival worldview, is it more reasonable than not to believe that the existence of libertarian actions and agents are more at home in a naturalist worldview than a theistic worldview? What is the truth of the matter?[37]

God creating humanity in his image and likeness with the power to be rational and approximate to his perfect standard of knowledge—or to fail to do so—provides a much better explanation than a naturalistic story of the world. Libertarian freedom points to the existence of God, and this is

35. William Lane Craig, in Jowers, *Four Views*, 60.

36. J. P. Moreland, "Theism, Robust Naturalism, and Robust Libertarian Free Will," in Copan and Taliaferro, *Naturalness of Belief*, 220.

37. J. P. Moreland, "Theism, Robust Naturalism, and Robust Libertarian Free Will," in Copan and Taliaferro, *Naturalness of Belief*, 238.

a win for Team Theism. Unfortunately, divine determinists (many, if not most Calvinists) also find themselves in the same complications highlighted throughout this discussion but for different reasons, since God, on their view, determines all thoughts and beliefs.

Matthew J. Hart writes, "Calvinists . . . are theological determinists. They hold that God causes every contingent event, either directly or indirectly."[38] Since human thoughts and states of belief are contingent events, this means that God—according to divine determinism—causes every thought and belief, including our false and evil beliefs. In *The Providence of God*, Paul Helm writes, "Not only is every atom and molecule, every thought and desire, kept in being by God, but every twist and turn of each of these is under the direct control of God. He has not, as far as we know, delegated that control to anyone else."[39]

I do not believe Helm is correct. Scripture clearly suggests that we have some control of our thoughts and ultimately of our important beliefs. The apostle Paul commands us to take certain thoughts captive (2 Cor 10:5) before they take us (Col 2:8). If God determined us to affirm false beliefs, it would be impossible for us to take those false thoughts captive. The committed Calvinist/determinist might counter by saying they do not have the same problems as the naturalist, since all their thoughts and beliefs are determined by an omniscient "God of truth" who is the standard of perfect knowledge. But, unless they are going to claim to be infallible, this move is unsatisfactory, given that without infallible knowledge, it follows that every person affirms false beliefs. If this is the case, it follows that God determines all people—including all theists—to affirm false beliefs. But, if this is the case, then our Creator is not a "God of truth" but is rather a "deity of deception."

Christians should not make this move! A god who causally determines us to affirm false beliefs is not worthy of worship. If a deity of deception determines all your beliefs, then you have reason to doubt your beliefs, including your theological beliefs. Therefore, if exhaustive divine determinism

38. Hart, "Calvinism and the Problem," 248. Hart notes that Paul Helm—a leading Calvinistic philosopher today—is a theological determinist. One must add, however, that there are some Calvinists who affirm the libertarian freedom to choose among a range of options consistent with one's nature. Koukl, *Tactics*, 128–29; Crisp, *Deviant Calvinism*, 17; Muller, *Divine Will*, 30, quotes Crisp, noting that Reformed theology is "not necessarily committed to hard determinism" and allows for "free will in some sense." He continues and says that a "libertarian Calvinist" will affirm that God "ordains whatever comes to pass but does not either determine or cause all things: some human acts are merely foreseen and permitted." This Calvinist/Reformed view is quite compatible with Molinism.

39. Helm, *Providence of God*, 22.

(EDD) is true, then God determines all Christ followers to affirm at least one false theological belief (and we stand in no position to *know* which of our determined theological beliefs is false). It would follow, then, that not only do humans lose the power to rationally infer and affirm truth but that the deity of EDD is anything but the "God of truth." With that in mind, consider these additional arguments:

Part 1

1. If God determines Christians to affirm false theological beliefs, then God is a deity of deception.
2. If a deity of deception inspired Scripture, then Scripture is not trustworthy.
3. Scripture is trustworthy.
4. Therefore, a deity of deception did not inspire Scripture.
5. Therefore, God does not determine Christians to affirm false theological beliefs.

Part 2

1. If God does not determine Christians to affirm false theological beliefs and Christians affirm false theological beliefs, then EDD is false.
2. God does not determine Christians to affirm false theological beliefs.
3. Christians affirm false theological beliefs.
4. Therefore, EDD is false.

If you assume that something or someone else determines all your theological thoughts and beliefs, then you cannot rationally affirm your theological thoughts and beliefs. But of course, at least on this occasion, you can rationally affirm your theological thoughts and beliefs, because to argue otherwise affirms them. Therefore, something or someone else does not determine all your thoughts and beliefs and you are a libertarian freethinker. If you believe that you are a rational freethinker who is not ultimately "mind controlled" by something or someone else, then you should reject the determinism that follows from any form of determinism. You should affirm that a supernatural God exists and that you are a supernatural and immaterial active and rational thinking thing—a soul—created in God's image.[40]

40. Moreland, *Soul*, 53; 125–26; see also, Moreland, *Recalcitrant Imago Dei*.

The freethinking argument against naturalistic atheism naturally aligns with Molinism but is in opposition with divine determinism, as it deductively concludes that humans possess libertarian freedom. In reality, this argument from rationality is often attacked from both atheists who assume naturalism is true and Christians who assume exhaustive divine determinism is true. Christian determinists cannot appeal to this apologetic argument for the existence of the human soul created in God's image because it destroys their divine determinism.

Because of problems like these, a minority of Calvinists choose to reject *exhaustive* divine determinism. Greg Koukl states:

> The problem with [determinism] is that without freedom, rationality would have no room to operate. Arguments would not matter since no one would be able to base beliefs on adequate reasons. One could never judge between a good idea and a bad one. One would only hold beliefs because he had been [determined] to do so. . . . Although it is theoretically possible that determinism is true . . . no one could ever know it if it were. Every one of our thoughts, dispositions, and opinions would have been decided for us by factors completely out of our control. Therefore, in practice, arguments for determinism are self-defeating.[41]

On this reasoning, Molinism seems to be the most defensible framework by which we understand libertarian freedom, and libertarian freedom is necessary for the freethinking argument against naturalism to hold.

MOLINISM AND OTHER APOLOGETICS ARGUMENTS

The Kalam Cosmological Argument

I believe that the Kalam cosmological argument (KCA) can expand our understanding of God's middle knowledge and libertarian freedom. The rational inferences provided by the KCA demonstrate that God exists in a "static state of aseity" in which the universe (time and space) does not exist.[42] That is to say, prior to the beginning of the existence of the universe, God exists, "and then" (to use temporal language), God creates the universe. The KCA is typically crafted in the following manner:

41. Koukl, *Tactics*, 128–29.

42. Divine aseity is the idea that God does not derive his existence from any source outside himself. He is not dependent on someone or something to give him existence.

1. Whatever begins to exist has a cause.
2. The universe began to exist.
3. Therefore, the universe has a cause.

Once one unpacks what is meant by the universe, one can rationally infer that the cause and Creator of the universe is:

1. Supernatural
2. Timeless
3. Eternal
4. Without beginning
5. Spaceless
6. Immaterial
7. Enormously powerful
8. Volitional (possesses libertarian freedom)
9. Personal[43]

It is also inferred that this supernatural and powerful personal cause and Creator of the universe exists in a static state of aseity sans creation. Considering this static state of aseity it must be asked if God is maximally great in this state.

To answer this question, allow me to pose three of my own:

1. Is it true that God exists in a state of aseity prior to creating the universe (i.e., without the universe)?
2. In this state of aseity is God omnipotent, and does he possess the power to create creatures with libertarian freedom, even if he never does create them?
3. In this state of aseity, is God omniscient, and does he possess the knowledge of what these libertarian free creatures would freely do?

If one answers yes to all the above, then Molinism follows. If one affirms that God is both omnipotent and omniscient prior to the creation of the universe, then some form of Molinism must be true. At the very least, God must possess middle knowledge, because God would possess the power to create libertarian free creatures even if he never creates them, and God

43. Stratton, *Human Freedom, Divine Knowledge*, 266–67.

would "middle know" exactly how these free creatures would freely think, act, believe, and behave prior to his creative decree.

Molinism and the Moral Argument

The moral argument might be the most attention getting of all the arguments in the arsenal of the apologist, since virtually all humans make moral judgments every day. It is typically offered in the form of the following syllogism:

1. If God does not exist, then objective moral values and duties do not exist.
2. Objective moral values and duties do exist.
3. Therefore, God exists.

There are several reasons why the atheist struggles with the moral argument. One is that naturalists typically reject libertarian freedom. As Sam Harris argues:

> Free will is an illusion. Our wills are simply not of our own making. Thoughts and intentions emerge from background causes of which we are unaware and over which we exert no conscious control. We do not have the freedom we think we have. . . . Either our wills are determined by prior causes, and we are not responsible for them, or they are the product of chance, and we are not responsible for them.[44]

If Harris is correct, then it logically follows that humans never possess the opportunity to choose any action, including actions with so-called moral properties. If determinism is true, then these things were decided for humanity long before they existed. We are nothing but passive cogs with illusions of responsibility.

However, if Molinism is true, then humans possess the opportunity to exercise an ability to think and act freely (at least occasionally). Thus, if Molinism is true, then humans can be held morally responsible—in a desert sense (justifiably *deserving* praise or blame for a thought, belief, or action)—for our thoughts and actions, because we are not causally determined by anything external to us and we possessed the opportunity to have chosen otherwise (but failed to take advantage of this opportunity with which we

44. Harris, *Free Will*, 5.

were presented). This leads to what I like to call the "oughts" and thoughts argument:[45]

1. If determinism is true, then humanity does not possess libertarian freedom.
2. If humanity does not possess libertarian freedom, then humanity does not possess the power of libertarian freethinking.
3. If humanity does not possess the power of libertarian freethinking, then "oughts" about our thoughts are illusory (as one would be deterministically prevented—by something or someone else—from thinking otherwise).
4. "Oughts" about our thoughts are not illusory.
5. Therefore, humanity possesses the power of libertarian freethinking.
6. Therefore, humanity possesses libertarian freedom.
7. Therefore, determinism is false.

If someone rejects human libertarian freedom—and thus affirms that something or someone else determines all things about them—then how can one be held morally or rationally responsible (in a desert sense) for behaving in the only way in which one was causally determined? Determinism cannot logically answer this question. Molinism, however, provides a logical foundation for these arguments to deductively prove the existence of God. Since libertarian free will appears to be necessary for them to work, the Christian apologist *ought* to be a Molinist. The Molinist can defeat any PoE and demonstrate how the KCA (along with the divine omni-attributes) supports the existence of God's middle knowledge. Molinists can also demonstrate how the moral argument assumes the libertarian freedom of humanity.

The Fine-Tuning Argument

I believe that if a Christian apologist appeals to the fine-tuning argument for the existence of God, then they should also be open to the middle knowledge of Molinism. This syllogism, also known as the teleological argument, is usually stated in the following manner:

1. The fine-tuning of the universe is due either to physical necessity, chance, or design.

45. An, "ought" refers to a duty or obligation to act (mentally or physically) in one manner instead of another.

2. The fine-tuning is not due to physical necessity or chance.
3. Therefore, the fine-tuning of the universe is due to intelligent design.

This argument from intelligent design is focused upon the fine-tuned early stages of the universe—the initial conditions of the big bang. If the constants and quantities were not specifically dialed in "just right," then a life-permitting universe would not exist. From galaxies, stars, and planets to atoms and subatomic particles, the foundation and structure of our universe are determined by many "special" numbers. William Lane Craig commented on the significance of these special numbers and what it would entail if these numbers were not so "special" and slightly altered:

> These are the fundamental constants and quantities of the universe. Scientists have come to the shocking realization that each of these numbers have been carefully dialed to an astonishingly precise value—a value that falls within an exceedingly narrow, life-permitting range. If any one of these numbers were altered by even a hair's breadth, no physical, interactive life of any kind could exist anywhere. There'd be no stars, no life, no planets, no chemistry.[46]

This is relevant to Molinism in that, prior to creation, God possesses certain knowledge of what would occur in possible worlds if he were to fine-tune the initial conditions of the early universe with all the relevant "special numbers" and actualize this certain possible world. This also means that God possesses perfect counterfactual knowledge—not grounded in anything that actually exists—about what kind of nonlife-permitting universes would have come into existence if any of those numbers were slightly altered (i.e., a different possible world would have been the actual world). God chose these special numbers and thus intelligently designed a universe in which humanity could and would exist and come to know him. If these numbers were different, the universe would have been otherwise and humanity would not exist. The advocate of the fine-tuning argument affirms that God designed the initial conditions of the big bang to guarantee an environment where intelligent life could and would exist.

If God possessed knowledge of what would follow from a certain fine-tuned point of singularity logically prior to his creative decree to actualize this universe—and God could have adjusted these initial conditions otherwise to bring a different kind of universe into existence—then God possesses knowledge of what he could accomplish. Moreover, given this knowledge, God also knows what would have happened if the initial conditions of the

46. Craig, "Fine Tuning of Universe," para. 1.

big bang were not so finely tuned or tuned otherwise. God knew all that could happen and all that would happen prior to his decree and prior to the actual existence of the fine-tuned point of singularity.

If God possesses the power to create worlds other than the world that actually exists, and if God knows all that would happen in all these other worlds if the initial conditions of these other worlds had been different and actualized instead, then this seems to strongly suggest that God possesses the pre-decree knowledge advocated by Luis de Molina. Because of this, I contend that if one is an advocate of the fine-tuning argument for the existence of God, then he or she should also be a Molinist.

CONCLUSION

Molinism is the key to unlocking many theological mysteries. Since Molinism explains so much of the data, answers many of the big questions, and defangs so many objections raised against Christian theism, William Lane Craig declares: "Once one grasps the concept of [Molinism], one will find it astonishing in its subtlety and power. Indeed, I would venture to say that [Molinism] is the single most fruitful theological concept I have ever encountered."[47] I say amen to that! As mentioned above, even Frank Turek has appealed to Molinism in presentations on university campuses for good reason. Since a plethora of apologetics-based arguments are either compatible with Molinism or supported by Molinism, it only makes sense for Christian apologists to argue for the truth of Molinism. However, if a Christian apologist still thinks another view provides a better explanation—but sees Molinism as a mere possibility—they ought to keep Molinism in their back pockets to offer those struggling with the problem of evil or other related topics.[48]

Bibliography

Beilby, James K., and Paul R. Eddy. *Divine Foreknowledge: Four Views*. Downers Grove, IL: InterVarsity, 2001.

Bignon, Guillaume. "A Response to Kevin Timpe's Review of My Book." Theologui, Mar. 12, 2019. https://theologui.blogspot.com/2019/03/response-to-kevin-timpe.html.

Copan, Paul and Charles Taliaferro, eds. *The Naturalness of Belief: New Essays on Theism's Rationality*. Lexington, KY: Lexington, 2018.

47. Beilby and Eddy, *Divine Foreknowledge*, 125.

48. Important points of this chapter—and much more—can be found in the final chapter of Stratton, *Human Freedom, Divine Knowledge*.

Craig, William Lane. "Arguing Successfully about God: A Review Essay of Graham Oppy's *Arguing about Gods*." *Philosophia Christi* 10 (2008) 435–52.

———. "The Fine Tuning of the Universe." Fine Tuned Universe, n.d. http://www.finetuneduniverse.com/finetuned.html.

Crisp, Oliver D. *Deviant Calvinism: Broadening Reformed Theology*. Minneapolis: Fortress, 2004.

CrossExamined. "Does Molinism Have a Biblical Basis?" YouTube, July 23, 2018. https://www.youtube.com/watch?v=lYuxF5wHl9M&t=10s.

Draper, Paul. "The Skeptical Theist." In *The Evidential Argument from Evil*, edited by Daniel Howard-Snyder, 175–92. Bloomington: Indiana University Press, 1996.

Erasmus, Jacobus, and Timothy A. Stratton. "A Molinist Response to Schellenberg's Hiddenness Argument." *Perichoresis* 21 (2023) 39–51.

Evangel University. "Jerry Walls: What's Wrong with Calvinism, Part 1." YouTube, Feb. 19, 2013. https://youtu.be/Daomzm3nyIg.

Freethinking Ministries. "Is Molinism Biblical? Tim Stratton vs. James White." YouTube, Feb. 19, 2022. https://www.youtube.com/watch?v=mPKqfexUu7k&t=4077s.

Handler, Chelsea. "Does Neil deGrasse Tyson Believe in God?" YouTube, May 14, 2017. https://www.youtube.com/watch?v=jXAokvnv7Mc.

Harris, Sam. *Free Will*. New York: Free, 2012.

Hart, Matthew J. "Calvinism and the Problem of Hell." In *Calvinism and the Problem of Evil*, edited by David E. Alexander and Daniel M. Johnson, 248–72. Eugene, OR: Pickwick, 2016.

Helm, Paul. *The Providence of God: Contours of Christian Theology*. Downers Grove, IL: IVP Academic, 1994.

Jaros, Kurt. "A Molinist Solution to the Problem of the Unevangelized." Presentation at the Evangelical Philosophical Society, Nov. 18, 2021, Fort Worth, TX. https://kurtjaros.com/wp-content/uploads/2021/12/EPS-2021-Paper-Final.pdf.

Jowers, Dennis, ed. *Four Views on Divine Providence*. Counterpoints: Bible and Theology. Grand Rapids: Zondervan, 2011.

Koukl, Gregory. *Tactics: A Game Plan for Discussing Your Christian Convictions*. Grand Rapids: Zondervan, 2009.

MacGregor, Kirk R. *Luis de Molina: The Life and Theology of the Founder of Middle Knowledge*. Grand Rapids: Zondervan, 2015.

Moreland, J. P. *The Recalcitrant Imago Dei: Human Persons and the Failure of Naturalism*. London: SCM, 2009.

———. *The Soul: How We Know It's Real and Why It Matters*. Chicago: Moody, 2014.

Muller, Richard A. *Divine Will and Human Choice: Freedom, Contingency, and Necessity in Early Modern Reformed Thought*. Grand Rapids: Baker Academic, 2017.

Pink, Arthur W. *Sovereignty of God*. Gearhart, OR: Watchmaker, 2011.

Plantinga, Alvin. *God, Freedom, and Evil*. Grand Rapids: Eerdmans, 1974.

———. *Where the Conflict Really Lies: Science, Religion, and Naturalism*. Oxford: Oxford University Press, 2011.

Spalding, Kirsty L., et al. "Retrospective Birth Dating of Cells in Humans." *Cell* 122 (July 2005) 133–43. https://www.cell.com/fulltext/S0092-8674(05)00408-3.

Stratton, Timothy A. *Human Freedom, Divine Knowledge, and Mere Molinism: A Biblical, Historical, Theological, and Philosophical Analysis*. Eugene, OR: Wipf & Stock, 2020.

Stratton, Timothy A., and J. P. Moreland. "An Explanation and Defense of the Free Thinking Argument." *Religions* 13 (Oct. 2022) 1–25.

Van Inwagen, Peter. "C. S. Lewis's Argument against Naturalism." *Res Philosophica* 90 (2013) 113–24.

———. "The Problem of Evil, the Problem of Air, and the Problem of Silence." In *God, Knowledge, and Mystery: Essays in Philosophical Theology*, by Peter Van Inwagen, Cornell Studies in Political Economy, 66–95. Ithaca, NY: Cornell University Press, 1995.

The Bible

Christians are not supposed to "just have faith." Christians are commanded to know what they believe and why they believe it. They are commanded to give answers to those who ask (1 Pet. 3:15), and to demolish arguments against the Christian faith (2 Cor. 10:4–5).

—Norman L. Geisler and Frank Turek,
I Don't Have Enough Faith to Be an Atheist

The Jesus Hermeneutic: Historical Method or Modern Heresy?

Alisa Childers[1]

WHAT IS THE "JESUS HERMENEUTIC"?

Richard Rohr is a Franciscan priest, author of several books, and the founder of the Center for Action and Contemplation (CAC) in Albuquerque, New Mexico. The CAC website describes Rohr as "a globally recognized ecumenical teacher bearing witness to the universal awakening within Christian mysticism and the Perennial Tradition."[2] Rohr's teachings are gaining influence, especially among millennials who grew up in the Evangelical church.[3] Rohr is particularly influential in the progressive Christian movement and is referred to as a spiritual father, hero, and mentor by well-known progressive voices.[4] He refers to the Jewish Scriptures as being filled with inconsistencies and falsehoods, and characterizes the New Testament

1. Dr. Turek's writing and speaking ministry was one of the primary resources God used to rebuild my faith after a significant crisis I endured more than ten years ago. Since then, I have had the privilege to meet, be advised by, and minister alongside Dr. Turek. It is not an exaggeration to say that he was one of the main catalysts God used to help launch my own speaking and writing ministry. For that, I am deeply indebted to him. It was an honor to contribute to this book, and I pray that God blesses him and his family with many more years of faithful ministry.

2. See https://cac.org/richard-rohr/richard-rohr-ofm/.

3. Falsani, "For Millennials, Mysticism Shows."

4. Progressive leader Jen Hatmaker referred to Rohr as such in a podcast episode. Hatmaker, "Live Yourself." Rohr is also praised by progressive thought leaders Rob Bell and William Paul Young, both of whom have worked with, appeared alongside, and produced content with Rohr. See Bel and Rohr, "In the Beginning." Rohr also spoke at a conference, "Trinity: The Soul of Creation."

Gospels as accounts that conflict with one another, having "no one clear theology of God, Jesus, or history presented."[5] Rohr defends his perspective and interpretation of Scripture through what he calls the Jesus Hermeneutic. He writes:

> Scripture is a polyphonic symphony, a conversation with itself, where it plays melodies and dissonance—three steps forward, two steps back. The three steps finally and gradually win out; you see the momentum of our Holy Book and where it is leading history. And the text moves inexorably toward inclusivity, mercy, unconditional love, and forgiveness. I call it the "Jesus Hermeneutic." Just interpret Scripture the way Jesus did! He ignores, denies, or openly opposes his own Scriptures whenever they are imperialistic, punitive, exclusionary, or tribal.[6]

In this chapter I will analyze Rohr's Jesus Hermeneutic and interact with specific passages he offers to support his thesis and demonstrate that Jesus did not, in fact, ignore, deny, or oppose the Old Testament Scriptures. Then I will evaluate other passages that establish what Jesus actually said about the Scriptures. This will follow with an evaluation of passages that clearly demonstrate how Jesus perceived and interpreted the Scriptures, exposing Richard Rohr's Jesus Hermeneutic as a deceptive interpretive tool that elevates one's own feelings, thoughts, and preferences over the word of God as the final authority for truth.

DID JESUS EVER IGNORE, DENY, OR OPPOSE SCRIPTURE?

In his written work, Rohr never defines what he means when he uses the words "imperialistic, punitive, exclusionary, or tribal" as the criteria Jesus supposedly used to justify contradicting the Scriptures. For our purposes, we will take them at face value, focusing on "punitive" (having to do with punishment) and "exclusionary" (relating to the exclusion of someone or something). The only biblical data Rohr provides to support his hypothesis is found in a footnote listing Luke 4:18–19; Matt 5; Matt 12:1–8; and John 5:1–23.[7] Therefore, we will examine each citation in order.

5. Rohr, *Falling Upward*, 62–63.
6. Rohr and Morrell, *Divine Dance*, loc. 2825.
7. Rohr and Morrell, *Divine Dance*, loc. 2875.

Luke 4:18–19

The setting for this text is Jesus reading from the Isaiah scroll at the synagogue in Nazareth. The portion of Scripture Jesus quotes is found in Isa 61:1–2: "The Spirit of the Lord is upon me, because the Lord has anointed me to bring good news to the poor; he has sent me to bind up the brokenhearted, to proclaim liberty to the captives, and the opening of the prison to those who are bound, to proclaim the year of the Lord's favor." Rohr points out that according to Luke's Gospel, Jesus stops mid-sentence, ignoring the next eight words from the Isaiah prophecy: "and the day of vengeance of our God." He notes that, rather than condemning those outside the house of Israel, Jesus points out Old Testament examples of God passing over widows and lepers of Israel to send sustenance and healing to gentiles. Rohr goes on to contend that, rather than declaring foreigners to be God's enemies, Jesus includes them, and it is their anger "at his selective reading" that incites the people to attempt to throw Jesus from a cliff.[8]

Rohr is correct that Jesus did not read the Isaiah prophecy in full but only the portion noted above, followed by "Today this scripture is fulfilled in your hearing" (Luke 4:21). Jesus is communicating that the primary purpose for his first coming is to bring salvation and hope to the world. John 3:17 supports this idea, reading: "For God did not send his Son into the world to condemn the world, but in order that the world might be saved through him." However, this does not contradict the idea that the Jewish Messiah would eventually usher in this "day of vengeance." Jesus selectively read from the prophecy because the day of vengeance had not yet occurred. Put another way, it was not part of the prophecy he was fulfilling at that moment. As Darrell Bock writes, "The ultimate time of God's vengeance is not yet arrived in this coming of Jesus (9:51–56; 17:22–37; 21:5–37). The deliverance of judgment in God's plan, alluded to in the omission, is sorted out later in Luke."[9] Bock goes on to explain that this is part of the "already-not yet tension" of the eschatology found in the New Testament.[10] Additionally, Alec Motyer writes, "What Isaiah sees as a double-faceted ministry the Lord Jesus apportions respectively to his first and second comings, the work of the Servant, and of the Anointed Conqueror."[11]

Rohr is also correct in noting that Jesus is including the gentiles in God's plan of salvation. However, their inclusion is in harmony with the

8. Rohr and Morrell, *Divine Dance*, loc. 2875.

9. Bock, *Luke*, 1:166.

10. For a devotional treatment of the concept of "already/not yet," see Bridges, *Transforming Power of Gospel*, 116–21.

11. Motyer, *Prophecy of Isaiah*, 499.

Scriptures, not in contradiction. The Old Testament is peppered with hints of gentile inclusion. Genesis 12:3 describes "all the families of the earth" being blessed by Israel. In Gen 18:18 and Gen 22:18 we read that all the nations of the earth will be blessed through Abraham. Isaiah 42:6 describes Israel as being a "light for the nations." Isaiah 60:10–14 predicts that other nations will bring work, resources, and wealth to Israel. Exodus 12:48–49 offers instructions on how to integrate gentiles into the community to celebrate the Passover: "If a stranger shall sojourn with you and would keep the Passover to the Lord, let all his males be circumcised. Then he may come near and keep it; he shall be as a native of the land." Additionally, Num 9:14; Num 15:13–16; 1 Kgs 8:41–43; and Isa 56:6–8 all describe gentiles being welcomed among God's people when they submit to his rules and worship him alone.

Specific Old Testament examples of gentiles being included among God's people are Melchizedek, the non-Jewish worshiper of YHWH (Gen 14); Moses's father-in-law Jethro (Exod. 18); and Caleb, a Kenizzite (Num 32:12).[12] Other examples include Caleb's brother Othniel (Judg 3:9), Rahab the prostitute (Josh 2), Jael the Kenite housewife (Judg 4–5), and Ruth the Moabite (Ruth 1:4). One would also be remiss not to mention the entire population of Nineveh, which is said to have repented after Jonah preached to them (Jonah 3:10). In fact, the case for gentile inclusion is so strong that even the apostle Paul, in Rom 9:25–26, quotes from Hos 1:10 and 2:23 to refute those who were opposing God's message, writing, "Those who were not my people I will call 'my people,' and her who was not beloved I will call 'beloved.' And in the very place where it was said to them, 'You are not my people, there they will be called 'sons of the living God.'"

Despite Old Testament passages concerning the inclusion of gentiles, the Jews of Jesus's day were deeply offended by his suggestion that gentiles would be included in God's plan. Commenting on the attitude of Jews toward gentiles in the first century, F. F. Bruce notes, "For centuries the Gentiles had been looked upon by the chosen people, with but few exceptions, as 'vessels of wrath made for destruction'; and certainly, God had 'endured' them 'with much patience.'"[13] It is not difficult to imagine, then, why the Jewish crowd reacted with such anger toward Jesus's suggestion that God's mercy would be sent to the gentiles. Perhaps they were hoping Jesus would continue to quote the Isaiah prophecy and condemn the gentiles to be victims of "the day of vengeance of our God" (Isa 61:2), as Rohr suggests. Leon Morris agrees with Rohr in this regard, writing, "Now that he appealed to

12. The Kenizzites are listed among the Canaanite tribes in Gen 15:18–21.

13. Bruce, *Romans*, 191.

God's dealing with gentiles, that was too much. Anger swept over the whole congregation ('God for the Jews'!) and they set out to lynch Jesus."[14]

Therefore, Rohr is correct that Jesus quoted a portion of the prophecy, emphasizing that gentiles would be included in God's plan, and that the people responded angrily at this inclusion. However, Rohr's suggestion that Jesus was ignoring or contradicting the Scriptures is erroneous and foreign to the text. Jesus was correcting the Jews' misunderstanding of the Scriptures, not correcting the Scriptures themselves.

Matthew 5

The second example Rohr offers to support his thesis is from the Sermon on the Mount. He writes, "[Jesus] begins a series of teachings with, 'You have heard that it was said . . . ,' summarizing a key, accepted part of the Law, and contrasting it with 'But I say to you . . . ,' bringing his own—often subversive—take on it."[15]

In every instance, the context within which these sayings of Jesus are located is fundamental to a proper interpretation of what is said. Just before the first "You have heard it said" statement, Jesus makes a bold claim about the Old Testament Scriptures. Matthew 5:17–18 records Jesus as saying, "Do not think that I have come to abolish the Law or the Prophets; I have not come to abolish them but to fulfill them. For truly, I say to you, until heaven and earth pass away, not an iota, not a dot, will pass from the Law until all is accomplished." In v. 19 he continues, "Therefore whoever relaxes one of the least of these commandments and teaches others to do the same will be called least in the kingdom of heaven, but whoever does them and teaches them will be called great in the kingdom of heaven." The word translated as "fulfill" in English is the Greek word πληρώσαι (*plērōsai*). New Testament scholar and Matthew commentator R. T. France notes that πληρώσαι is a complicated and nuanced word. He explains that, in this context, the meaning is that "Jesus is bringing that to which the Old Testament looked forward; his teaching will transcend the Old Testament revelation, but far from abolishing it, is itself its intended culmination."[16] Jesus has not come to ignore or oppose the Scriptures. He tells us plainly that he came to fulfill

14. Morris, *Luke*, 128.

15. Rohr and Morrell, *Divine Dance*, loc. 2887.

16. France, *Matthew*, 120; Dr. Craig Evans of Houston Baptist University interprets Jesus's use of "fulfill" differently than France, arguing that he has come to "obey" the law. See Evans, *Matthew*, 115.

the Scriptures, not deny them, even outlining the penalty for teachers who relax the commandments of the word of God.

Jesus goes on to make six statements following a "You have heard it said . . . but I say to you" pattern. In the first, found in Matt 5:21, Jesus says, "You have heard that it was said to those of old, You shall not murder; and whoever murders will be liable to judgment. But I say to you that everyone who is angry with his brother will be liable to judgment." Here Jesus is referring to the commands of the law regarding murder, but rather than denying them, he makes them even more difficult to uphold. In this way, he is not subverting the Old Testament moral law but strengthening it. While affirming that murder is a sin, Jesus exposes the fact that this sin festers in the heart of every man. His next five statements follow a similar pattern, dealing with the issues of lust (Matt 5:27–30), divorce (5:31–32), the taking of oaths (5:33–36), retaliation (5:38–42), and the treatment of enemies (5:43–48). Of these six statements, France writes, "It is in each case more demanding, more far-reaching in its application, more at variance with the ethics of man without God."[17]

Of the six, the only two statements that could potentially be interpreted as being subversive or in contradiction to the Old Testament are the final two, dealing with retaliation and the treatment of enemies. However, these supposed contradictions are resolved when the context is examined more closely. In Matt 5:38 Jesus says, "You have heard that it was said, An eye for an eye and a tooth for a tooth. But I say to you, do not resist the one who is evil." While the Old Testament does teach the concept of "an eye for an eye" in Exod 21:24; Deut 19:21; and Lev 24:20, the original intent of the law was not to give individual Israelites permission to exact revenge on their enemies but to give the authorities the jurisdiction to impose a just sentence. This prevented the punishment from exceeding the crime and ensured that a just outcome would be secured in the case of a violent dispute.

In his commentary on the Gospel of Matthew, Craig Blomberg remarks, "This law originally prohibited the formal exaction of an overly severe punishment that did not fit a crime as well as informal, self-appointed vigilante action. Now Jesus teaches the principle that Christian kindness should transcend even straightforward tit-for-tat retribution."[18] France notes that by the time of Jesus, financial penalties had replaced physical damages, so Jesus wasn't necessarily talking physical retribution. Jesus was making the broader point that we should not demand our just due but should show

17. France, *Matthew*, 123.

18. Blomberg, *Matthew*, 113.

mercy.[19] So, rather than opposing or denying the Old Testament, Jesus is, once again, calling people to go above and beyond what was technically permitted by Old Testament case law. Stuart Weber writes, "The scribes and Pharisees of Jesus's day must have taken the 'eye for an eye' passages (Exod 21:24; Lev 24:19–20; Deut 19:21) as justification for hurting others at least as badly as they had been hurt."[20] Yet, in a culture in which it appears many Jews were using these Old Testament passages as a free pass to take revenge on their enemies, Jesus calls his audience to an even higher standard.

In Matt 5:43–44, Jesus says, "You have heard that it was said, You shall love your neighbor and hate your enemy. But I say to you, love your enemies and pray for those who persecute you." This statement of Jesus is slightly unique in this series, because, in this case, he is not quoting solely from the Old Testament but also from the traditions of the Pharisees and scribes. "You shall love your neighbor as yourself" is found in Lev 19:18. But nowhere in the Old Testament does God instruct his people to hate their enemies. In fact, Prov 25:21 says, "If your enemy is hungry, give him bread to eat, and if he is thirsty, give him water to drink." Exodus 23:4–5 instructs the Israelites to go out of their way to help an enemy when their ox wanders away or is lying helpless under its load. Leviticus 19:18 declares that you should not take vengeance but should love your neighbor as yourself. There are complicated passages in which God commands Israel to go to war against an enemy nation, exacting his judgment for their sin (Deut 7:2), and the psalmist declares that he hates those whom God hates (Ps 139:21–22), but here Jesus isn't denying or opposing the Scriptures; he's actually denying and opposing a misinterpretation of the Scriptures. It wasn't the Scriptures that recommended hating our enemies but human tradition.

Matthew 12:1–8

In the Matt 12 passage, Jesus and his disciples are wandering through the fields of grain on the Sabbath day. Being hungry, the disciples begin to pluck the heads from the wheat and eat them. Seeing this, the Pharisees criticize the disciples for plucking heads of grain to eat on the Sabbath, accusing them of breaking the law. However, the disciples did not break the law. In fact, Deut 23:25 states of the Sabbath, "If you go into your neighbor's standing grain, you may pluck the ears with your hand, but you shall not put a sickle to your neighbor's standing grain." What the disciples broke was the traditions and misinterpretations that had been added to the law.

19. France, *Matthew*, 130.

20. Weber, *Matthew*, 69.

In the second century, an edited collection of previously oral teachings on the Torah, or Jewish law, was compiled. This collection is called the Mishnah, which means "study by repetition," and thus served as a study guide for the law. Though it was not written down until one century after Christ, it is likely that many of the teachings found in it were present in Jesus's day and age, and it serves as an excellent reference for understanding the Jewish interpretation of the Torah. In Mishnah Shabbat 7, or the seventh teaching concerning the Sabbath, we read that thirty-nine categories of labor were prohibited on the Sabbath. Regarding wheat, the prohibition is against "one who sows, and one who plows, and one who reaps, and one who gathers sheaves into a pile, and one who threshes, removing the kernel from the husk, and one who winnows threshed grain in the wind."[21] It is likely, then, that the Pharisees were interpreting the disciples' actions as a type of winnowing.

As we see above in the book of Deuteronomy, the disciples were within the bounds of the Torah, as it was written, even if they were possibly out of the bounds of its oral interpretation. Jesus rebukes the Pharisees using an example of King David and his men but closes by saying, "The Son of Man is lord of the Sabbath" (Matt 12:8). This title, "Son of Man," is one of Jesus's preferred self-designations, which means that he is telling the Pharisees that he is the one who rules over the Sabbath. All this to say that the Pharisees were applying a human understanding of the divinely given law over people rather than letting the Torah speak for itself. Therefore, contrary to Rohr's claims, Jesus did not ignore, deny, or oppose *the Scriptures* but rather the faulty interpretation of them.

John 5:1–23

Here, Jesus heals a man who had been an invalid for thirty-eight years. The man in question spent his time lying on a mat, begging, so when Jesus heals him, he also commands him to "take up [his] bed and walk" (John 5:8). Jesus performs this miracle on the Sabbath, and therefore the man picking up his bed and walking away with it constitute a violation of the law, in the eyes of the Jewish leadership. This is another command found in the Mishnah mentioned above. The fact that Jesus's healing prompts the violation, as well as his command to do so, makes Jesus an accessory in their eyes.

As with the example in Matthew, we again find Jesus opposing the misinterpretation of the Jewish leaders over what constituted "work" rather than opposing the Scriptures themselves. The leaders were so focused on

21. *m. Shab.* 7:2. See https://www.sefaria.org/Mishnah_Shabbat.7.2?lang=bi.

the man carrying his mat that they failed to even acknowledge a miraculous healing from God that also occurred! According to John, this was an example of the Jews "persecuting" Jesus (John 5:16), not an example of Jesus breaking the law. In fact, we find Jesus in complete agreement with the Old Testament Scriptures.

When examined within their cultural and biblical contexts, none of the passages Rohr offers to support his thesis hold water. Jesus never "ignored, denied, or opposed the Scriptures." Rather, he held them to be the highest authority. What Jesus opposed and often corrected was the religious leaders' traditions, faulty interpretations, and expansions to the divinely inspired word of God.

WHAT DID JESUS SAY ABOUT SCRIPTURE?

If we are going to look to Jesus to inform our hermeneutics, as Rohr suggests, we should understand what Jesus actually taught about the Old Testament; during his life on earth, he had quite a bit to say. He affirmed on multiple occasions that the Scriptures were the word of God. In Mark 7:8–13, he criticizes the Pharisees for leaving "the commandment of God" and adding their own traditions to Scripture. He tells them that they "void the *word of God* by [their] tradition." In Matt 22:31–32, just before quoting Exod 3:6, Jesus says, "Have you not read what God said to you?" In Matt 15:3, he chastises the religious leaders for breaking the commandment of God. He says in v. 4, "For God commanded, 'Honor your father and your mother,' and, 'Whoever reviles father or mother must surely die'"—referring to the prophecies of Exod 20:12; Lev 19:3; and Deut 5:16. Notice that Jesus quotes three separate Old Testament books and states, "For God commanded." Compare this with the criteria Rohr uses in his so-called Jesus Hermeneutic, which claims that Jesus contradicted Scripture whenever it was "imperialistic, punitive, exclusionary, or tribal." Matthew 15:4 provides a clear example of Jesus affirming a section of Scripture that is both exclusionary and punitive, on the basis that God commanded the punishment.

Jesus believed that the Old Testament was inspired by God. One day, Jesus is teaching a large crowd in the temple courts, and he encounters some Pharisees with whom he has an exchange of words. Jesus appeals to the inspiration of Scripture to help them understand that the Messiah is more than just a descendant of David. He says, "How is it then that David, speaking by the Spirit, called him [the Messiah] 'Lord'?" (Matt 22:43). Here, Jesus himself gives a definition for divine inspiration. He affirms that David, along with the other biblical writers, was "speaking by the Spirit" when he wrote Scripture. John Wenham notes that whenever Jesus says, "It is written," he is also appealing to the inspiration of Scripture. According to Wenham, "It is clear that Jesus understood 'It is written' to be equivalent to 'God says.'"[22] In fact, Jesus and his apostles quote the Old Testament by using the phrase "It is written" (or its equivalent) more than ninety times in the New Testament.[23]

Jesus believed that the Old Testament is authoritative for Christians as the objective source for truth. When Jesus is tempted by the devil in the wilderness, he appeals to the authority of the Scriptures to fend off the attack. As God incarnate, Jesus could have called down a legion of angels or employed any means of defense to ward off the temptation of the enemy. Instead, he chooses to quote Scripture. Leon Morris notes that when Jesus responds to the devil with "It is written," this "points to the reliability and unchangeability of Scripture. For Jesus, to have found a passage in the Bible that bears on the current problem is to end all discussion."[24] Jesus's high view of the authority of the Scriptures stands in contrast to Rohr's claim that Jesus routinely opposed them.

Jesus affirmed that the Scriptures were historically reliable. He continually referred to Old Testament characters as actual people who lived in real times and places throughout history. He spoke of Abel (Luke 11:51), Noah (Matt 24:37–3; Luke 17:26–27), Abraham (John 8:56), Lot (Luke 17:28–29), Isaac (Matt 8:11), Jacob (Luke 13:28), Moses (John 7:22), David (Matt 12:3–4; Matt 22:43; Mark 12:36; Luke 20:42), Solomon (Matt 6:29; Matt 12:42; Luke 11:31; Luke 12:27), Elijah (Luke 4:25–26), Elisha (Luke 4:27), Jonah (Matt 12:39–42; Luke 11:29–30, 32), and Zechariah (Luke 11:51).

He also described events such as the institution of circumcision (John 7:22), the judgment of Sodom and Gomorrah (Matt 10:15), the miracle of manna (John 6:31), Moses lifting the snake in the wilderness (John 3:14), and David eating the shewbread (Matt 12:3–4; Mark 2:25–26; Luke 6:3–4) as real history. If that were not enough, Jesus affirmed two of the most disputed Old Testament stories: the great flood and Jonah in the belly of the great fish. Some skeptics claim that the great flood and the story of Jonah and the fish never actually happened, yet Jesus spoke of both as historical occurrences (Matt 24:37–38; Matt 12:40). In fact, he compared the historicity of the story of Jonah with the historicity of his own resurrection, a historical event that the apostle Paul claimed could support or discredit all of Christianity based on its veracity (1 Cor 15:14). While it is also common for

22. Wenham, *Christ and the Bible*, 28.

23. Geisler and Turek, *I Don't Have Enough*, 357.

24. Morris, *Gospel According to Matthew*, 75.

skeptics to claim that Daniel could not have really been a prophet because some of his predictions were too accurate to have been written before the events they describe,[25] Jesus affirmed that Daniel was an actual person and a real prophet (Matt 24:15).

Jesus also introduced the idea that the Scriptures are without error. In Matt 22, the Sadducees, a group that did not believe in the resurrection of the dead, try to trap Jesus with a question about the afterlife. Jesus corrects them in v. 29 by stating, "You are wrong, because you know neither the Scriptures nor the power of God." Jesus viewed the Scriptures as the inerrant standard for truth by comparing the perfect word of God with the errant conclusions of the Sadducees. This is further supported by a statement Jesus makes when he is about to be stoned by the Jews for claiming to be one with the Father. In John 10:35, he says, "Scripture cannot be broken," thus claiming that the Scriptures were the infallible standard for truth. The very statement "Scripture cannot be broken" should be sufficient to refute the Jesus Hermeneutic, because it demonstrates that Jesus believed the Scriptures were never to be ignored, denied, or opposed.

Jesus affirmed the idea that God's word will never pass away, a common theme found in both the Old and New Testaments. He could not endorsed this tenet more plainly than he does in Matt 5:17–18. He says, "Do not think that I have come to abolish the Law or the Prophets [the Old Testament]; I have not come to abolish them but to fulfill them. For truly, I say to you, until heaven and earth pass away, not an iota, not a dot, will pass from the Law until all is accomplished." This speaks to the imperishability of the Old Testament. Jesus also says, "It is easier for heaven and earth to pass away than for one dot of the Law to become void" (Luke 16:17). Once again, Jesus repeatedly asserts that he did not come to ignore, deny, or oppose the Scriptures but to fulfill them completely.

Shortly after his resurrection, we find Jesus on the road to Emmaus where he encounters two of his followers who don't recognize him (Luke 24:13–35). They begin talking about how disappointed they are that Jesus has been crucified and how they had hoped he would have been the one to redeem Israel. In v. 25 Jesus scolds them for being "slow of heart to believe all that the prophets have spoken." Then v. 27 explains, "And beginning with Moses and all the Prophets, he interpreted to them in all the Scriptures the things concerning himself." It is important to note that the first thing Jesus wanted these followers to know following his resurrection is that everything

25. One of the earliest recorded objections to the prophecies of Daniel is from the third-century philosopher Porphyry. Jerome states that Porphyry claimed that the prophecies were written at the time of Antiochus Epiphanies, not at the time of Daniel. Jerome, *Commentary on Daniel*, 491.

Moses and the prophets recorded in Scripture was about him. He placed the utmost importance on the reliability of the Old Testament Scriptures and the events they prophesied.

In contrast to Rohr's Jesus Hermeneutic, the Gospels record Jesus himself using language that is highly exclusionary and punitive. In Luke 12:51, Jesus says, "Do you think that I have come to give peace on earth? No, I tell you, but rather division." In Matt 10:34, he says, "Do not think I have come to bring peace to the earth. I have not come to bring peace, but a sword." He continues in vv. 35–38 that he has come to "set a man against his father, and a daughter against her mother." He describes what life will be like for those who choose to follow him. He predicts that following him will cause enemies to be found in the same household. He requires believers to deny themselves, take up their crosses, and follow him—even going so far as to say that anyone who does not do this is not worthy of him.

In several of the parables describing the kingdom of heaven, Jesus concludes with people being excluded. In Matt 25:1–13, Jesus tells the parable of the ten virgins who were all invited to meet the bridegroom for a marriage feast. Five were wise and brought oil for their lamps, but five were foolish, bringing no oil to replenish their lamps. When the bridegroom comes to open the door, the five foolish virgins have gone to buy oil and missed the opportunity to go into the marriage feast. At that point, Jesus explains that the door closes, leaving the foolish virgins excluded from the feast. Even after they come back and plead to be let in, the bridegroom sends them away.

In Matt 25:14–30 Jesus tells the parable of the ten talents, which ends with a similar exclusion of the servant who hid his talent in the ground. In this case, the wicked servant is not only excluded from "entering the joy of your master" but is cast into outer darkness where there will be weeping and gnashing of teeth. Just after the parable of the ten talents, Jesus describes the final judgment, in which he will separate people into two groups: sheep and goats. To the sheep on his right, he will say, "Come, you who are blessed by my Father, inherit the kingdom prepared for you from the foundation of the world." But to the goats on his left, he will say, "Depart from me, you cursed, into the eternal fire prepared for the devil and his angels."

These three parables demonstrate that not only did Jesus not ignore, deny, or oppose the Scriptures whenever they were punitive or exclusionary, he commonly used language himself that was both exclusionary—with many people being excluded from his kingdom on judgment day—and punitive—with people being cast into outer darkness and eternal fire.

Not being limited to punitive and exclusionary language, Jesus also performed punitive and exclusionary acts. In Matt 21:12–17 and John 2:13–22, he physically drives the money changers out of the temple for making

God's house a "den of robbers," even using a handmade whip, according to John's account. In Luke 10:13–15, Jesus pronounces "woe" on the cities of Chorazin, Bethsaida, and Capernaum for not repenting even after mighty works have been done in them. He compares these cities to Sodom and Gomorrah, which were destroyed by God for their blatant rejection of God's ways. Jesus tells them that judgment day will even be more tolerable for Sodom and Gomorrah than it will be for them. In the Sermon on the Mount in Matt 7:21–23, Jesus states plainly that not everyone who says to him, "Lord, Lord," will be allowed to enter the kingdom of heaven. To those who do not do the will of his Father in heaven, he will exclude them by saying, "I never knew you; depart from me, you workers of lawlessness."

One often-overlooked source for Jesus's words is the book of Revelation. In his letter to the church in Pergamum, in Rev 2:12–17, Jesus urges the Christians to repent for their sin of eating food sacrificed to idols and for their sexual immorality. If they do not repent, Jesus promises to "war against them with the sword of my mouth" (v. 16). To the church in Thyatira, Jesus declares that he will cast the woman Jezebel on a sickbed and strike her children dead for leading Christians into sexual immorality (v. 22). These are hardly the words of someone seeking to ignore, deny, or oppose anything that is punitive or exclusionary.

CONCLUSION

Rohr claims that Jesus ignored, denied, or openly opposed his own Scriptures whenever they were imperialistic, punitive, exclusionary, or tribal. The passages of Scripture he uses to defend this view are Luke 4:18–19; Matt 5; Matt 12:1–8; and John 5:1–23. As we have seen, Luke 4:18–19 fails to support Rohr's thesis, because Jesus is not ignoring the rest of the Isaiah prophecy by ending his reading where he does. In fact, his next statement, "Today this scripture is fulfilled in your hearing," communicates that he is currently fulfilling the prophecy he has just read. The next part of the Isaiah prophecy will be fulfilled later in history, at his second coming.

The six "You have heard it said . . . but I say to you" statements of Jesus in Matt 5 also fail to support Rohr's position, because Jesus is not contradicting Scripture. Instead, he is making the Old Testament commands more difficult to uphold.

The final two passages depict Jesus and his disciples being confronted by the religious leaders for breaking the Sabbath. However, according to Old Testament law, they are not breaking the Sabbath but simply breaking the misinterpretations and traditions the leadership has added to the law.

All four passages fail to support the idea that Jesus ever contradicted the Scriptures.

When we investigate what Jesus actually said about Scripture, we find that he affirmed the Old Testament to be the inspired, authoritative, historically reliable, inerrant, infallible, imperishable word of God that was all about himself. Not only did Jesus not ignore, deny, or oppose Scripture, but he also did and said things that were exclusionary and punitive. He said on more than one occasion that he did not come to bring peace but a sword, promising that even family members would be divided against each other because of him. His parables present a picture of a heavenly kingdom that is not only exclusionary but also punitive to those who reject him. He physically drives the money changers out of the temple and pronounces "woe" on three cities; and in the book of Revelation, he urges Christians to repent for their sins to avoid punishment. Richard Rohr's Jesus Hermeneutic not only fails to have any Scriptural support, but taken as a whole, the biblical data portrays an entirely opposite view of how Jesus handled the Scriptures. A more accurate Jesus Hermeneutic would be to interpret Scripture the way Jesus did! He acknowledges, affirms, and openly declares his own Scriptures to be authoritative and unbreakable even when they seem to be "imperialistic, punitive, exclusionary, or tribal." The truth is that Jesus never once declared or implied that the Scriptures were anything but fully truthful and should be obeyed.

If a Christian were to adopt Rohr's hermeneutic, they would be left with nothing but their own personal conscience, moral compass, thoughts, feelings, and preferences to guide them as they tried to discover what in Scripture is true and what is false. This would no doubt lead to a God constructed in their own image. But Scripture warns in Jer 17:9 that the human heart is "deceitful above all things, and desperately sick; who can understand it?" Christians would be wise to reject Rohr's Jesus Hermeneutic in favor of what Jesus actually said about Scripture: that it is the inspired and authoritative word of God.

Bibliography

Bell, Rob, and Richard Rohr. "In the Beginning: Six Hours with Rob Bell and Richard Rohr." https://store.cac.org/products/in-the-beginning-six-hours-with-rob-bell-and-richard-rohr-cd.

Blomberg, Craig. *Matthew.* New American Commentary 22. Nashville: Broadman & Holman, 1992.

Bock, Darrel L. *Luke.* 2 vols. Baker Exegetical Commentary on the New Testament. Grand Rapids: Baker Academic, 1996.

Bridges, Jerry. *The Transforming Power of the Gospel.* Colorado Springs: NavPress, 2012.

Bruce, F. F. *Romans: An Introduction and Commentary.* Downers Grove, IL: InterVarsity, 1985.

Evans, Craig. *Matthew.* New Cambridge Bible Commentary. Cambridge: Cambridge University Press, 2012.

Falsani, Cathleen. "For Millennials, Mysticism Shows a Path to their Home Faiths." *National Catholic Reporter*, Apr. 24, 2019. https://www.ncronline.org/news/millennials-mysticism-shows-path-their-home-faiths.

France, R. T. *Matthew: An Introduction and Commentary.* Vol. 1. Downers Grove, IL: InterVarsity, 1985.

Geisler, Norman L., and Frank Turek. *I Don't Have Enough Faith to Be an Atheist.* Wheaton, IL: Crossway, 2004.

Hatmaker, Jen. "Live Yourself into a New Way of Thinking: Richard Rohr." Jen Hatmaker, episode 5, series 16. https://jenhatmaker.com/podcasts/series-16/live-yourself-into-a-new-way-of-thinking-richard-rohr/.

Jerome. *Commentary on Daniel.* Translated by Gleason L. Archer. Eugene, OR: Wipf & Stock, 2009.

Morris, Leon. *The Gospel According to Matthew.* Downers Grove, IL: InterVarsity, 2020.

———. *Luke: An Introduction and Commentary.* Vol. 3. Downers Grove, IL: InterVarsity, 1988.

Motyer, J. Alec. *The Prophecy of Isaiah: An Introduction and Commentary.* Downers Grove, IL: InterVarsity, 2015.

Rohr, Richard. *Falling Upward: A Spirituality for the Two Halves of Life.* San Francisco: Jossey-Bass, 2011.

Rohr, Richard, and Mike Morrell. *The Divine Dance: The Trinity and Your Transformation.* New Kensington, PA: Whitaker, 2016. Kindle.

Weber, S. K. *Matthew.* Vol. 1. Nashville: Broadman & Holman, 2000.

Wenham, John. *Christ and the Bible.* Eugene, OR: Wipf & Stock, 2009.

Does the Resurrection of Jesus Prove He is the Jewish Messiah?

Eric Chabot[1]

Nearly twenty years ago God ignited a passion in me to engage with college students about the Christian worldview. This journey began at The Ohio State University. My initial outreach approach on the campus was the "cold turkey" approach, which involved stopping students in public and trying to initiate faith-based conversations. As I gained more experience and grew in my comfort level, I pivoted to asking students if they would participate in a five-question spiritual survey. Though I was fairly equipped in Christian apologetics, the university environment brought a new set of questions. Christian ministries on campus rarely emphasized the need for apologetics, and within two years, literature from New Atheist authors like Daniel Dennett, Christopher Hitchens, and Richard Dawkins was entering the public sphere, and the secular humanist group on campus was becoming the new Evangelicals. To combat these issues, I enrolled as a graduate student at Southern Evangelical Seminary.

Christianity is an evangelistic faith. One of the hallmarks of being a devoted follower of Jesus is to be committed to sharing the message that Jesus is indeed the Savior of the world and that people need to repent and accept him as their Lord and Savior. In its first-century context, a crucial

1. Dr. Turek was one of the first people to show me the need for a faithful Christian witness and defense to the outside world. His work on college campuses around the country inspired me to begin my work with Ratio Christi many years ago, and I have continued to serve in college ministry since. There aren't enough words to thank him for the impact he has had on my life and the lives of others, including the students at Ratio Christi. It is my honor and pleasure to write this chapter as an appreciation for him and his ministry.

element of this acceptance was embracing him as the promised Messiah of Israel and the nations. Scholar Michael Bird explains this further:

> The statement that "Jesus is the Messiah" presupposes a certain way of reading Israel's Scriptures and assumes a certain hermeneutical approach that finds in Jesus the unifying thread and the supreme goal of Israel's sacred literature. A messiah can only be a messiah from Israel and for Israel. The story of the Messiah can only be understood as part of the story of Israel. Paul arguably says as much to a largely Gentile audience in Rome: "For I tell you that [Messiah] has become a servant of the circumcised, to show God's truthfulness of God in order to confirm the promises given to the patriarchs, and in order that the Gentiles might glorify God for his mercy" (Rom. 15:8–9).[2]

Here in Columbus, Ohio, I am the director of two apologetic ministries known for bringing well-known apologists and scholars to speak on campus about a variety of topics. Being that I have always had a heart and calling toward the Jewish people, several years ago, we decided to host a lecture by premier messianic apologist Dr. Michael Brown, called "Is Jesus the Jewish Messiah?" While promoting the event we handed out flyers, which prompted several Christians to ask us if we were suggesting that Jesus was not the Christian Messiah. Conversely, some Jewish students would tell us that Jesus is definitely not the Jewish Messiah. These interactions clarified in my mind that many Christians did not see the clear connection between Judaism and the messianic status of Jesus.

MESSIANIC PROPHECY

In 1994 I was a new believer, and my faith was extremely exciting to me. I would tell friends and strangers about Jesus the Messiah. It was not long before I realized that many of my Jewish and non-Jewish friends did not share my enthusiasm toward Jesus. I was barraged with questions about my faith, and though I knew that God had given me a natural ability to initiate conversations about Jesus, my lack of knowledge was hindering me from communicating

I started searching through local Christian bookstores for theology and apologetic resources but also noticed a trend in the literature. Most Christian apologetic books mention more than three hundred messianic prophecies that are fulfilled in Jesus as a means to demonstrate that the God

2. Bird, *Are You the One*, 163.

of the Bible is active in human history and the one, true God. At the time I thought this was a convincing evidential apologetic for believing that Jesus is the promised Messiah of Israel and the world. However, as the years have gone by, I have come to realize that this approach needs refining.

Messianic Prophecy in the Early Messianic Community

Undoubtedly, when many people hear the word *prophecy* it brings to mind people like Nostradamus, Harold Camping, or apocalyptic bestsellers sitting on the shelves of the local bookstore. Cynicism aside, the Bible portrays prophecy as God's preferred method for proving that he is the one true God (Deut 18:15; Isa 41:21–24; 42:8–9; 43:9–13; 44:6–8, 24–28; 45:11–13, 20–22; 46:8–11; 48:3–7, 12–16). Even Jesus used messianic prophecy in two post-resurrection appearances (Luke 24:25–27; 24:44–46), rebuking the disciples on the road to Emmaus for being slow to believe in all that the prophets spoke (Luke 24:25).

The apostles often appealed to messianic prophecy when proclaiming the gospel of Jesus and the resurrection. Luke records that Paul reasoned with his Jewish audience by "explaining and proving" that Jesus was the Jewish Messiah foretold in the Hebrew Bible (Acts 17:2–3). The book of Acts records that "every Sabbath [Paul] reasoned in the synagogue and tried to persuade Jews and Greeks" (Acts 18:4). Even Peter, when making his defense before the Sanhedrin for healing a lame man, applied messianic prophecy to Jesus in order to explain how he had the power to heal, and asserted that the Jewish council's rejection of Jesus was the fulfillment of the Hebrew Bible. Acts records the apostle saying, "This Jesus is the stone that was rejected by you, the builders, which has become the cornerstone" (Acts 4:11). Stephen made mention of messianic prophecy in his case before the Sanhedrin (Acts 7), and Philip used messianic prophecy when an Ethiopian official (Acts 8:26–40), inquired of whom Isaiah spoke in Isa 53. Philip answered that the prophet was speaking of Jesus, directly associating Jesus's identity with the Jewish Messiah (vv. 34–35).

The Hebrew word מָשִׁיחַ (*mashiach*, "messiah") is derived from the verb מָשַׁח, which has the general meaning of "to rub something" or, more specifically, "to anoint someone."[3] The Hebrew Bible uses this word for those who were "anointed" for a specific purpose, such as priests (Exod 28:41; 29:7, 29; 30:30; Lev 7:36; 8:12; 16:32), kings (Judg 9:8, 15; 1 Sam 9:16; 10:1; 15:1, 17; 16:3, 12–13; 2 Sam 2:4, 7; 3:39; 5:3; 1 Kgs 1:34, 39, 45; 5:15; 19:15–16; 2 Kgs 9:3, 6, 12; 11:12; 23:30; 1 Chr 5:17; 11:3; 2 Chr 22:7; 23:11; 29:22; Ps 89:2),

3. F. Brown et al., *Hebrew and English Lexicon*, 602, מָשַׁח.

and even prophets (1 Kgs 19:16; 1 Chr 16:22; Ps 105:15). As Walter Kaiser notes, "Even though *mashiach* occurs thirty-nine times in the Old Testament, only nine of those instances have a possible reference to the coming Messiah."[4] In Isa 41 and 45 God even "anoints" the pagan king Cyrus for the task to restore Israel while they were in exile (Isa 41:2–4) For this reason it is important to remember that the Hebrew Bible does not reveal a monolithic "messianic concept." This lack of a monolithic messianic expectation continues into the intertestamental and New Testament period and into their respective literature. Stanley Porter says:

> Intertestamental and New Testament literature suggests that the expectation was all over the map. Some Jewish people did not expect a Messiah. Others thought that the Messiah would be a priestly figure, still others a royal deliverer. Some scholars interpret the evidence to suggest that at least one group of Jewish thinkers believed there would be two messiahs, one priestly and one royal. From what we know we can be certain that the New Testament did not create the idea of the Messiah. But we can also be sure that there was nothing like a commonly agreed delineation of what the Messiah would be like. The latter point means that modern-day Christians who shake their heads about why the Jewish people did not universally recognize the Messiah, considering all the fulfilled prophecy, really do not understand Old Testament literature.[5]

Messianic Prophecy and the Resurrection of Jesus Christ

The resurrection of Jesus Christ is the fundamental element of the Christian faith. Therefore, if Jesus has not risen from the dead, several consequences follow:

1. We are still dead in our sins (1 Cor 15:1–17; Eph 2:1–6).
2. There could not have been an ascension (Acts 1:9–11).
3. Without the ascension, the Holy Spirit could not have been sent (John 7:37–39; 14:26; 15:26; 16:7).
4. Without the sending of the Spirit, the local church cannot flourish (Eph 4:10–13).

4. These references are 1 Sam 2:10, 35; Pss 2:2; 89:51; 132:10, 17; Dan 9:25–26; Hab 3:13. Kaiser, *Recovering Unity of Bible*, 71.

5. Porter, *Messiah*, 29.

5. There is no new birth/supernatural regeneration (John 3:3–7).
6. There is no new covenant (Jer 31:31–34).
7. Jesus cannot fulfill the role of our advocate and intercessor (Rom 8:34; 1 John 2:2).
8. Jesus is a false prophet (Deut 18:22; Matt 12:38–40).
9. Jesus cannot be the everlasting and eternal Davidic King (2 Sam 7:16; Pss 21:14; 72:17; 89:36–37; Jer 33:17; Rom 1:1–5).
10. Jesus cannot be installed as Son of God in power (Rom 1:4), universal Lord (Rom 14:9; Eph 1:20; Phil 2:9–11), and Judge of the living and the dead (Acts 17:31).
11. There will not be a second coming (Zech 14:1–21; Acts 1:11).
12 There is no daily victory over sin (Rom 6:1–11).

Though the resurrection is foundational to Christian belief, as it relates to messianic prophecy, we might rightly ask if the Old Testament ever says that the Messiah will rise from the dead. Or, within the history of Jewish thought, has there ever been any teaching that states that resurrection is a messianic qualification? In one of the most important New Testament passages on the resurrection, Paul writes, "For I delivered to you as of first importance what I also received: that Christ died for our sins in accordance with the Scriptures, that he was buried, that he was raised on the third day *in accordance with the Scriptures*" (1 Cor 15:3–4).

Jesus repeats a similar theme in Luke 24:46 when he says, "Thus, *it is written*, that the Christ should suffer and on the third day rise from the dead." Clearly, Christians believe that Jesus rose on the third day. But where does it say in the Old Testament that the Messiah will rise on the third day? The short answer is that there is no text that specifically says the Messiah will rise on the third day. What, then, is the explanation for what Jesus and Paul have said? Are they playing fast and loose with the sacred Scriptures? Were they simply confused or perhaps employing an early Jewish hermeneutic? Dr. Michael Brown believes that the importance of these passages rests on their use of "the third day." He notes that at several points in the Jewish Scriptures God uses the third day to do something incredibly special. In Hosea, we read, "Come, let us return to the LORD; for he has torn us, that he may heal us; he has struck us down, and he will bind us up. After two days he will revive us; *on the third day* he will raise us up, that we may live before him" (Hos 6:1–2). In this passage Israel is promised a full restoration, even a type of resurrection, on the third day.

Also, according to Gen 22:4, it was *on the third day* that Abraham arrived at Mount Moriah and prepared to sacrifice his son Isaac, whom the author of Hebrews speaks of as being resurrected in a way (Heb 11:19). Furthermore, God told the children of Israel assembled at Mount Sinai to be ready for *the third day*, "for on the third day the LORD will come down on Mount Sinai in the sight of all the people" (Exod 19:11). We also see another passage in Genesis on the topic:

> *On the third day* after Joseph interpreted the dreams of two of his fellow prisoners—both of whose dreams included a symbolic "three"—one of the men was hung and the other man restored to his former position. (Gen 40:1–23)[6]

The Hebrew Bible reveals a pattern of God working in a significant way in the life of Israel *on the third day*—whether it be a restoration or a symbol of God's divine activity.

The Use of Ps 16:8–11 in Acts 2:25–28

The apostles appealed to fulfilled prophecy and the resurrection as evidence of Jesus's messiahship (Acts 2:14–39; 3:6–16, 4:8–14; 17:1–4; 26:26). Immediately following the filling of the Holy Spirit at Pentecost, the apostle Peter proclaimed:

> Men of Israel, hear these words: Jesus of Nazareth, a man attested to you by God with mighty works and wonders and signs that God did through him in your midst, as you yourselves know—this Jesus, delivered up according to the definite plan and foreknowledge of God, you crucified and killed by the hands of lawless men. God raised him up, loosing the pangs of death, because it was not possible for him to be held by it. For David says concerning him, "I saw the Lord always before me, for He is at my right hand that I may not be shaken; therefore my heart was glad, and my tongue rejoiced; my flesh also will dwell in hope. For you will not abandon my soul to Hades or let you Holy One see corruption. You have made known to me the paths of life; you will make me full of gladness with your presence." (Acts 2:22–28)

Craig Keener notes here that Peter "underlines the point that the Scripture, which must be fulfilled, had not applied literally and fully to David and

6. M. Brown, *Answering Jewish Objections*, 181–83.

hence must apply to someone else of whom David would have spoken."[7] Therefore, Peter seems to be saying the resurrection was necessary because death could not hold Jesus. Thus, as David himself did not escape decay, this confidence in God's faithfulness to his "Holy One" is prophetically speaking about Jesus the Messiah. In contrast, most scholars are more comfortable with a typological approach to the text. Rather than Peter seeing the original setting as speaking about an obvious forward referent (i.e., Jesus), the Holy Spirit opened Peter's eyes to see how Ps 16:8–11, while originally speaking about David, now speaks to the possibility of a new and more complete referent, which is Jesus the Messiah.

The Messianic Prophecy of Isa 53:10

It is, at times, debated whether the end of Isa 53 teaches a personal vindication or resurrection of the servant of the Lord. The text reads:

> Yet it was the will of the LORD to crush him; he has put him to grief; when his soul, makes an offering for guilt, he shall see his offspring; he shall prolong his days; the will of the LORD shall prosper in his hand. (Isa 53:10)

The late Jewish scholar David Flusser of Hebrew University said the following about Isa 53:

> Although no Jewish interpretation of this passage, which would explain that the Servant will be a prophet or the Messiah who will be killed, is preserved, such an interpretation could have existed. If an interpretation of Isa [53] in this vein ever existed in Judaism, this would have been important for the concept that the prophet will again come to life. Though the Servant "was pierced for our transgressions, tortured for our iniquities" (v.5), he "shall enjoy long life and see his children's children (v.10). So, Isa [53] could be understood not only as speaking about the death of the Servant, but implicitly about his resurrection.[8]

One way or the other, there is little in the Old Testament that says that a chief sign of the coming Messiah is that he will rise again from the dead.

7. Keener, *Acts*, 950.

8. Flusser, *Judaism and the Origins*, 423.

Messianic Expectations of the Hebrew People

Having established that the Old Testament does not explicitly predict the Messiah will rise from the dead, it is clear why many Jewish thinkers do not see the resurrection as being a messianic qualification. Let us look at some of the traditional messianic expectations by Jewish thinkers and some of their objections to the claim Jesus is the Jewish Messiah:

> The state of the world must prove that the Messiah has come; not a tract. Don't you think that when the Messiah arrives, it should not be necessary for his identity to be subject to debate—for the world should be so drastically changed for the better that it should be absolutely incontestable! Why should it be necessary to prove him at all? If the Messiah has come, why should anyone have any doubt?[9]

According to David Berger and Michael Wyschogrod, the only way to define "the Messiah" is as the king who will rule during what we call the messianic age.

The central criterion for evaluating a Messiah must therefore be a single question: Has the messianic age come? It is only in terms of this question that "the Messiah" means anything. What, then, does the Bible say about the messianic age? Here is a brief description by a famous Christian scholar: "The recovery of independence and power, an era of peace and prosperity, of fidelity to God and his law, of justice and fair dealing and brotherly love among men, and of personal rectitude and piety."[10] If we think about this sentence just for a moment in the light of the last two thousand years, we will begin to see what enormous obstacles must be overcome if we are to believe in the messianic mission of Jesus. If Jesus was the Messiah, why have suffering and evil continued and even increased in the many centuries since his death?[11]

Amy Jill Levine, a Jewish scholar who specializes in New Testament studies, says the following:

> Did Jews reject Jesus because he wasn't the Messiah they were expecting? That claim that Jews rejected Jesus because he counseled peace and all Jews were looking for some warrior Messiah whose job it would be to get the Romans out of the country misses the variety of messianic ideas that were floating around

9. Rabbi Chaim Richman, as quoted in Milavec, *Salvation Is from Jews*, 128.

10. Moore, *Judaism in First Centuries*, 2:324.

11. Berger and Wyschogrod, *Jews and "Jewish Christianity,"* 20, as cited in Skarsaune, *In Shadow of Temple*, 302.

> in the first century. The majority of Jews did not accept Jesus as a Messiah because most Jews thought that the Messiah and the messianic age came together. The messianic age meant peace on earth and the end of war, death, disease, and poverty, the ingathering of the exiles, a general resurrection of the dead. When that didn't happen, I suspect quite a number of Jews who were highly attracted to Jesus' message of the kingdom of heaven thought: That's a good message, but we have to keep waiting.[12]

These quotes make it evident that the Messiah ushering in the messianic age and building an earthly kingdom is one of the most traditional Jewish messianic expectations. Several truths in the Hebrew Bible must be taken into consideration:

1. The Jewish people are regathered to their land both before and after the exile (Isa 11:10–16; Jer 3:11–20; 12:14–17; 30:1–11; Ezek 11:14–20; 36:16–36).
2. The Jewish people are ruled by their Messiah with Jerusalem as its capital (Jer 23:5–6; 33:17; Ezek 37:22, 24; Zech 9:10; 14:9).
3. Israel is recognized by the nations as being blessed (Isa 62:2; 66:18; Ezek 36:23; 37:28; Mal. 3:12).
4. The nations go to Jerusalem to worship God (Isa 2:2–4, 56; 62:9–11; Jer 16:19; Zeph 3:9; Zech 9:16; 14:16–18).
5. The temple is rebuilt with the presence of God in it (Isa 56:6; Ezek 37:26–28, 40–48; 43:1–7; 48:35).

It is also evident from these quotes that that none of them mention an expectation that the Messiah must be personally resurrected. Eugene Borowitz discusses why the resurrection of Jesus is of relative insignificance in modern Jewish belief:

> Jews can see that the story of Jesus' resurrection is told against the background of Pharisaic belief. Despite this, our people have never had difficulty rejecting it. Our Bible is quite clear that the chief sign of the coming of the Messiah is a world of justice and peace. No prophet says the Messiah will die and then be resurrected as a sign to all humanity. Except for the small number of converts to Christianity, Jews in ancient times did not believe Jesus had actually been resurrected. Modern Jews, who believe

12. Levine, "Jewish Take on Jesus," para. 34.

> in the immortality of the soul or in no afterlife at all, similarly reject the Christian claim.[13]

With this in mind, we must ask that, if the Old Testament does not explicitly affirm that the Messiah must be personally resurrected and many Jewish thinkers do not see the resurrection as a messianic qualification, how does Jesus qualify as being the Jewish Messiah?

The Miracle of the Resurrection

Jesus demonstrated that a visible sign following his inauguration of the kingdom of God was the ability to perform miracles. Thus, if the kingdom is breaking into human history, then the King has come. If the messianic age has arrived, then the Messiah must be present. However, some Jewish scholars do not believe that miracles prove that Jesus is the Jewish Messiah:

> According to the Gospel of Mark, which makes no mention of Jonah, Jesus' contemporaries ask him for a sign: they want some sort of proof that he is the Messiah. Healings, resuscitations, and nature miracles do not prove messianic status, for ancient prophets such as Elijah and Elisha, and contemporary Jewish charismatic figures such as Haninah ben Dosa and Honi the Circle Drawer, do the same. Wise teaching does not prove messianic status, as the stories of Solomon and biblical wisdom literature show. How can one "prove" messianic status? The people were expecting universal changes: a general resurrection from the dead where everyone returns to life, a final judgment, and peace on earth. The request is understandable: assertion needs to be backed up with action.[14]

In contrast, I believe there is a compelling reason why the resurrection of Jesus does, in fact, provide ample support for his messianic status.

CAN A DEAD MESSIAH LEAD GENTILES TO EMBRACE THE ONE, TRUE GOD?

In the first century, there were several Jewish sects—the Sadducees, Pharisees, the Zealots, and the Essenes. The word *sect* is what Josephus used to distinguish the different Jewish groups at this time.[15] It is believed there

13. Borowitz, *Liberal Judaism*, 216.

14. Levine and Brettler, *Bible with and without*, 317.

15 Josephus, *War* 2:119–66; *Ant* 18:11–15.

may have been more than twenty sects, groups, or subgroups at the time of Jesus, including the followers of Jesus or what was called the "sect of the Nazarenes" (Acts 24:5), the followers of "the Way."[16] Out of the Jewish sects mentioned, only two of them still exist today: the Pharisees and the followers of "the Way." The Pharisees eventually evolved into what is called rabbinic Judaism, and "the Way" eventually became Christianity. Currently, some Jewish followers of Jesus embrace messianic Judaism, which, given that the first followers of Jesus were Jewish, is not a new phenomenon. The question is what caused this sect of Judaism, known as "the Way," to eventually become an avenue for gentiles to have a relationship with the God of Abraham, Isaac, and Jacob.

Jesus and the Inclusion of the Gentiles

The Hebrew word for covenant is בְּרִית (*berit*), which means "agreement" or "arrangement."[17] Primarily a legal term, the Hebrew Bible often portrays the act of "covenanting" as an arrangement either between God and individuals, or God and the nation of Israel as their descendants. We see this unique arrangement clearly in the Abrahamic covenant. The promise to Abraham in Gen 12:3 exhibits God's plan to bless the nations. All peoples of all the earth would be beneficiaries of the promise (Gen 12:2–3; cf. 22:18; 26:4; 28:14). God intended to use Abraham in such a way that he would be a channel of blessing to *the entire world*. The election of Israel was for *a universal goal*—the redemption of humanity—not to be a blessing to herself alone. Therefore, through her witness, the gentile world would either be repelled or drawn toward the God of Abraham, Isaac, and Jacob. "Gentile," which stems from the Hebrew term גּוֹי (*goy*) and its plural form הַגּוֹיִם (*ha-goyim*), or "the nations," refers to the nations of the world that are not Jewish.

Concerning the prophets, Isaiah spoke about how the nations are to be drawn to Israel, saying:

> It shall come to pass in the latter days that the mountain of the house of the LORD shall be established as the highest of the mountains, and shall be lifted up above the hills; and all the nations shall flow to it, and many peoples shall come, and say: Come, let us go up to the mountain of the LORD, to the house of the God of Jacob, that he may teach us his ways and that we may

16. Charlesworth, *Historical Jesus*, 46.

17. F. Brown et al., *Hebrew and English Lexicon*, בְּרִית, 136–37.

> walk in his paths. For out of Zion shall go the law, and the word of the LORD from Jerusalem. (Isa 2:2–4)

And,

> Arise, shine, for your light has come, and the glory of the LORD has risen upon you. For behold, darkness shall cover the earth, and thick darkness the peoples; but the LORD will arise upon you, and his glory will be seen upon you. And nations shall come to your light, and kings to the brightness of your rising. (Isa 60:1–3)

When Solomon dedicated the temple, it was to be a holy place where the Jewish people would offer prayers and worship to God. However, it was also meant to be a place of prayer and worship for the gentiles as well:

> Likewise, when a foreigner, who is not of your people Israel, comes from a far country for your name's sake (for they shall hear of your great name and your mighty hand, and of your outstretched arm), when he comes and prays toward this house, hear in heaven your dwelling place and do according to all for which the foreigner calls to you, in order that all the peoples of the earth may know your name and fear you, as do your people Israel, and that they may know that this house that I have built is called by your name. (1 Kgs 8:41–43)

The Old Testament reveals that gentiles would be restored to God because of Israel's eschatological restoration and be united to them. The prophet Micah spoke of a time when the nations would go to a restored temple to learn about God (Mic 4:15). Amos spoke of all the nations coming to the God of Israel (Amos 9:12), and other prophets spoke of the inclusion of the gentiles into God's redemptive plan (Ezek 17:23; 31:6; Dan 4:9–21). Even Jewish writers agree that the Messiah will open the door to the nations of the world to have a relationship with God:

> The Jewish concept of the Messiah is that which is clearly taught in the prophets of the Bible. He is a leader of the Jews, strong in wisdom and power and spirit. It is he who will bring complete redemption to the Jewish people both spiritually and physically. Along with this, he will bring eternal love, prosperity, and moral perfection to the world. Most important, the Jewish Messiah will bring all peoples to God. This is expressed most clearly in the Alenu prayer, which concludes all three daily services: "May the world be perfected under the kingdom of the Almighty. Let all the humans call upon Your Name and turn all the world's

> evildoers to You. Let everyone on earth know that every knee must bow to You . . . and let them all accept the yoke of Your Kingdom."[18]

But here we see the problem. It is evident in Israel's history that God's goal is that Israel is loyal to him so that the other nations will take notice and be drawn to the one true God (Deut 4:6). We can see this did not happen, but God had a plan to redeem this problem: to raise up a specific figure to act as Israel's ideal representative.

Within the book of Isaiah, there are several passages that speak of the "servant of the Lord." Some of these passages are about the nation of Israel (Isa 41:8–9; 42:19; 43:10; 44:21; 45:4; 48:20), while others present the servant of the Lord as a righteous individual. Two passages that stand out are as follows:

> Behold my servant, whom I uphold, my chosen, in whom my soul delights; I have put my Spirit upon him; he will bring forth justice to the nations. He will not cry aloud or lift up his voice, or make it heard in the street; a bruised reed he will not break, and a faintly burning wick he will not quench; he will faithfully bring forth justice. He will not grow faint or be discouraged till he has established justice in the earth; and the coastlands wait for his law. Thus says God, the Lord, who created the heavens and stretched them out, who spread out the earth and what comes from it, who gives breath to the people on it and spirit to those who walk in it: "I am the Lord; I have called you in righteousness; I will take you by the hand and keep you; I will give you as a covenant for the people, a light for the nations, to open the eyes that are blind, to bring out the prisoners from the dungeon, from the prison those who sit in darkness." (Isa 42:1–7)

> Listen to me, O coastlands, and give attention, you peoples from afar, The Lord called me from the womb, from the body of my mother he named my name. He made my mouth like a sharp sword; in the shadow of his hand he hid me; he made me a polished arrow; in his quiver he hid me away. And he said to me, You are my servant, Israel, in whom I will be glorified. But I said, "I have labored in vain; I have spent my strength for nothing and vanity; yet surely my right is with the Lord, and my recompense with my God." And now the Lord says, he who formed me from the womb to be his servant, to bring Jacob back to him; and that Israel might be gathered to him—for I am honored in the eyes

18. Kaplan, *Real Messiah*, 27–28.

> of the Lord, and my God has become my strength—he says: It is too light a thing that you should be my servant to raise up the tribes of Jacob and to bring back the preserved of Israel; I will make you as a light for the nations, that my salvation may reach to the end of the earth. Thus says the Lord, the Redeemer of Israel and his Holy One, to one deeply despised, abhorred by the nation, to the servant of rulers: Kings shall see and arise; princes, and they shall prostrate themselves; because of the Lord, who is faithful, the Holy One of Israel who has chosen you. (Isa 49:1–7)

The first passage (Isa 42:1–7) is clearly speaking of an individual who will be "a light for the nations." In Isa 49:1–7, the servant is called "Israel" (v.3), but it appears to be an individual (vv. 5–7), distinct from Israel, who will bring the nation back to God. Thus, the servant will be "despised" and "abhorred" by Israel. However, this passage repeats a theme similar to Isa 42:1–7, where this figure will also be used to take salvation to the nations outside of Israel. Later on, the New Testament applies this role to the Messiah:

> Now there was a man in Jerusalem, whose name was Simeon, and this man was righteous and devout, waiting for the consolation of Israel, and the Holy Spirit was upon him. And it had been revealed to him by the Holy Spirit that he would not see death before he had seen the Lord's Christ. And he came in the Spirit into the temple, and when the parents brought in the child Jesus, to do for him according to the custom of the Law, he took him up in his arms and blessed God and said, "Lord, now you are letting your servant depart in peace, according to your word; for my eyes have seen your salvation that you have prepared in the presence of all peoples, a light for revelation to the Gentiles, and for glory to your people Israel." (Luke 2:25–32)

This connection is vital to the recognition of Jesus as the Jewish Messiah because Jesus is the only messianic figure that has opened a door for gentile people to come to know the one true God. Just as Israel is called to be a light for the entire world (Gen 12:3), the Messiah's mission is to be a "light for the nations." In relation to Jesus's messiahship, while a remnant believed in him, the modern church is predominately comprised of gentiles. Gentiles who had been previously polytheistic idolators are now offered a relationship with the one true God. Just as Paul was praising the Thessalonians for having "turned to God from idols to serve the living and true God" (1 Thess 1:9), gentiles across the world have come to know the God of Abraham, Isaac, and Jacob. But the question is whether a dead, crucified, messianic figure could open the door for the nations to come into a relationship with the true God.

JESUS THE CRIMINAL

Despised and executed criminals are not likely candidates for becoming major figures in world history, so the odds that Jesus could overcome these severe handicaps and still become a worldwide religious leader would be difficult.[19] On this point, there is a significant comment made in the book of Acts by Gamaliel I—a key rabbinic leader and member of the Sanhedrin:

> But a Pharisee in the council named Gamaliel, a teacher of the Law held in honor by all the people, stood up and gave orders to put the men outside for a little while. And he said to them, "Men of Israel, take care what you are about to do with these men. For before these days Theudas rose up, claiming to be somebody, and a number of men, about four hundred, joined him. He was killed, and all who followed him were dispersed and came to nothing. After him, Judas the Galilean rose up in the days of the census and drew away some of the people after him. He too perished, and all those who followed him were scattered. So in the present case I tell you, keep away from these men and let them alone, for if this plan or this undertaking is of man, it will fail; but if it is of God, you will not be able to overthrow them. You might even be found opposing God!" (Acts 5:34–39)

Clearly Gamaliel knew of other Jewish revolts that featured a messianic element, but these revolts had all failed. The Jewish historian Josephus mentioned that Judas of Galilee had rebelled against Quirinius's census and was defeated.[20] Additionally, Josephus lists figures who claimed royal prerogatives between 4 BC and AD 68–70 but are not called "the" or "a" Messiah:

1. In Galilee, 4 BC: Judas, son of bandit leader Ezekias[21]
2. In Perea, 4 BC: Simon the Herodian slave[22]
3. In Judea, 4 BC: Athronges, the shepherd[23]

19. Robert C. Newman, "Fulfilled Prophecy as Miracle," in Geivett and Habermas, *In Defense of Miracles*, 221–23.

20. Josephus, *Ant.* 18:1.

21. Josephus, *War* 2:56; *Ant.* 17:271–72.

22. Josephus, *War* 2:57–59; *Ant.* 17:273–77.

23. Josephus, *War* 2:60–65; *Ant.* 17:278–84.

4. Menahem: grandson of Judas the Galilean[24]
5. Simon, son of Gioras (bar Giora)[25]

There are other messianic figures throughout Jewish history as well:

Simon Bar Kochba

Simon Bar Kochba was another Jewish leader who had messianic undertones. Some say he made an open proclamation to be the real Messiah who would take over Rome and enable the Jewish people to regain their self-rule (AD 132–135). Even a prominent rabbi called Rabbi Akiba affirmed him as the Messiah. Justin Martyr noted that Bar Kokhba commanded Christians to be led away to terrible punishment unless they denied Jesus as their Messiah.[26] Bar Kochba's revolt failed, and as a result both he and Rabbi Akiba were slain.[27]

Sabbatai Sevi

Sevi was a seventeenth-century Jewish teacher who claimed to be the Messiah and was heralded by a contemporary named Nathan. It is said that after Sevi's death in 1676 his brother found his tomb empty but full of light. If anything, the Sevi story sounds like it was borrowed from the resurrection story about Jesus. The Sevi story has little historical backing. What is more ironic is that Sevi later left the Jewish faith for Islam.[28]

Rabbi Menachem Mendel Schneerson

Within Judaism, there is a sect known as Hasidic Judaism. A rabbi who is considered to be a leader in the movement is called a צַדִּיק (*tzaddik*), which is Hebrew for "righteous man." A *tzaddik* is sometimes viewed as a רַבִּי (rabbi), meaning "master" or "teacher." In the book of Acts, during Stephen's famous speech, the deacon refers to Jesus as a *tzaddik*, saying: "Which of the prophets did your fathers not persecute? And they killed those who

24. Josephus, *War* 2:433–48.

25. Josephus, *War* 2:521, 625–54; 4:503–10, 529; 7:26–36, 154. See Zannoni, *Jews and Christians Speak*, 113–14.

26. *Apo.* 31:6.

27. Bockmuehl and Paget, *Redemption and Resistance*, 156.

28. Geisler, *Big Book*, 502.

had announced beforehand the coming of the Righteous One, whom you have now betrayed and murdered" (Acts 7:52). An example of a present-day *tzaddik* is Rabbi Menachem Mendel Schneerson (1951–1994), the leader of the Chabad Lubavitch Hasidim. Some of the followers of Rabbi Schneerson think he was the Messiah and ironically, after Schneerson died in 1994, some asserted that Isa 53 could be used as a proof text that the Messiah will rise from the dead. Of course, this has led to great controversy.

What do all these messianic figures have in common? They are all dead! Furthermore, we can empirically verify that none of them has bought more than one billion gentiles into a relationship with the one true God by the life they lived. Regarding the significance of this in relation to Jesus, Jewish author Michael Kogan writes:

> Has Jesus brought redemption to Israel? No, but he has brought the means of redemption to the gentiles—and that in the name of Israel's God—thus helping Israel to fulfill its calling to be a blessing to all peoples. A Jewish Messiah for the gentiles! Perhaps, as I have suggested, an inversion of Cyrus's role as a gentile Messiah for the Jews. Israel is redeemed by engaging in redemptive work. Perhaps redemption is not a final state but a process, a life devoted to bringing oneself and others before God. To live a life in relationship to the Holy One and to help the world to understand itself as the Kingdom of God—which it, all unknowingly, already is—is to participate in redemption, to live a redemptive life. This has been Israel's calling from the beginning.[29]

A potential objection is that I am appealing to large numbers as the primary apologetic as to why Jesus must be the Messiah. Of course, the growth of a new religious movement does not determine its truth. Muslims, for instance, have tried to convince me that Islam is the fastest-growing religion in the world—"Therefore, Islam must be true." My point is that we have a prophetic element that is discussed in the Old Testament that speaks of the need for a Jewish Messiah who provides redemption to the gentile world, and of all the messianic figures in Jewish history, only Jesus has accomplished this—and he has accomplished it on a large scale.

Historians are concerned with causality—the examination of cause and effect. Thus, they ask cause-effect questions. They ask what caused the first-century Jesus movement to expand from a Jewish sect to a largely gentile-based religious movement. Once again, given the negative views of

29. Kogan, *Opening the Covenant*, 68.

the crucifixion and a dying Messiah, the early Jesus movement prior to AD 70 should have ended very quickly.

Roman crucifixion was viewed as a punishment for those of lower status—dangerous criminals, slaves, or anyone who caused a threat to Roman order and authority. Crucifixion was the worst form of death. Given that Jewish nationalism was quite prevalent in the first century, the Romans also used crucifixion to quell uprisings. In the Hebrew Bible we read: "And if a man has committed a crime punishable by death and is he is put to death, and you hang him on a tree, his body shall not remain all night on the tree, but you shall bury him on the same day, for a hanged man is cursed by God. You shall not defile your land which the LORD your God is giving you for an inheritance" (Deut 21:22–23).

In these verses it is not the execution itself but what is done to the body after the person is executed—displaying it as a warning to others. Returning to Paul's claim in 1 Cor 15, Jewish people at that time would have viewed someone crucified as either a victim or a villain. If the latter, the person being condemned as a criminal would be considered cursed by God because of their actions. If the former, they could hardly be the Savior of Israel. Crucifixion was undoubtably seen in a negative light within Judaism. Therefore, since the birth of the Christian faith and hope for the future starts with the crucifixion of Jesus, Jesus's movement should have died out rather quickly. However, the opposite happened, because his earliest followers understood his crucifixion as being vindicated by his resurrection from the dead.

CONCLUSION

We have surveyed the Old Testament and attempted to find specific messianic predictions that the Messiah will rise again from the dead. While there is no specific text that points to a resurrected Messiah, there are several passages that discuss the role of gentiles being drawn to Israel and the role of the servant of the Lord as God's agent to bring salvation to gentile nations. Jesus is the only messianic figure who has accomplished the mission of Israel through his own life and work, specifically by fulfilling the promise of the Abrahamic covenant to the nations. Since this could not be accomplished by a dead, crucified Messiah, the resurrection clearly served as the reason for the Jesus movement's survival and how Jesus could bring the nations into a relationship with the one true God. Only the true Messiah can bring salvation to the nations, and only through his resurrection has Jesus done so, making the resurrection of Jesus a necessary qualification for his messiahship. Thus, we conclude with the following comment by N. T. Wright:

> If nothing happened to the body of Jesus, I cannot see why any of his explicit or implicit claims should be regarded as true. What is more, I cannot as a historian, see why anyone would have continued to belong to his movement and to regard him as the Messiah. There were several other Messianic or quasi-Messianic movements within a hundred years either side of Jesus. Routinely, they ended with the leader being killed by authorities, or by a rival group. If your Messiah is killed, you conclude that he was not the Messiah. Some of those movements continued to exist; where they did, they took a new leader from the same family. (But note: Nobody ever said that James, the brother of Jesus, was the Messiah.) Such groups did not go around saying that their Messiah had been raised from the dead. What is more, I cannot make sense of the whole picture, historically or theologically, unless they were telling the truth.[30]

Bibliography

Bird, Michael F. *Are You the One Who Is to Come? The Historical Jesus and the Messianic Question*. Grand Rapids: Baker, 2009.

Bockmuehl, Markus, and Jameson Carleton Paget. *Redemption and Resistance: The Messianic Hopes and Christians in Antiquity*. New York: T&T Clark, 2009.

Borowitz, Eugene B. *Liberal Judaism*. New York: Behrman, 1984.

Brown, Francis, et al. *A Hebrew and English Lexicon of the Old Testament with an Appendix Containing the Biblical Aramaic*. Oxford: Clarendon, 1966.

Brown, Michael L. *Answering Jewish Objections to Jesus*. Vol. 3. Grand Rapids: Baker, 2003.

Charlesworth, James H. *The Historical Jesus: An Essential Guide*. Nashville: Abingdon, 2008.

Crossan, John Dominic, and N. T. Wright. *The Resurrection of Jesus: John Dominic Crossan and N. T. Wright in Dialogue*. Edited by Robert B. Stewart. Minneapolis: Fortress, 2006.

Flusser, David. *Judaism and the Origins of Christianity*. Jerusalem: Magnes, 1988.

Geisler, Norman L. *The Big Book of Christian Apologetics: An A to Z Guide*. Grand Rapids: Baker, 2012.

Geivett, R. Douglas, and Gary R. Habermas. *In Defense of Miracles: A Comprehensive Case for God's Actions in Human History*. Downers Grove, IL: InterVarsity, 1997.

Kaiser, Walter C. *Recovering the Unity of the Bible: One Continuous Story, Plan, and Purpose*. Grand Rapids: Zondervan, 2010.

Kaplan, Aryeh, et al. *The Real Messiah: A Jewish Response to Missionaries*. New York: National Conference of Synagogue Youth, 2000.

Keener, Craig S. *Acts: An Exegetical Commentary*. Vol. 1. Grand Rapids: Baker Academic, 2012.

30. Crossan and Wright, *Resurrection of Jesus*, 71.

Kogan, Michael S. *Opening the Covenant: A Jewish Theology of Christianity*. Oxford: Oxford University Press, 2007.

Levine, Amy-Jill. "A Jewish Take on Jesus: Amy-Jill Levine Talks the Gospel." U.S. Catholic, Sept. 24, 2012. https://uscatholic.org/articles/201209/a-jewish-take-on-jesus-amy-jill-levine-talks-the-gospels/.

Levine, Amy-Jill, and Marc Zvi Brettler. *The Bible with and without Jesus: How Christians and Jews Read the Same Stories Differently*. New York: Harper One, 2020.

Milavec, Aaron. *Salvation Is from the Jews: Saving Grace in Judaism and Messianic Hope in Christianity*. Collegeville, MN: Liturgical, 2007.

Moore, George Foot. *Judaism in the First Centuries of the Christian Era: The Age of the Tannaim*. 3 vols. Cambridge, MA: Harvard University Press, 1955.

Porter, Stanley. *The Messiah in the Old and New Testaments*. Grand Rapids: Eerdmans, 2007.

Skarsaune, Oskar. *In the Shadow of the Temple: Jewish Influences on Early Christianity*. Downers Grove, IL: InterVarsity, 2002.

Zannoni, Arthur E. *Jews and Christians Speak of Jesus*. Minneapolis: Fortress, 1994.

What Do You Mean by Reliable? Navigating the Question behind the Question

Clark R. Bates[1]

A popular saying in modern Evangelicalism is that Christianity is not based on a book, but a person.[2] Some say that God did not send us a book; he sent us his Son. Statements like these are intended to emphasize the historical reality of the life, death, and resurrection of Jesus of Nazareth, as opposed to preferencing the Bible at the expense of the one to whom the Bible points. While this sentiment is admirable, it is an inescapable reality that much of what Christians can know about Jesus, and the Christian faith, comes from the book we call the Bible.

It is this inevitability that leads many to ask questions about the Bible's reliability. Apologists in general will face questions about the historical reliability of events in the Old Testament (OT) as well as the New, accusations

1. I first became aware of Dr. Turek's ministry sixteen years ago, as a young man coming back to the Christian faith. My wife and I were working to reconcile our marriage after a near-divorce, and I had rejected the simplistic fundamentalism that I grew up with. I found out about *I Don't Have Enough Faith to Be an Atheist* through a footnote in another book and was quickly drawn into the radio broadcast of the same name. Dr. Turek helped draw me back to a faith that I could reasonably defend and claim as my own. I met him in 2016 at the CrossExamined Instructor Academy, not knowing what to expect. I found a man larger than life but willing to sit and listen to my questions patiently and lovingly. He helped me ascertain that what I was passionate about defending was the Bible, particularly the New Testament, and now, as I write this, I am months away from defending my PhD in that same field. I am deeply grateful for Dr. Turek and his heartfelt desire to spread the gospel. This book is a small way of saying thank you.

2. Burchard, "Does Jesus Want You," para. 6; Robertson, "Run to God," paras. 4–5.

against the historicity of the exodus, doubts about miracles, or even the existence of a historical Jesus. Others will challenge the legitimacy of the text itself, its transmission, and even one's ability to know what the Bible said in its original form. For this reason, Christians must be prepared to answer these questions to the best of their ability, but the number of questions and the breadth of knowledge required, often across several, very technical academic disciplines, can be daunting.

No Christian should feel compelled to be an expert in every discipline to defend their faith, but they should be aware of ways to answer various kinds of questions. As it relates to reliability, the question being asked is one of trust and confidence, and ultimately all questions about—and accusations against—the text and the historicity of the Bible mask an underlying question; a question behind the questions, if you will. When someone asks about biblical manuscripts, or about the existence of Sodom and Gomorrah, what they are really asking is, "Can I trust this book to be an accurate guide for my life?" They are seeking a trustworthy voice outside themselves. Understanding this underlying question casts skeptical interlocutors in a different light, and if Christians seek to answer this question above all, engagements can be less about being right and more about speaking truth in love. In this chapter I will approach the Bible from three categories of reliability: historical, textual, and what I will call epistemological. I will walk through some common objections aimed at the former two categories, to help answer the question of the third—the question that is ultimately being asked by those who interrogate the other two.

I OBJECT!

Over the years, countless claims have been made against the Bible's historicity. These objections are not limited to miraculous or divine occurrences but include the existence of places, people groups, practices, and individuals. It was once argued that the biblical King David did not exist, though numerous archaeological discoveries have been unearthed supporting circumstances around the biblical narrative—not least of which is the ninth-century Tel Dan inscription believed to read "house of David."[3] It is still argued no evidence exists for the mass immigration of the Israelites out of Egypt, though many of these oppositions rely heavily on a late-dating model of the exodus.[4] The Hittite people were, at one time, believed not to

3. Knoppers, "Historical Study of Monarchy," 220–21; Windle, "Top Ten Discoveries."

4. For an overview of the different approaches, see Chavalas and Adamthwaite, "Archaeological Light," 78–96. Also consider what evidence one should reasonably expect.

exist, and Pontius Pilate, the infamous procurator that condemned Jesus to death, was once thought to be fictional. In every case, evidence has been discovered, pushing back against these objections.[5]

Questions about historicity are necessarily linked to reliability, and though some might suggest that the moral or ethical truths of Scripture are still valuable even if the Bible should not be considered historical, these truths are inextricably joined to the historical context within which each book takes place.[6] To pick which piece of a biblical book is true and which is in error reduces the Christian faith to a kind of spiritual pick 'n' mix, wherein there is no objective truth, only preferred flavors. Nevertheless, there are good reasons to trust the historicity of Scripture. Because an exhaustive response to every challenge against biblical historicity is impossible here, I have fashioned this section on historical reliability to respond to specific objections in the hope that by answering some questions, readers will be both encouraged in their faith and motivated to investigate answers for other objections on their own.

The Old Testament

Objection: No Sufficient Written Language Existed at the Time of the Biblical Patriarchs

On its face this does not seem like much of an objection. After all, the OT never says that Abraham, Isaac, or Jacob ever wrote anything. Historically, Moses was believed to have written the records of the patriarchs, but modern historians prefer to place the writing of the Torah sometime after the sixth century. An objection like this suggests that the Genesis accounts could not have been recorded contemporaneously to the events they depict, let alone by Moses, and thus the stories are unreliable. However, the study of linguistics in tandem with archaeological efforts has shed a great deal of light on the evolution of language in the world.

Recently, a team of independent researchers alongside academics from the University of Durham and University College London published

The biblical depiction of the exodus involves a people group thoroughly inculcated in Egyptian culture and "plundering" the Egyptians prior to leaving. If this is the case, many remains left behind, if discovered, would appear Egyptian, not Semitic.

5. Beckman, "Hittite Administration in Syria." For a transcription of the Pontius Pilate Stone, see https://library.brown.edu/iip/viewinscr/caes0043/.

6. Psychologist Jordan B. Peterson is famous for this conviction, though he appears to be accepting more of the historicity of the Bible as time goes on. His lectures are visible here: https://www.jordanbpeterson.com/bible-series/.

findings on the existence of a Paleolithic protowriting system from approximately four hundred caves across Europe. The team determined that the non-pictographic symbols found in these caves constituted a communication system relaying the seasonal behavior of animal breeds 21,000 years ago.[7] Whether this qualifies as a written "language" in the strictest sense is up for debate, but knowing that the transition from rudimentary cave paintings to a systematic and intentional message began this far into our past immediately weakens any accusation that written abilities or alphabetic systems did not exist at the time depicted in most of the book of Genesis.

The Sumerian epic *Enmerkar and the Lord of Aratta* (2000–1700 BC) suggests that King Enmerkar invented writing.[8] Prior to this, Egyptian hieroglyphs have been found as far back as 4000 BC, with additional discoveries of alphabetic characters on clay cylinders dated to 2300 BC.[9] The earliest alphabet comes from Egypt in 1700 BC, followed shortly after by the Ugaritic alphabet in 1300 BC, roughly one century after the earliest dating for the exodus. Between 1200 and 980 BC—within the latest dating of the exodus—a linear alphabet was in demonstrable use.

While a post-Babylonian exile date for the composition of Genesis is popular among modern academics, it cannot be said that the lack of written language or ability was a reason. Additionally, this data provides a reason to believe that the stories of the biblical patriarchs could have been recorded in the writing style of an ancient alphabetical system like that found in Syria or Egypt. The existence of Egyptian alphabetical systems supports the case for Mosaic authorship in a tangential way, given Moses's Egyptian upbringing. Being raised by Pharaoh's daughter would have provided Moses with the education used by Egyptians to train scribes and the ability to read texts in the writing systems of that time.

Most recently, Christian media has publicized the finding of a lead curse tablet in the West Bank. This tablet is reported to have been found through a wet sifting technique and contains a curse in Hebrew that includes the name of Yahweh. This find is significant in that it was found in the location of Mt. Ebal, where the Israelites were commanded to proclaim the curses of Yahweh against disobedience (Deut 27–28), and because it becomes one of the earliest inscriptions to contain the divine name.[10] The discovery has

7. Bacon et al., "Upper Palaeolithic Proto-Writing System."

8. Meade and Gurry, *Scribes and Scriptures*, 29.

9. Glenn M. Schwartz, "Non-Cuneiform Writing at Third-Millennium Umm el-Marra, Syria: Evidence of an Early Alphabetic Tradition?," as cited in Meade and Gurry, *Scribes and Scriptures*, 39.

10. Some examples: https://www.premierchristianity.com/opinion/is-this-biblical-curse-tablet-the-most-significant-discovery-in-recent-history/12803.article; https://

not completed academic peer review at the time of this writing, however, and until this takes place, the claims being made are tentative. I share it to point out two important, concluding facts: (1) the OT has faced objections to its historicity for centuries, if not millennia, and it has overcome them every time; and (2) in our rush to "prove" the Bible historically, we must be cautious in accepting every purported discovery that comes along. Not all evidence is equal. Do we have answers to every historical objection against the OT? No, but we possess enough answers to have sufficient reason to trust its accounts, even when the physical evidence has not yet been found.

The New Testament

Objection: The Authors of the New Testament (NT) Were Unscientific

This claim is generally followed by arguments that the NT authors believed the earth was flat or that they did not understand the world in the scientific way moderns do.[11] Because of this, they were prone to mistakenly believing in the supernatural. It is true that the apostles Peter and John are said to be "uneducated"—in Greek ἀγράμματος (*agrammatos*)—when they are examined by the Pharisees (Acts 4:13), but the meaning of this term is debatable.[12] Literally, it means "unlettered" or "illiterate," but the context of the interrogation in Acts is in response to the apostles' preaching. The Pharisees are amazed at their boldness and their message, given that they were ἀγράμματοι (*agrammatoi)*—uneducated—presumably, in the ways of the law. If this is correct, the text does not suggest the apostles were illiterate but merely lacked formal religious instruction.

We must concede that the Bible does not provide any scientific details to determine the authors' knowledge, but neither is it completely silent. The idea that the NT authors believed in a flat earth comes from a claim that they believed the universe consisted of three flat disks—the "things on earth," "things above the earth," and "things below the earth" (Phil 2:10). This was a demonstrably popular view in Mesopotamia and in the Ancient Near East, but the NT was not written by men steeped in Mesopotamian worldviews. The culture at the time of the NT was decidedly Greco-Roman.

---

www.christianpost.com/news/biblical-researchers-decipher-curse-tablet.html; https://www.livescience.com/ancient-curse-tablet-early-hebrew.

11. Evans, *Inspired*, xvii.

12. See Hilton, *Illiterate Apostles*, 95–98. Hilton accepted the meaning of "illiterate" but recognizes that the purpose of pointing this out is something greatly debated.

That the area in which Jesus and his disciples worked was more Hellenic than Jewish is proven by the infamous Maccabean revolt of 160–167 BC, which fought back against the threat of losing Jewish distinctiveness in the face of overwhelming Hellenization. Neither did this Hellenization occur by force. Because of Alexander the Great's conquest of the known world, any hope of economic and social survival required the adoption of the Greek language and much of the Greek lifestyle.

In 1914, a trove of papyri consisting of supply lists, official correspondence, and account ledgers was discovered in the Fayum region of Egypt.[13] These papyri recorded life in and around the ancient city of Philadelphia in the third century BC. Rather than being written in Aramaic, Hebrew, or other local dialects, almost all were written in Greek. Apart from Jewish tomb, ossuary, and synagogue inscriptions, most Palestinian writing from the third century was in Greek.[14] Herod the Great famously undertook large-scale architectural projects in Israel and the surrounding regions, utilizing Greek style and technique, even in the region of the temple. Therefore, despite being first-century Jews, the authors of the NT inhabited a world more Greek than Hebrew, and their understanding would have been steeped in Greek science and philosophy, even if they lacked formal training.

To explain the worldview of the NT authors, one is better served by looking at the Grecian world. Thales of Miletus (seventh century BC) was the earliest recorded scientist and believed in a spherical universe, a belief found throughout Greek philosophy. The Greek philosopher Aristarchus (third century BC) is the first to have proposed that the Earth orbited the sun, thousands of years before Copernicus. The mathematical ability of Greek astronomers even enabled them to accurately determine the circumference of the earth within 160 km! It would be implausible to suggest that the apostles and NT authors were not aware of these teachings, and even less likely that they believed in a flat earth. The fact that Paul and others wrote of things being above and below the earth is not meant scientifically but metaphysically, referring to angelic and demonic beings, ultimately acting as a figure of speech referring to all of creation.

At least one Gospel author can be tested against this theory. Luke is referred to as the "beloved physician" in Col 4:14. The Greeks made substantial breakthroughs in the world of medicine, leaving a wealth of medical terminology still used today. It is estimated that of the sixty thousand words

13. Papyrus is an early form of writing material like paper but developed from a plant grown in various regions of the ancient world. Later manuscripts were written on animal skin known as vellum or on paper after its popularity increased in the thirteenth century.

14. Hengel, *Judaism and Hellenism*, 58.

in the modern medical dictionary, 68 percent are Greek.[15] If Luke was indeed a physician, we should expect to find Greek medical terminology in his writing. As we might expect, Luke's Gospel records multiple accounts of healings performed by Jesus that can be examined.

In Luke 4:38–39 Jesus heals Peter's mother-in-law. The parallel accounts in Matt 8:14–15 and Mark 1:30–31 say she is "lying sick with a fever," but in Luke we read that she is "suffering from a high fever." This phrase—συνεχομένη πυρετῷ μεγάλῳ (*sunechomenē piretō megalō*), unique to Luke, is a medical term found more than 7,800 times in Greek texts, describing someone in the grip of a sickness.[16] In Luke 13:11–13, Jesus heals a crippled woman who is "bent over and could not straighten herself." Again, the Lucan language was also used by the famous physicians Galen and Hippocrates to describe the shifting of vertebrae. Lastly, in Luke 14:2 we read of a man "whose body was swollen with fluid," otherwise known as edema. The author describes the disease as ὑδρωπικός (*hidrōpikos*), a term that occurs 267 times in Greek literature, almost exclusively in medical texts referring to modern-day edema. Similar medical terminology is also found in the healing accounts of the book of Acts, long believed to have been penned by Luke.

Though I am using only one NT author as my example, this is merely to prove the point that the authors of the NT lived with an understanding of the natural world that was far more advanced than is often believed in popular circles. While they might have lacked the detailed scientific expertise that we possess in the era of the electron microscope, that did not make them barbarians in relation to science. The authors of the NT were not scientists to be sure, but neither were they "flat-earthers."

Objection: The Gospel Stories Are Invented

Recently, I listened to a debate regarding the historicity of the Gospels in which the skeptic repeatedly stated that he was interested only in the most parsimonious solution to the claims of Christianity. He felt the most complete answer to his doubts was the one most likely to have occurred within a naturalistic framework. Most skeptics phrase their objections in similar ways, ultimately rejecting the reliability of the NT based on anti-supernatural bias. Many, like this skeptic, readily accept that the NT may contain historical truth but reject anything metaphysical. Because of this strong aversion to the supernatural, even when the collective evidence of

15. Konstantinidis, *Οἰκουμενική Δίασταση*, 3.

16. Caragounis, *New Testament Investigations*, 78–79.

historical information is incontrovertible, the existence of the miraculous makes the story of Jesus more likely a myth wrapped in history than eyewitness testimony.

This objection to the miraculous cannot be brushed off. After all, despite the abundance of historical support, we do not believe in Christianity because of the historical details in the Bible; we believe in it because of the miracle of the resurrection. Amassing historical details takes the argument only so far. Too often when Christians debate skeptics on this matter, they continue to press the historical data without hearing the skeptic say that it is not the history of the material that troubles them. Dr. Peter J. Williams of Tyndale House, Cambridge, writes, "Were it not for the many miraculous reports in the Gospels, most historians would be very happy to treat their accounts as generally historically reliable. This itself is no small thing."[17] What often holds most back from the story of Jesus is their presupposed naturalism, not the actual reliability of the Bible.

Christians must realize and communicate that when we speak of our faith as historical, it is built upon a cumulative case. It is not merely that we have archaeological evidence of the accuracy of the Gospels, but that we have this, along with very accurate reporting of cultural conditions, political life, geography, botany, social customs, and religious life. It is not that there are random miracles contained within Scripture, but that these miracles fall with an ordered pattern, the accumulation of which point in a particular direction: toward the identity of Jesus. This pattern connects the OT with the NT, making it even more difficult to fabricate. For the skeptic to consider all the evidence and still be convinced that the story of Jesus is an invention within a historical narrative, they must admit that the biblical authors were the most creative authors of their time—something few will acknowledge.

These authors would have to have demanded of themselves an attention to detail of historical matters down to the minutiae of every aspect in their stories, only to invent miraculous healings and a physical resurrection that no Jewish writer prior had anticipated. They would have been the literary groundbreakers of their respective centuries and cultures. This hardly seems to be the most parsimonious of explanations, even with the miraculous occurrences. Considering the complexity of this task, Dr. Williams says:

> If the presentation of Jesus in the Gospels is wrong, one faces many intellectual hurdles to explain why so many historical details are right or plausible. One has to explain how the various layers of textual material arose in the Gospels, all of which

17. Williams, *Can We Trust Gospels*, 133.

> display signs of abundant familiarity with the time of Jesus and show the features one would expect from the earliest Jewish layers of tradition. One needs to explain the origin of the parables, the original teaching, and the range of cases where one Gospel is most simply explained by assuming the truth of another. One has to explain how the movement of Jesus' followers took off numerically in a manner for which historians cannot agree on an explanation.[18]

Given the limitless ingenuity of the human mind, even this is not likely to convince, but it cannot be ignored. The fundamental objection is that belief in the supernatural is more complicated than belief in the natural, but when the entirety of the Bible is taken into consideration, the simplest, or most parsimonious, explanation is that the story of Jesus's life, ministry, death, and resurrection are true. If Jesus is who he claimed to be in the Gospels, both the narrative of Israel in the Hebrew Bible and the spread of Christianity after his death make sense. If he is not, nothing does.

LET'S TALK ABOUT TEXTS, BABY

In the city of St. Louis, Missouri, there is a basilica. Its construction began in 1907, but the interior would not be completed until 1988. The St. Louis Basilica is roughly 83,000 sq. ft. inside and is decorated with more than 41.5 million squares of glass. Individually, each square is nothing more than a colorful trinket of gold, green, blue, red, etc., but when the squares are combined in the appropriate pattern, they create some of the most beautiful images found in an American cathedral. Entering the basilica, one cannot help but stand in awe as one's eyes are drawn upward to the top of the dome, encompassed in golden images of angels, apostles, prophets, and the Lord. It is beautiful on a heavenly scale. Now, it could be possible for someone to look at all the various mosaic tiles individually and say that, because they are all different, you can never be certain what image they really comprise, but this would be nonsensical given the nature of a mosaic is a single image made by intentionally placed individual pieces. To focus only on the individual pieces ignores the nature of the art. In a way, biblical manuscripts are like the individual pieces of glass in a mosaic, and the practice of textual criticism seeks to place each manuscript in the proper place to discover the original image.

18. Williams, *Can We Trust Gospels*, 137.

The Old Testament

When textual critics speak of scribes and scribal habits, many people immediately picture large rooms of monks copying from manuscripts at a desk or listening attentively to a single monk reading from a master copy as they transcribe every word. While this might have some selective historical truth in the Middle Ages, the history of biblical scribes is less structured. We read about Hebrew scribes in the pages of the OT itself—most prominently Ezra (Ezra 7:6, 11–12). Ezra is referred to as both a "priestly scribe" and "skilled in the law of Moses." His being a priestly scribe might indicate that he worked in and around the domain of the temple, which, in the ancient world, functioned as a repository for various administrative, legal, and sacral texts, not unlike the Library of Congress in the United States.

The book of Deuteronomy records that copies of the law were placed inside the ark of the covenant (Deut 31:24–26), which would later be stored in the temple. In the eighteenth year of the reign of King Josiah, Hilkiah the high priest discovered a copy of the law in the "house of the LORD" (2 Kgs 22:8), i.e., the temple. The regions closest to the temple would often possess the most accurate copies of texts. The further from the temple one got, the more varied copies would generally become. This can be helpful when we read of variations between the manuscripts of the Dead Sea Scrolls (DSS) found in Qumran, some twenty-two miles from the Temple Mount, and those in other Hebrew manuscripts used for our English Bibles. Knowing this about the culture surrounding the writing and compilation of the OT is very important when thinking through reliability, precisely because the material evidence for the OT is much farther removed from any "autographs" than the NT.[19]

Manuscripts of the Old Testament

Hebrew manuscripts can be categorized into three epochs: the time of the DSS, the "silent period," and the Masoretic period.[20] The time of the DSS dates to approximately 250 BC, from which 210 fragmentary manuscripts of the OT—minus the book of Esther—can be identified.[21] The so-called silent period lasted between the third and eighth century AD and is so called because only fragments of the Torah, Kings, and Job are extant. It is here

19. Autograph refers to an original manuscript (e.g., the first manuscript of Isaiah).

20. Meade and Gurry, *Scribes & Scriptures*, 54.

21. Bear in mind that this period ranges from 250 BC to AD 130, so not all the manuscripts discovered in Qumran date to the earliest period. To suggest that they do, even implicitly, is unethical.

that a shift to the consonantal text known as Masoretic begins, with the handwriting on these manuscripts referred to as "proto-Masoretic." The last period, and most abundant in terms of manuscript production, is the Masoretic period. With all fragments and full manuscripts combined, there are approximately thirty-five thousand copies dated to this epoch. It's no wonder that the Masoretic period, and the handwriting known as the Masoretic Text, is the primary source for all English translations of the OT. This stage begins in the ninth century AD and lasts until the end of the Middle Ages.

The Masoretic period and its text are named after a group of Jewish scribes known, unsurprisingly, as the Masoretes. Their name means "transmitters of tradition," and they applied a vowel system to the existing Hebrew alphabet. During this time, copying enters a formal, controlled stage, and large units of variation between manuscripts decrease. Manuscripts of the OT also exist in translations, including Greek as early as the second century BC, Syriac in the second century AD, Latin in the fourth century AD, and Aramaic in the later centuries. Because of this wealth of evidence, even from manuscripts further removed from the originals than with the NT, textual critics can compare the texts with each other and confidently identify areas of stability and uncertainty. Lest we think that this uncertainty should lead to doubt about the reliability of the text, Dr. John Meade answers:

> The witnesses do not present a uniform picture, . . . but that is not to say that the textual pluriformity discovered in the earliest period presents a picture of chaos or a chance process. Rather it displays a beautiful mosaic. The evidence shows three kinds of copying: (1) conservative, (2) free, and (3) careless. Conservative copying means that a scribe copied his exemplar . . . strictly, letter by letter. Free copying means that the scribe updated the text's spelling, grammar, and vocabulary, and even adapted it according to the community's interpretations and needs. Careless copying . . . accounts for simple, accidental mistakes that all scribes make.[22]

While this pluriformity in the manuscript tradition of the OT has led some to conclude that there was no "fixed" Hebrew Bible until the Masoretic period, and thus no way to know what the early Israelites believed, Christians need not be led down this same alley. On the contrary, the words of Jesus himself imply a stable understanding of the "law and prophets" in Israel during his ministry—nearly a millennium before the Masoretic period. As

22. Meade and Gurry, *Scribes & Scriptures*, 69. I am indebted to Dr. John D. Meade for his years of instruction and support related to understanding Old Testament textual criticism and the canonization of the Hebrew Bible.

Jesus read from the prophet Isaiah, quoted the psalmist, or even asserted that Moses "wrote," "said," or "commanded" something to the people, there was the expectation that the audience knew of what Jesus spoke. There was no need to clarify which book was canonical or which version of Isaiah was meant. When Jesus related his teaching to the OT, the Israelites simply conceded the accuracy of the text in question. Therefore, rather than being thrust into doubt about the textual reliability of the OT because of the manuscript evidence, Christians should stand in awe of the mosaic of witnesses that the evidence presents us and be grateful to the providence of God for its preservation.

The New Testament

Inevitably, when a conversation about the reliability of the NT ensues, the discussion turns to the number of manuscripts. Every apologist has heard and said that there are more manuscripts of the NT than any other ancient literary work. This is very true. By current estimates, there are more than 5,000 NT manuscripts in Greek alone, with approximately 20,000 when combined the other languages. When this is compared with the few hundred existing manuscripts of classical works, the numbers look very impressive. However, we must be careful with what we are trying to prove with these numbers.

Generally, when we trot out the totals, we often include the age of the manuscripts with the number. The argument often goes that we have "*more* manuscripts than any other work *and earlier* copies to the original." While this is true enough, it gives the mistaken impression that we have complete copies of NT books as early as the second or third century, when almost all the earliest manuscripts of NT books prior to the fourth century are fragmentary. They can be as small as a playing card or as large as a standard sheet of printer paper, but even then, they're riddled with holes and damage. The reality is that the earliest full manuscripts of the NT come three hundred to four hundred years after the originals, and if our argument is that we have confidence in the NT because we have so many manuscripts *and* that they are early, then our confidence in the OT would have to be less, since its manuscript evidence is much farther removed from the originals and fewer in number.[23]

23. Consider that prior to the discovery of the Dead Sea Scrolls in 1947 the earliest OT manuscripts were in the Greek codices of the fourth century AD, and even after their being found, the earliest of those date to the second century BC. Depending on when one dates the composition of various OT books, even at the most liberal dating,

Am I saying we should not have confidence in the text of our Bible? No, absolutely not! I am merely saying that we need to think very clearly about what we mean when we use arguments about manuscripts. It is still true that we have a larger number of manuscripts for both the OT and the NT than for other works of antiquity. It is also true that we have a portion of manuscripts for the NT that are considerably closer to the originals than any other classical work. But all this means is that it can explain the number of textual variants used by critics to challenge the reliability of the Bible and can be used to better determine the earliest text of both Testaments.[24] For instance, when someone claims that there are "more variants in the NT than there are words," this is precisely because there are so many manuscripts to choose from. Additionally, if someone claims that a particular reading is not original to the Bible, they must assume a knowledge of the original reading. To suggest that we cannot know what the NT originally said requires the belief that in 20,000 manuscripts no original readings are contained in any, but Homer's original can be found in roughly 1,500 manuscripts of the *Iliad*.

It is precisely because we have so many manuscripts, covering so large a span of time, that textual critics are able to determine how most variant readings come to exist. Doing this makes it possible to find the initial text from which the readings diverge.[25] And while some become concerned by the idea that academics are "determining" the text of their Bibles, bear in mind that no teaching of the Christian faith is determined by any one verse. This is because—thanks to the plurality of Christian doctrine—no doctrinal belief is isolated to a single passage of Scripture. There is "no Christian doctrine or practice, major or minor, *determined* by a textually difficult passage."[26]

---

this makes our earliest OT texts several centuries removed from any originals—if we use the dating promoted in evangelical circles, more than one thousand years removed.

24. Prothro, "Myths about Classical Literature," 82.

25. In German, "initial text" is read as *Ausgangstext* and is the preferred way most textual critics refer to what we may think of as the original biblical text. Textual critics use this slightly differently than most lay people, as they see it as the earliest text that can be recovered from which all other readings come. However, even the Institute for New Testament Textual Research in Muenster, Germany (the heart of German textual criticism), admits that there is likely no discernible difference between what they call the initial text and the original text.

26. Gurry, "Myths about Variants," 208.

Manuscripts of the New Testament

In the earliest stages of the Christian church, the message of Jesus and the apostles was transmitted orally. In 1 Cor 15:3 Paul writes that he "handed on to [the Corinthian church] as of first importance what in turn [he] had received," but by the time 1 Timothy and 2 Peter were written (AD 64–150 and 60–125) we find a citation from the Gospel of Luke and recognition of a Pauline letter collection, respectively.[27] Even if one accepts the latest possible dates for these letters, the written tradition of the last NT books had begun circulating within the early second century. As these texts were converted from oral to written testimony, they were copied by hand and transmitted throughout the various regions in which the Christian faith spread.

The earliest period of this transmission took place between the first/second century and the seventh century. As many textual critics note, "This early proliferation of copies took place freely and with few regulations, which caused variation in readings to be introduced into the texts. Such variation would of course then be reproduced in further copies and enter into the manuscript tradition."[28] While the unregulated copying of this period prior to the fourth century is used by skeptics as a reason to doubt the reliability of the NT, these claims are largely overstated.

By the eighth century a transition in copying practices took place throughout the Greek-speaking world. Prior to this, the Greek language was written exclusively in what we would consider capital letters, or majuscule, deriving from the practice of etching Greek words and phrases into stone. As the centuries progressed, a need for a faster, more fluid form of writing grew, shifting the written style into a type of cursive, and eventually into a "lowercase" form known as minuscule. This new style of writing meant that book production could be accomplished at a higher rate than before, and with this change a "Cambrian explosion" of sorts occurred in Greek NT manuscripts.[29] From this period until the seventeenth century, thousands of Greek manuscripts were copied by hand. Monasteries developed standardized rules for copyists, and scriptoriums were created wherein multiple scribes copied NT books simultaneously. This more-regulated copying

27. In 1 Tim 5:18, the author writes that "scripture says . . . 'The laborer deserves to be paid.'" This is a phrase found only in Luke 10:7. This clarifies possible dating for this epistle as well. Additionally, in 2 Pet 3:15–16 we read that "Paul wrote to you according to the wisdom given him, speaking of this as he does in all his letters." At the close of v. 16 these letters are referred to as "scripture." The dating of these epistles is a difficult knot to untangle, which is why I have provided the large ranges here. A very helpful discussion of these dates is found in Bernier, *Rethinking the Dates*, 172–79 and 224–29.

28. Anderson and Widder, *Textual Criticism of Bible*, 116.

29. Bates, "Studios," 12.

system enabled adjustments to manuscripts to be made *en masse*, creating a largely homogeneous text eventually called the Byzantine Text.

Church fathers as early as the second century also acknowledge variant readings in their NT books. Some authors prefer one reading over another, while others theologize how both readings point to spiritual truths. While it remains popular to thrust differences in manuscripts upon believers as if it is something heretofore unknown, the church has long known of these differences. Variations between manuscripts is a necessary consequence of their being handwritten, and large numbers of variation are expected given the sheer quantity of manuscripts. The only way a manuscript could exist without variation is if it were the only one in existence; but if it were the only one in existence, it would be impossible to know if its text were accurate, and we would have every reason to doubt its reliability! Therefore, just as the early church was not troubled by these different readings, neither should we be. Instead, we should recognize that these variations help us identify the earliest text and *increase* our trust in its reliability, rather than cause us to doubt it.

Methodology and Theology in Textual Criticism

While it might be easy for me to pontificate about the confidence I have in the text of the Bible, this does not do much for the skeptic—or the Christian in the pew—wondering how they can have the same confidence, given the real differences between manuscripts in both Testaments. The way through this maze is simply to understand the importance of these differences and the impact they have on the overall text of the Bible. As Dr. Dirk Jongkind of Tyndale House, Cambridge has said, "Clearly, many of the differences affect how we read a particular sentence and how the text says what it says. But the actual content of a paragraph or a chapter—let alone that of the whole book—stands firm regardless. The message that is communicated comes across clearly even though there is interfering noise."[30]

Methodology

Scholars compare manuscripts of a verse or verses to identify places where they differ. Variations can be word insertions or omissions, repetition of words or phrases, or even spelling. While some may claim that these are intentional, theologically motivated changes, the reality is far more

30. Jongkind, *Introduction to the Greek*, 21.

mundane. One can never know the mind of a scribe when a change is made to a manuscript. One person's accident may be another's intent. Famously, Dr. Bart Ehrman has argued that many of the oldest, most reliable Greek manuscripts of the Gospel according to Mark omit the title "Son of God" in the first verse. For Dr. Ehrman, this omission is evidence that Jesus was not seen as a divine figure by the earliest Christian groups.[31] There are, of course, alternative explanations, particularly the fact that the words "Jesus Christ," which appear before "Son of God" in the verse, end with the same two letters in Greek as "Son of God." A common scribal error was to visually skip over a word, or words, when looking between the master copy and their manuscript, when those words had similar endings. It happens all the time. What makes this variant even less theologically motivated is that Jesus is declared to be God's Son in the eleventh verse of the same chapter without variation between manuscripts. If this were theologically motivated, why would the scribe omit it only at the first verse?

The most recent survey of textual variations estimates that there are approximately five hundred thousand variants in NT manuscripts.[32] While some involve many verses and have caused no shortage of debate, the vast majority make no consequential difference to the message of your Bible. The truth is that when someone asks if textual variants are important, the answer you get will depend on who you ask. For the textual critic, every variation matters, because textual scholars are interested in finding the earliest recoverable text in every, minute detail. The skeptic might also say the majority matter, because they believe the number of variants impacts the reliability of the text. But when you ask how many variants matter to the message of the Bible, both skeptical and religious scholars generally agree that few do.[33] Decisions on which reading is original are generally based on four factors: distribution of the evidence, knowledge of the individual manuscripts, knowledge of groupings of manuscripts, and knowledge of scribal behavior.[34]

31. Ehrman, *Orthodox Corruption of Scripture*, 72–74.

32. Gurry, "Number of Variants."

33. An excellent, and lengthy, Twitter thread on this subject was published by Dr. Stephen C. Carlson from the Australian Catholic University. In it, Dr. Carlson summarizes every variant in the Epistle to the Galatians and its importance to the text. The link is available here: https://twitter.com/sccarlson/status/1587611302406815745.

34. Jongkind, *Introduction to the Greek*, 66–67.

Distribution of Evidence

It might seem sensible that, where differences in manuscripts are found, the reading found in the largest number of manuscripts should be the reading preferred. However, as mentioned above, most biblical manuscripts are written after the eighth century and generally in a controlled environment where variant readings are changed to conform to the master copy being used. Most manuscripts are not only much later than the originals, but they are likely to have been changed to match a later reading from a later master copy. This is not always the case, but it illustrates why the "majority reading" cannot always be accepted. Nor is it always acceptable to choose the reading that occurs in the oldest manuscripts, because many of them contain scribal errors and were copied without the same levels of care. Because of this, what scholars are looking for are readings that have a wide distribution between manuscripts of all eras. Careful attention is paid to readings in earlier manuscripts that might explain how a change occurred in the same location in later manuscripts.[35]

Knowledge of Individual Manuscripts

Every person you meet in life has different features and characteristics. They have mannerisms and personalities all their own. Manuscripts, being products of people, also have their own set of unique characteristics and features. This is especially true of earlier manuscripts. Some features, like notational systems for church use or identifying themes of chapters, are inherited from an earlier copy, while others, like patterns of adding or removing material or abbreviating certain words, can be created by the scribe. Knowing the patterns that arise in an individual manuscript helps determine how different readings might have occurred, in the same way that knowing a person's character might help explain an action they take.

35. An example of how this works can be seen in Mark 1:2 where the OT quotation that follows is said to be written either "in Isaiah the prophet" or "in the prophets" depending on the Greek manuscripts. The current Greek edition of the NT, and most English Bibles, reads "in Isaiah the prophet." Both readings are found in early and late Greek manuscripts and in early church fathers, but since the OT reference is actually an amalgamation of two prophets and not just Isaiah, it is more likely that later scribes would have changed the text to read "the prophets" rather than strictly Isaiah. Therefore, the reading found in most English Bibles reflects the reading that not only experiences wide distribution but also helps explain the variant reading.

Knowledge of Groups of Manuscripts

Just as individuals can have their own characteristics, groups of people can become largely homogenous. Most readers are likely familiar with how adolescent groups tend to match each other in speech, clothing, and behavior. Similarly, groups of manuscripts can adopt similar characteristics. This stems from their being copied from a common master or from intentional harmonization with one another. The best example of this is the aforementioned Byzantine Text. As Dr. Jongkind writes, "The later Byzantine text is formed by many near-identical manuscripts from the early and late Middle Ages. In these, the influence of the church liturgy is clearly visible. The Byzantine text also tends to be more consistent in the details of grammar and spelling than the original authors were." Understanding the purpose or activity of a group of people can help understand why they do what they do, and knowing that individual manuscripts belong to a group of manuscripts that all feature the same changes can explain why a variant reading occurs.

Knowledge of Scribal Behavior

In most cases, scribes did nothing more than copy the text in front of them. However, even when a scribe strove for accuracy, mistakes were often made. A simple misreading of a text can introduce errors into a copy. When a Gospel passage is found in more than one of the Gospels, a scribe can easily add material from memory that is found in a different Gospel. Similar-sounding words can create issues, particularly if the scribe is writing while someone else is reading the master copy, and even a scribe's ability to read Greek can lead to variant readings. Knowing as much as possible about the way scribes act is an invaluable tool in understanding where different readings come from.

These four factors are held in balance, as best is possible, by scholars examining the textual evidence for the Bible. While certain biases will naturally creep into these decisions, they are tempered by the existence of multiple, critical editions of the OT and NT developed with different methodologies. In the same way you might compare various English versions of a verse to see how different committees chose to translate it, the same is done with the editions made from the original languages. These tools create an impressive system of checks and balances guarding the reliability of our Bible.

Theology

But what about something like verbal inspiration? How do Christians deal with our belief that, according to 2 Pet 1:21, the words of the Bible were written by men who "spoke from God, carried along by the Holy Spirit"? Some in the Christian community would rather dismiss the idea that manuscripts differ and prefer to argue that if God inspired his word, then the true version of it must contain no differences. This leads them to select a particular set of Greek manuscripts, or even a specific English translation. The reality is that God did inspire his word *and* there are differences in the copies of that inspired word. Therefore, rather than try to project what we might think God *should have* or *would have* done, we should start with what the evidence shows that God *did* do.

God, in his infinite wisdom, chose not to give us perfect copies of the Bible. He chose not to give us exhaustive knowledge of all the copies. He chose to communicate his words through fallible humans, from the earliest days of the prophets to the days of scribes. This is God's choice. He could have controlled every step of this communication in such a way that no textual criticism was necessary, but the pattern of the God of the Bible is to use humanity as the communicative vessel for his will, his plan, and his purposes. Lest we forget, the book of the law for the Israelites was lost for many generations until it was discovered in the temple, under the reign of King Josiah (2 Kgs 22). Contemplate that for a moment. God allowed his people to lose his word for years! As it relates to inspiration, remember that, in God's providence, he orchestrated the structuring of his word in such a way that the inspired message contained within it did not rely on any single verse or chapter and, in so doing, guarded that message from being lost on the basis of any single difference between manuscripts.

In the days leading up to the Babylonian exile of Israel, the prophet Jeremiah is told by God that God will make a "new covenant" with his people that will be written on their hearts (Jer 31:33). No longer would the covenant be inscribed on stone tablets or kept in the temple, copied by kings. It would be for all the people. This new covenant was realized in the coming of Jesus Christ and the subsequent communication of the Holy Spirit after Jesus's death, resurrection, and ascension (John 14:26). As the church grew, the books of the old covenant took on new, fulfilled meaning in Jesus and this message began to spread. As the age of the apostles ended, the need to copy these texts increased, and copies spread throughout Christian communities. As God grew his church and his people spread across the globe, more copies, in more languages, were needed. God's central plan to save the world and make for himself a people from every tribe and nation has existed from before creation (Eph 1:4; 1 Pet 1:20), and a consequence of this eternal plan is the proliferation of God's word. It is the spreading of this word across the world that builds the church, and with that spread comes differences in its copies. One does not happen without the other, and the very existence of these differences enables us to ensure the reliability of the message we share.

THE QUESTION BEHIND THE QUESTION

I've used considerable space defending various aspects of biblical reliability in order to provide readers with a certain degree of comfort in knowing that what they find in the text of Scripture can withstand the test of history, accuracy, and textual stability. All of that is ultimately meant to lead here, to deal with the real question that lies behind the other questions. What I am about to say may seem bold, but it is nonetheless true. Despite what you might find on the internet, when considered objectively, based on the data we have today, the historical and textual reliability of the Bible is without question.

While skeptics, critics, or even fellow Christians may ask about the historical or textual reliability of the Bible, what they are really asking is, "Can I trust my life to the Bible? Can it reliably answer why anything exists at all?" This is what I call questions of "epistemological" reliability. In philosophy, epistemology involves the nature of determining truth. I am using it here to refer to the question of whether the Bible can reliably define and guide our existence. Even if one denies it intellectually or verbally, the very questions of the Bible's truthfulness or reliability reveal a recognition that, if it is reliable, it becomes more than a book. It becomes a lens through which the reader must learn to live, act, and see themselves and others.

If epistemological reliability is the real question, how do we, as apologists, get to that question? It must be granted at the outset that every interaction one has with someone asking these questions will be unique. Certainly, the questions may overlap, and the answers will be the same, but the actual method or opportunity used to move to deeper questions will vary. With that in mind, what follows is conveyed in generalities, but the key to all interactions, no matter how difficult, is to love our interlocutors as image-bearers of God.

A large portion of this chapter on reliability has revolved around the development and transmission of language. Therefore, it seems only natural that language becomes the key to the question behind the question. The nineteenth-century philosopher of language Ludwig Wittgenstein argued that while all that exists in the world is the propositions of natural science—the language of the world, if you will—there is no one speaking these propositions from outside the natural world. Paradoxically, he also recognized that mankind desperately needed more than naturalistic propositions, yearning for meaning, values, and ethics, yet there was no "voice" speaking these needs into our lives. At the core of his argument was the realization that for mankind to know anything, something must be spoken to us, but since there is no one speaking to mankind, we must speak to each other and ourselves. This has become the standard core of most naturalistic worldviews. We are our own guides in this world and must find our own values, ethics, and purpose. Of course, this is an entirely circular proposition. We cannot at the same time be our guide in life while also being the one seeking guidance. That is the very definition of "the blind leading the blind."

The individual asking honest and legitimate questions about the reliability of the Bible is admitting that they are seeking a guide for their life. They are looking for the voice that will speak into their reality and give them purpose, value, morality, and wholeness. The mere act of asking questions about the Bible reveals that this is the case. On the other hand, the one making accusations against its reliability is in one of two possible positions: they are either reacting to painful, past experiences from within the Christian community and, while wanting a reliable guide for life, do not want it to be the God of the Bible; or they are not seeking, only reacting. They are voicing an internal desire to be their own guide and prefer—like Wittgenstein—to deny anything speaking outside themselves. Knowing which of these types of individuals you're interacting with is crucial to answering their questions.

Yes, the critics and skeptics may rage against any idea that they are seeking a voice to guide them, but if this is not what is at stake, the questions of historicity or textual stability are pointless. The skeptic should not care if the Bible is historical. They should not care if the text has been changed. If the Bible is just a book, it means nothing and contains nothing of overarching value. Most of us do not demand evidence that *Romeo and Juliet* be historical before we enjoy it as a play,, and knowing that most of Shakespeare's plays exist in wildly divergent copies does not impact our lives beyond the intellectual exercise of studying the Bard at work. But when an attack against the reliability of the Bible is made, it comes with a ferocity not seen elsewhere—something evident in many of the videos of Dr. Frank Turek's talks on college campuses. This is because one's presuppositions ultimately determine whether one will hear the answer to the real question one is asking. According to Francis Schaeffer:

> If I am completely committed without question to the uniformity of natural causes in a closed system, then whether I express myself in philosophical or religious terms is irrelevant.

> Propositional, verbalized revelation—knowledge that man has from God—is a totally unthinkable concept. This is because, by definition, everything is a machine, so naturally there is no knowledge from outside, from God. If this is your worldview, and you refuse to consider the possibility of any other, even though your naturalistic worldview leads to the dehumanization of man and is against the facts that we know about man and things, you are at a dead-end.[36]

Dr. Turek's work across the country seeks to break down these presuppositions in order to move hearers away from the despair of a naturalistic "dead end," and this should be the goal of all Christians, let alone apologists contending for the faith. Understanding that challenges to the Bible are, at their core, cries for evidence of a guide to a lost world prevents us from merely seeking to win an argument and orients our hearts toward shining light on a darkened soul.

CONCLUSION

The Christian worldview is not reliable because it offers an idealistic, romantic, or fanciful notion of how the world is, or how mankind should exist within it. It is reliable because it is realistic. The message communicated in the pages of the Bible is set in the real world—in space and time—within an historical context. It communicates that there is truth and it is knowable, but above all else, it believes that there is One who is speaking into our lives. It rejects the silence of naturalistic philosophy and offers a hope that cannot be found elsewhere. As Christians, we possess the answers to the questions of reality, purpose, and existence, but we do not invent these answers out of our own minds. These answers have been communicated to us by God, through his revelation—the primary vehicle of which is the two Testaments of the Christian Bible.

In this chapter I have sought to defend the reasonableness of trusting the Bible historically as well as textually, and to define what I believe it means to trust the Bible epistemologically. However, the reliability of the Bible is not the sole reason for trusting the Christian faith; it is only one line of evidence. Christianity is not more believable or more reliable because of one piece of evidence but because of the accumulation of evidence from all aspects of life—as this book seeks to demonstrate. The Christian worldview is unique among all others in that its biblical message remains internally consistent with itself, while also being externally consistent with

36. Schaeffer, *He Is There*, 322–23.

the observable world. This is precisely what makes the Bible epistemologically reliable. When questions about the reliability of the Bible are brought to our feet, it is this consistency that we must endeavor to show, so that we, like Jesus, can give an answer to the question that rests behind all other questions: Can I trust my life to the hands of Christ?

Bibliography

Anderson, Amy, and Wendy Widder. *Textual Criticism of the Bible*. Bellingham, WA: Lexham, 2018.

Bacon, Bennett, et al. "An Upper Palaeolithic Proto-Writing System and Phenological Calendar." *Cambridge Archaeological Journal* 33 (2023) 371–89. doi:10.1017/S0959774322000415.

Bates, Clark R. "Studios: The Convergence of History, Palaeography, and Textual Criticism on the Greek Miniscule Hand." *Diogenes* 11 (June 2021) 1–20.

Beckman, G. "Hittite Administration in Syria in Light of the Texts from Hattusa, Ugarit, and Emar." In *New Horizons in the Study of Ancient Syria*, edited by Mark Chavalas and John L. Hayes, 41–49. Malibu: Undena, 1992.

Bernier, Jonathan. *Rethinking the Dates of the New Testament: The Evidence for Early Composition*. Grand Rapids: Baker Academic, 2022.

Burchard, Kenny. "Does Jesus Want You to Follow the Bible? Actually, No." Church Plants, Nov. 2015. https://churchplants.com/articles/10698-does-jesus-want-you-to-follow-the-bible-actually-no.html.

Caragounis, Chrys C. *New Testament Investigations: A Diachronic Perspective*. Wissenschaftliche Untersuchungen zum Neuen Testament 487. Tübingen, Germ.: Mohr Siebeck, 2022.

Chavalas, Mark W., and Murray R. Adamthwaite. "Archaeological Light on the Old Testament." In *The Face of Old Testament Studies: A Survey of Contemporary Approaches*, edited by David W. Baker and Bill T. Arnold, 59–96. Grand Rapids: Baker Academic, 1999.

Ehrman, Bart D. *The Orthodox Corruption of Scripture: The Effect of Early Christological Controversies on the Text of the New Testament*. Oxford: Oxford University Press, 2011.

Evans, Rachel Held. *Inspired: Slaying Giants, Walking on Water, and Learning to Love the Bible Again*. Nashville: Nelson, 2018.

Gurry, Peter J. "Myths about Variants: Why Most Variants Are Insignificant and Why Some Can't Be Ignored." In *Myths and Mistakes in New Testament Textual Criticism*, edited by Elijah Hixson and Peter J. Gurry, 191–210. Downers Grove, IL: IVP Academic, 2019.

———. "The Number of Variants in the Greek New Testament: A Proposed Estimate." *New Testament Studies* 62 (2016) 97–121.

Hengel, Martin. *Judaism and Hellenism: Studies in Their Encounter in Palestine during the Early Hellenistic Period*. Translated by John Bowden. Reprint, Eugene, OR: Wipf & Stock, 2003.

Hilton, Allen R. *Illiterate Apostles: Uneducated Early Christians and the Literates That Loved Them*. The Library of New Testament Studies 541. London: T&T Clark, 2018.

Jongkind, Dirk. *An Introduction to the Greek New Testament: Produced at Tyndale House, Cambridge*. Wheaton, IL: Crossway, 2019.

Knoppers, Gary. "The Historical Study of the Monarchy: Developments and Detours." In *The Face of Old Testament Studies: A Survey of Contemporary Approaches*, edited by David W. Baker and Bill T. Arnold, 207–36. Grand Rapids: Baker Academic, 1999.

Konstantinidis, A. E. *Ἡ Οἰκουμενικὴ Δίασταση τῆς Ἑλληνικῆς Γλώσσας* [The ecumencal dimension of the Greek language]. Thessaloniki: Konstantinidis, 2006.

Meade, John D. and Peter J. Gurry. *Scribes & Scripture: The Amazing Story of How We Got the Bible*. Wheaton, IL: Crossway, 2022.

Prothro, James B. "Myths about Classical Literature: Responsibly Comparing the New Testament to Ancient Works." In *Myths and Mistakes in New Testament Textual Criticism*, edited by Elijah Hixson and Peter J. Gurry, 70–89. Downers Grove, IL: IVP Academic, 2019.

Robertson, Brandan. "Run to God, Not to the Bible." *Huffington Post*, Dec. 8, 2015; updated Dec. 7, 2016. https://www.huffpost.com/entry/run-to-god-not-to-the-bib_b_8746588.

Schaeffer, Francis. "He Is There and He Is Not Silent." In *The Francis A. Schaeffer Trilogy: The Three Essential Books in One Volume*, 275–342. Wheaton, IL: Crossway, 1990.

Williams, Peter J. *Can We Trust the Gospels?* Wheaton, IL: Crossway, 2018.

Windle, Bryan. "Top Ten Discoveries Related to David." Bible Archaeology Report, June 11, 2021. https://biblearchaeologyreport.com/2021/06/11/top-ten-discoveries-related-to-david/.

The Church

> If Christians continue to rely on emotion and ignore evidence, they will continue to lose their children to secularism . . . a tepid Christianity cannot withstand a rabid secularism. And make no mistake—secularism is rabid. The world isn't neutral out there. Today's culture is becoming increasingly anti-Christian.
>
> —Frank Turek, *Stealing from God*

The Spiritual Sin Pervading Christianity

MELISSA DOUGHERTY[1]

IN THE MODERN CHRISTIAN life, spiritual stumbling blocks are plentiful. A day barely goes by without hearing of a pastor being removed for moral failings, a Christian executive embezzling money, or even a brother or sister in the Lord adopting social views that reject biblical authority. There is one stumbling block that is sweeping through American churches today more than any other, but it is almost completely unnoticed. This stumbling block might even be happening in your church or your life, and it is not just sinful, it is harmful. I am speaking of the idolatry of seeking supernatural experiences. This desire is becoming a growing trend in secular and religious communities and is hurting people. It is hurtful because it is built on bad theology, and bad theology hurts people.

Before going any further, let me assert my view that the Christian worldview is, indeed, a supernatural one. Where would Christianity be without the miracles of Jesus in the Gospels and the signs and wonders in the book of Acts? The very core of Christianity is the greatest supernatural event of all, the resurrection of Jesus. In the Old Testament, we have numerous extraordinary acts of God, such as the plagues in Egypt, the parting of the Red Sea, floating axe heads, and a fiery furnace. Even the desire for the supernatural has a rightful place in Scripture. In 2 Kgs 2:9, Elisha asks for a double portion of Elijah's spirit, but this is a request made with pure

1. Dr. Turek has been inspirational in my life. Being part of the CrossExamined Instructor Academy helped hone my abilities to present a clear message of the beauty and reliability of the Christian faith and create effective methods of communication. After I met Frank, my videos began to be shared through CrossExamined and my platform grew exponentially. Frank has been so much more than an instructor and guide. He is a mentor and friend, and I can never thank him enough for the impact he has had on my life and ministry.

motives, not so that he can have these "magic" powers or draw attention to himself. Elisha asks for this "double portion" so that he can continue in the footsteps of his mentor, both to worship and serve God himself.

We have a supernatural God who works miracles, heals, and moves in unexplainable ways. He's a relational God. He's not distant and angry. I believe that most Christians would readily concede this truth. According to philosopher J. P. Moreland, "Without question, the overwhelming majority of believers around the world are not cessationists."[2] But even cessationist brothers and sisters would acknowledge that the Bible records many miracles and healings from a supernatural God. I do not personally hold to cessationism.[3] Therefore the perspective of this chapter is from my position as a continuationist—someone who believes God works supernaturally and that spiritual gifts are still present today. I am continually humbled by many of my charismatic and cessationist brothers and sisters who have taught me a great deal about these perspectives, and I am certain they would gladly join hands in agreement with me that something is amiss in many of our churches.

Human beings long for more than just a physical experience of life. Ecclesiastes 3:11 says that God has "put eternity into man's heart," and consequently, as image-bearers of God, we deeply long to go beyond this simple human experience. I believe this is by design in order to create a yearning for something divine. Romans 1:18–23 explains this:

> For the wrath of God is revealed from heaven against all ungodliness and unrighteousness of men, who by their unrighteousness suppress the truth. For what can be known about God is plain to them, because God has shown it to them. For his invisible attributes, namely, his eternal power and divine nature, have been clearly perceived, ever since the creation of the world, in the things that have been made. So they are without excuse. For although they knew God, they did not honor him as God or give thanks to him, but they became futile in their thinking, and their foolish hearts were darkened. Claiming to be wise, they became fools, and exchanged the glory of the immortal God for images resembling mortal man and birds and animals and creeping things.

2. Moreland, *Simple Guide to Experience*, 101.

3. Cessationism is the position within Christianity that the charismatic spiritual gifts (speaking in tongues, word of knowledge, word of wisdom, interpretation of tongues, etc.) ceased with the closing of the canon of Scripture and/or the death of the last apostle.

We are creations of God, and as creations of God, we bear witness to a Creator. This then bears witness to a supernatural reality outside of our own. In fact, in v. 18 above, Paul says that for anyone to deny this, one must suppress the truth willfully. In other words, this yearning for something beyond our human experience is so powerful that we must actually make a deliberate decision to ignore it![4]

So, I am not here to tell Christians they need to shove *all* experiences, emotions, feelings, and moments with God into the bin, especially if they are in line with, and tested by, Scripture. There is no doubt that it is normal, if not healthy, to realize that a supernatural God created us and we should seek him out. As beings created by a supernatural being, we should not be surprised that secularism leaves us empty and hollow, looking beyond our material world for something more. However, what happens when this goes too far? What happens when churches, pastors, and teachers put supernatural experiences on a pedestal? What I am proposing is that there is a dangerous movement within Evangelical Christianity, particularly within the hyper-charismatic movement, that is relying on mystical experiences to not only to define faith, but that those trapped in this movement rely on mystical experiences to inform their theological beliefs, sometimes going beyond biblical parameters. In this chapter, I will attempt to point out the issues within this movement and what can be done about them.

A PENDULUM PROBLEM

I once had the same set of two Mormon missionaries meet with me for nine months. Missionaries from the LDS church rotate very often, and it is rare to see the same pair for any extended period. During our conversations, one topic we discussed at length was evidence versus experience. Mormons base the truth of their religion not on evidence but on feelings. "I *know* the [LDS] Church is true," they would say, when I would push back with evidence against some of their claims. I learned to expect it whenever I knew they had doubts but fell back on their feelings. Their *Doctrine and Covenants Student Manual* says, "The Lord will cause the feeling of security and truth to take hold of the individual and burn within the bosom, and there will be an overwhelming feeling that the thing is right."[5] This burning in their bosom testifies to them, internally, that the Church of Jesus Christ of Latter-day Saints is the one, true church.

4. Heiser, *Supernatural*, 18.

5. *Doctrine and Covenants*, sect. 9.8.

Mormonism serves as a parallel here because it is not only demonstrably and evidentially false, but because its means of determining truth is similar to what I see in many Christian churches today: truth by *experience.* For the missionaries, their fail-safe plan was to rely on their subjective interpretation of how they felt; but if this is the acceptable standard, *everyone's* religion must equally be true!

I am thankful that Christianity is evidence based. I am glad there seems to be a growing army of theologians and apologists combatting bad theology and equipping the saints. But I am also increasingly concerned about how some Christians evaluate truth claims. Sometimes we fail to process truth claims rationally. Instead of assessing the evidence and drawing the most reasonable inference, we rely explicitly on personal experience, emotional responses, and "blind faith."[6] When applied to objective truth or spirituality, this is an extreme view. We would not apply this reasoning in other, important areas of our lives, such as deciding the financial benefits of gambling based on how we feel. And it is a view that I see more and more. One thing I have learned from Christians much smarter than I, who have been trustworthy sources of biblical wisdom, is to *avoid extremes.*

When it comes to extremes, there are always two sides to this pendulum. Some churches have what I would consider a balanced and level-headed view of Scripture and experience, with a constant emphasis on testing experiences through a biblical lens. However, on one side of the pendulum there are those who think *any* reference to the supernatural is, at best, from your mind or exaggerated or, at worst, demonic and should be rejected.[7] On the other side of the pendulum, there are those who would consider cessationists as "putting God in a box" or "missing out" on what God has to offer because they are not seeking constant encounters with God. In communities like this, these encounters are often extreme and go far beyond seeking God's will or looking for answered prayer. In these churches, Christians are encouraged to seek out visitations by angels, visions and dreams, and even out-of-body experiences to visit heaven.[8] There are even some prominent church leaders teaching that believers can and should employ New Age practices because those practices supposedly belong to the church. The most recognizable church in America that is known for this kind of teaching is called Bethel Church, located in Redding, California. In the book *Physics of Heaven*, editors and contributors Judy Franklin and Ellyn Davis write:

6. Wallace, *Forensic Faith*, 24.

7. Though I'm in agreement with many teachings from John MacArthur and similar teachers, he, and other leaders sympathetic to his teachings, would reject many supernatural claims of Christians.

8. Mills, "Encountering the Angels."

> Many in the church have tended to write off all dabblings into quantum mysticism as blasphemous and demonically inspired. However, there are a few courageous Christians who are beginning to speak up and say, "Wait a minute, there may be some God truth there that really belongs to us and that we should know about!" These Christians are spearheading an effort to extract the precious from the worthless and make those truths available to the church at large. . . . [The contributors of this book] all agree that there are precious truths hidden in the New Age that belong to us as Christians and need to be extracted from the worthless.[9]

What are these teachings that need to be redeemed? Author Jonathan Welton answers in chapter 6:

> I have found throughout Scripture at least 75 examples of things that the New Age has counterfeited, such as having a spirit guide, trances, meditation, auras, power objects, clairvoyance, clairaudience, and more. *These actually belong to the church*, but they have been stolen and cleverly repackaged.[10]

This is a clear and startlingly forward admission from someone entering into New Age practices in order to have more supernatural experiences, and while this is a far side of the spiritual pendulum, many Christians find it attractive because of what it promises.

Frankly, they are exchanging *godly* experiences for *supernatural* experiences. They are abandoning the regulative principle of worship set down in the Bible for how we should relate to God and adopting a counterfeit spirituality. Scripture teaches that the imitation of pagan practices is evil (3 John 1:11). God clearly says to have nothing to do with these things. At the same time, we are to test them. In 1 Thess 5:20–22, Paul gives instructions on how to test prophetic words. He begins in v. 21 by saying that we should not "quench the Spirit" and that we should not "despise prophecies, but test everything." We are never given instruction to sift through pagan faiths and try to pick out what is good from them, but rather what Paul is saying in regard to prophecies is essentially "Test this intrinsically good practice God has ordained to ensure the prophets are speaking the truth." Ways to test what is true in this regard is if what something is saying is hermeneutically in harmony with the rest of Scripture, is not perpetuating a false gospel or false god, and corresponds to reality. Paul is not saying,

9. Franklin and Davis, *Physics of Heaven*, 16, 18.

10. Franklin and Davis, *Physics of Heaven*, 49 (emphasis added).

"Test these intrinsically demonic practices to find some helpful elements in them." We do not redeem these practices. We *divorce* them.

But this brings up another layer of this issue. I cannot help but think: *Why?* Why does this happen? How does this happen? Why would any Christian venture into spiritual darkness thinking that there is anything good to be found there? At its core, I believe it has to do with idolatry.

DESPERATION

Idolatry is something few in the modern age recognize. It's often associated with carved statues and shrines, and most Christians do not have anything like this in their homes. But, biblically speaking, idolatry is not limited to figurines and shrines. Anything can be an idol if it takes from God the honor and glory that he deserves. Even Christians can become idolaters, though often unintentionally and without realizing it. For most of us, the real difficulty is in identifying the idols in our lives—especially when they appear to be something perfectly reasonable. In the case above, wanting to experience God is good and reasonable, but when Christians depart from Scripture in an effort to force a spiritual experience, what was good and reasonable becomes sinful and idolatrous.

In the second century the church father Irenaeus, seeking to defend the orthodox faith, wrote against various heretical Christian groups. Concerning a particular group, he writes:

> Such, then, is their system, which neither the prophets announced, nor the Lord taught, nor the apostles delivered. . . . They gather their views from other sources than the Scriptures; and, to use a common proverb, they strive to weave ropes of sand, while they endeavor to adapt with an air of probability to their own peculiar assertions the parables of the Lord, the sayings of the prophets, and the words of the apostles, in order that their scheme may not seem altogether without support. In doing so, however, they disregard the order and the connection of the Scriptures, and so far as in them lies, dismember and destroy the truth. By transferring passages, and dressing them up anew, and making one thing out of another, they succeed in deluding many through their wicked art in adapting the oracles of the Lord to their opinions. Their manner of acting is just as if one, when a beautiful image of a king has been constructed by some skillful artist out of precious jewels, should then take this likeness of the man all to pieces, should rearrange the gems, and so fit them together as to make them into the form of a

> dog or of a fox, and even that but poorly executed; and should then maintain and declare that this was the beautiful image of the king which the skillful artist constructed, pointing to the jewels which had been admirably fitted together by the first artist to form the image of the king, but have been with bad effect transferred by the latter one to the shape of a dog, and by thus exhibiting the jewels, should deceive the ignorant who had no conception what a king's form was like, and persuade them that that miserable likeness of the fox was, in fact, the beautiful image of the king.[11]

In a similar way, most of the experiences encouraged by Bethel Church are not based on Scripture itself, but at best, are supported with biblical verses cherry-picked from their context and glued together to make the church's own mosaic of how they want Scripture to look. They are selling a "new" approach to Scripture that is nothing more than an old heresy. They are putting pagan, spiritual experience above God's design for worship and communion with him—and anything placed above God is an idol. I believe this desire for experience comes from a mixture of things. Perhaps it is a yearning to control a situation. Perhaps it stems from the belief that we have the same creative power as God, as taught by the Word of Faith movement. Perhaps some Christians are simply not satisfied with having a Christian walk that is not saturated with supernatural stories and spiritual encounters. Perhaps they are simply desperate for something more.

Supernatural encounters should be examined on a case-by-case basis. The source should be considered and tested against Scripture, and wisdom should be exercised when we either have an experience or hear of one secondhand. It is at this point that our greatest enemy becomes confirmation bias. Confirmation bias is the tendency to engage only with information that already conforms to our preexisting beliefs. Many people are so desperate for an encounter with God that they'll search for, notice, and recall only the information that confirms their beliefs while disregarding alternative evidence.[12] Many in the hyper-charismatic movement do not want to "miss out" on anything from God, so there is a tendency to view one's subjective interpretation as a divine act and ignore contrary evidence.

To experience a miracle, the movement encourages the individual to have faith with no doubt. This is then paired with a desperate attempt to hear from, or experience, God. When this fails, some resort to unbiblical solutions for answers. Of course, this is not a new phenomenon. We read of

11. Irenaeus, *Against Heresies*, 8.1.

12. Moreland, *Simple Guide to Experience*, 72.

a similar event in 1 Samuel with Saul and the witch of Endor. When Saul did not get the answer he wanted from God, instead of considering his folly and submitting to God's will, he resorted to witchcraft (1 Sam 28:7–25). In Acts 8:9–24, Simon the sorcerer received salvation but was enticed by what he saw the Holy Spirit do through the apostles. He offered the apostles money in exchange for the ability to lay hands on someone and have them receive the Holy Spirit, for which Peter harshly rebuked him and declared that his heart was not right with God. This is an apropos rebuke, considering many hyper-charismatic ministries charge money to "activate" one's spiritual gifts to get closer to God.[13]

It is not just confirmation bias that can distort people's concept of God and how he works. When people hear fantastic stories of healings, signs, wonders, and miracles and are told that this should permeate their life, what are they to think when they don't experience this? They think, "Why is everyone talking about these constant miracles and healings when I am not receiving anything like this?" I submit that this is not just an idolatry of supernatural experiences but a *lust* for them. People are addicted to them.

TWITTERPATED

Bambi is not one of my favorite Disney films. I know that it is a classic, but my crushed childhood would disagree. (And Simba's dad? Come on!) Even so, there is a particular scene in that movie that lives rent-free in my head and is one of the best examples to describe the danger of living from one supernatural high to another. In the movie, after our hearts were crushed when Bambi's mom died, springtime came. Bambi and his friends noticed that the birds were acting strangely, and Owl explained to them that the birds were under a strange and awful spell. They were "twitterpated," and Bambi and his friends had better watch out, or it would happen to them too! Sure enough, it did. They fell under the twitterpated enchantment, losing all sense of control. Adults often laugh at this part of the film because it is a feeling we know all too well. It is the feeling of falling in love. Think of a time when you fell madly in love. Do you remember how it felt at first? Do you remember the euphoric, intoxicating bliss of it all? Do you remember the passion and excitement that rushed through your body at the very thought of them? Do you remember the stupidity?

Being "twitterpated" is actually a chemical response to stimulus that develops in the brain. When activated, your brain produces an organic chemical known as dopamine; this can lead to an increase in heart rate and

13. Pivec and Geivett, *Counterfeit Kingdom*, 36.

blood pressure and produce a sense of pleasure. When we think back to that first love we can recognize the potency of this chemical and our need for more. However, just like a synthetic drug that can lead to withdrawals, we can become hooked on our own dopamine response.

The problem is that this feeling does not last. Like most addictions, unless you have your "fix," you will be in a constant state of yearning, and you can resist for only so long until your next emotional drag. As time goes on, this "twitterpated" fog that we loved living in begins to fade and, with it, many of the feelings that were being suppressed. Before long, we begin to notice that our love interest is a real person with flaws and can be difficult and frustrating to be with at times. Our body reacts, motivating us to either flee the situation or find a way to return to our emotional cloud nine. It is here that a choice must be made. You can either remain with this person, grow together, and realize that real relationships are not like romance novels or Cinderella stories; or you can leave this person to chase after the next dopamine fix. God has designed real relationships to be delightful and fulfilling in deep, unexplainable ways, but they take work. They are not always indwelled with fervent, zealous emotion. They must be infused with respect, truth, selflessness, forgiveness, and friendship. Romance is wonderful, but it is only one part of God's design for relationships. Biblical godly love is filled with a decision to love in perfect love.

Particularly in new and undeveloped relationships, an almost toxic cycle develops to keep those early feelings alive. The feeling becomes the priority. The logic often goes, "As long as I feel this way, then I am loved!," and in order to keep this feeling at its peak, people will resort to destructive measures. This can manifest through fighting, with the goal of breaking up and subsequently "making up," only to reignite the feeling. Sometimes there are unnecessarily dramatic displays of jealousy, or romantic gestures that mirror a supposedly undying love. It is an exhausting and unsustainable cycle designed to maintain a constant state of pleasure and excitement, but instead of freeing them to feel love, it imprisons them in a state of emotionalism and experience. The experience becomes the means to gauge love, and if they are not constantly "twitterpated," *then the object of their affection must not love them.*

This growing habit of seeking spiritual experiences throughout Christian churches in pursuit of God's love and approval parallels the romantic notions above. Do you remember when you first became a Christian? Do you remember when it felt as though it was just you and God, and you felt brand new and loved—possibly for the first time? Perhaps you were a zealous new believer, telling everyone from the stranger in the grocery store to your dentist about your new relationship with Jesus. You were "twitterpated," practically prancing in a hypothetical field of daisies, enamored with the spiritual high of your newly saved soul! However, after a few months go by, life starts breaking in. Worship songs that once made you weep do not feel the same as they used to. Your prayer time is not as saturated with the divine closeness you originally felt. Simply put, you stop feeling warm and fuzzy all the time. But what does this mean? Has God abandoned you? You might even ask, "Why can't I feel him the same way anymore?" At that stage of faith, we may not yet understand that the Christian life is a process of growth and spiritual maturity, and this process happens only *after* the early stages of our divine romance wear off. Sadly, many Christians never want to leave the safety of the "twitterpated" phase because it feels good, and they would do anything to maintain that experience.

While this can parallel what happens with those who idolize the supernatural, it can also apply in less extreme situations. In daily life, some Christians rely more on their feelings and subjective experiences than they do on Scripture. They believe that what they are experiencing must be from God because it *feels* a certain way, and that feeling is confirmation of the message God is sending to them. If it feels good, it is from God. If it feels bad, it is not, and this emotional high equates to an intimate communion with God—they have his favor and love. As we have already seen, our emotions are an unreliable, and unbiblical, litmus test for intimacy with our Creator.

It should be restated that feelings are not bad or wrong, in and of themselves. Our emotions are an incredible gift from God designed to help us process our daily lives—both horizontally with one another and vertically with him. In Matt 22:37, Jesus tells us to "love the Lord [our] God with all [our] heart and with all [our] soul," but he also tells us to love the Lord "with all [our] mind." Therefore, wisdom dictates that we should include our minds alongside our feelings to discern reality. Both play their part and dance a lovely dance together. Jesus himself displayed strong emotions but never remained in them. Jesus says in Matt 15:19 that evil things proceed from our hearts, and in Jer 17:9–10, the prophet states that our hearts are sick and deceitful. If the heart does not have the same mind as its dance partner, it will cause us to trip and fall on our faces. The interpretation of spiritual truth involves more than just "following our hearts." We should position ourselves to understand God through deep love and awe but tether this to what we know with our minds. It is suspected that individuals with an overactive production of dopamine can become schizophrenic, while those with an underactive production of dopamine can be diagnosed with attention deficit disorders. In the same way, too much of one over the other can be unfruitful and damaging. Balance is needed, and neither should be neglected entirely.

A dangerous theological and emotional imbalance occurs when Christians are taught that sensationalism and emotionalism are accurate guides to test what is true about God. One prominent hyper-charismatic leader teaches that the mind is an offense and a deterrent to experiencing God. Christians are praised for suspending their intellect to experience God. From this leader's perspective, theology has been exalted at the expense of encounters and belief: academic assessment has replaced supernatural experience, and Christians should not let the mind dictate their beliefs.[14] A corresponding doctrine in this community is that the mind is offended by the works of the Spirit, which is to say that Christians must suspend logic to experience the presence of God. However, if you suspend your mind, your ability to discern what is actually from God relies on your heart, which we have already seen comes with a stark warning in Scripture.

On a more pastoral level, a very real, potential consequence of this approach is to mistake an experience or desire as being from God when it is a self-generated deception. If a person acts on this experience and fails, they could blame God and—in extreme cases—even leave the faith altogether. Being taught that not receiving constant supernatural experiences from God—be they dreams, visions, visitations from angels, healings, miracles, signs, or something else—means there is something lacking in one's faith can lead to spiritual overload, just like the body can experience with a physical overload of dopamine. The spiritual euphoria one must chase in order to maintain this distortion of the Christian life must be constant, because without it, the worshipper feels as though they are not loved by God. "Twitterpation" leads to shipwreck.

FORCE, FAKE, AND FLAUNT

Imagine being a child again but an orphan. You long for a family to provide you with a loving home. One day, a powerful and loving man comes into the orphanage and adopts every child, including you. You have brothers and sisters, a wonderful house to live in, and a loving and kind father. Not only this, but he also gives his children fascinating gifts that allow the children to have supernatural abilities. He tells you that the only requirement to receive these gifts is to believe and accept them. You are meant to have them! As his child, you can receive power from him that only his children can have and do greater things than even he can do, but there is a catch. Because this is based on your faith, if you do not receive them, then it is not his fault, but yours—for not having enough faith. If others receive gifts, it is because their

14. Johnson, *Supernatural Power*, 36.

faith is stronger and the father's blessing is upon them. Therefore, if you do not receive your special abilities, you are left to feel like a second-class child. One day, he walks around to everyone, giving them power and supernatural abilities, but when he gets to you, he keeps walking, giving you nothing. This leaves you feeling confused, vulnerable, and left out, thinking, "Why am I not receiving what everyone else is receiving? Did I do something wrong? Why has my father ignored me? Does he love me less than these other children? They are getting fascinating power and experiences with our father! What have I done wrong? I must not have enough faith. I am desperate to receive from my father what I deserve, so I must do more to show that I am loved and accepted!"

This is, of course, fantasy, but the illustration presented is like what many Christians struggle with when they are not constantly filled with the Holy Spirit or continuously walking in the supernatural. Logically, if you are not receiving more from God, it follows that there must be something wrong with your faith. Divine encounters should be commonplace for the average Christian. Christians who do not live in the supernatural or are skeptical of what they see can be labeled as "carnal" or accused of having a "religious spirit."[15] This can be a very damaging thought for Christians who want to experience God the same way they observe other Christians supposedly experiencing God, and some end up believing that God loves them less if they do not regularly have these experiences.

I believe this desperation to be seen, even by themselves, as "spiritual enough" is why many Christians seek out unbiblical practices like those above. They are frustrated with the lack of supernatural encounters they think they should be having. So, they either force it, fake it, or flaunt it. Desperate for a revival, healing, or miracle, they seek out forbidden occultic practices. They are taught that it is never God's will for Christians to be sick, poor, or not to dwell constantly in the supernatural. As a result, they embellish or fake it, mimicking those around them to create a semblance of being a part of the "gifted." They are taught that during his earthly ministry Jesus demonstrated that they could do what he did—and more![16] The flaunting of these displays of supernatural favor is nothing more than an attempt to prove this.

15. This is a derogatory term used in some charismatic circles to imply that a Christian has a demonic spirit attached to them that influences a person, or group of people, to replace a genuine relationship with God with works and traditions. The implication is that they have the same attitude as the Pharisees did if they're skeptical of some supernatural reports and behaviors.

16. Johnson, *Supernatural Power*, 42–43.

This inevitably results in the creation of a type of spiritual "caste system." One member has visions and dreams and can hear God's literal voice, while another speaks to angels and can heal at will, but if the only "gift" another one can demonstrate is a desire to defend the faith with their mind, then they must lack something. Simply reading the Bible and living a Christian life equates to not walking in the power of God. In the apostle Paul's day, the Corinthian church faced a similar problem. A caste system was developing in their church on the basis of whom they were baptized by. In 1 Cor 1:12 we read that some in the church were claiming to be better than others because they were baptized by Apollos while others claimed Peter (Cephas), and Paul's response is that this type of division is wrong because Christ is not divided. Demanding spiritual experiences of a body of believers where all cannot have them divides the body of Christ—something the Bible explicitly rejects.

Lastly, an additional consequence of this kind of teaching is that believers are often deterred from reading and studying their Bibles. Being able to make regular visits to heaven, see angels, or have prophetic revelations eliminates the need to pick up that dusty book on the shelf. While some will say that we should not put God in a box, I say that it is God who has put us in a box—a box that defines how we are to know, serve, and worship him. This box is the Bible.

THE CORE OF THE ISSUE

The allure of the supernatural is something that I deeply understand. I empathize with those who feel this yearning for God. In my youth I was obsessed with the supernatural. I was saved at sixteen years old but for many reasons was dissatisfied with my Christian walk, both experientially and theologically. However, there was a core reason why I wanted supernatural experiences. It took many years for me to realize this, but my motivation for wanting to experience the supernatural was not because I had more faith but because of my *lack of faith*.

Early in my Christian walk, I loved the "twitterpated" stage. It was probably the best time of my entire life, but when I ceased to feel that way, the disappointment was palpable. Life became boring, and I wanted more. Beyond this, I had serious questions. I looked around and saw the sin and suffering of the world, what I thought were inconsistencies in the Bible, the problem of evil, and persistent questions about hell. I wondered where God was, and I did not look to the Bible for answers because I thought it was not reliable. So, asking God to show himself to me became my idol. I willingly embraced occultic practices, thinking that the experiences I was having were godly and therefore good, and those experiences became my confirmation. I attributed every supernatural experience to God's favor, and since even the negative experiences gave me that spiritual high I craved, it no longer mattered what the results were. They were my spiritual dopamine fix but always left me wanting more. Reflecting on it now, I know that I opened doors that should have remained closed, all for the rush of finding an enticing spiritual world.

At the time, the Bible was nothing more than an accessory. None of these experiences were tested by Scripture because I always rationalized that my salvation prevented me from being deceived. I thought that experience was God's blessing. Not only did I believe in occultic practices masquerading as things that Jesus taught, but I also elevated these experiences above Scripture. Without a firm foundation in Scripture and the application of proper hermeneutical principles, the Bible can be, and often is, used to say anything. An objective standard must exist in order to test experiences; otherwise, any experiences can claim to be the truth. They did for me, and they are still doing it for Christians around the world.

DEMOTING GOD TO ELEVATE MAN

Marty Sampson. Jon Steingard. Michael and Lisa Gungor. Jerry and Esther Hicks. All have either left Christianity because spiritual experience was all they had—all style and no substance—or embraced supernatural experience as their ultimate truth, abandoning biblical Christianity. The common denominator was personal experience over Scripture. Sampson, Steingard, and the Gungors were well known in the Christian world. Each claimed to have had powerful spiritual experiences throughout their Christian walk, and that was the apologetic for their beliefs. The Hicks were the other way around. They were Christians that wanted more beyond just their "boring" Christian experience. Esther Hicks became involved with spirit channeling and decided that the Bible must be wrong regarding these practices. She now channels a group of entities who call themselves "Abraham." It is not that everyone who struggles with this temptation will end up the same, but if we do not have a firm grounding in what is true about God rather than how we feel about God, then we will ultimately, though slowly, begin to bring him down to our level.

It is this demoting of God that makes it a sin. The idolizing of fleeting, emotional experiences leads to foolish actions in an attempt to reignite what we think is God's love for us. When these feelings ultimately fail, we feel lost, alone, and abandoned, thinking God did not follow through with a promise that, in reality, he likely never made. This is the point where many people deconstruct and abandon their faith, which, tragically, was nothing more than an imposter Christianity, not the one, true faith.

Scripture teaches that God is pleased when we believe even when we don't see. In John 20:29, Jesus tells Thomas that Thomas believes because he sees, but that those who don't see yet still believe are *blessed*. Hebrews 11:1 says that without faith, it is impossible to please God, and God rewards those who earnestly seek him. This is not blind, unfounded faith but rather a faith balanced with evidence, reason, and belief. In 2 Cor 12:2–4 the apostle Paul even speaks of having visited heaven, but unlike the leaders of these movements, encouraging others to do the same, he writes that no one should know what he saw. Scripture routinely points Christians away from a reliance on experience for our foundation and towards a trust in the words of the Bible.

As followers of Jesus, we are commissioned to spread the gospel, and if that is the only "power" we have, it is the most supernatural experience I can think of worth sharing with others. When Jesus sent out seventy-two disciples in Luke 10:1–20 to spread the good news, we read that they came back rejoicing. I was always stunned at Jesus's response. It says that they returned, rejoicing that even the demons listened to them, but Jesus reproved them. He told them that they were reveling in their power over demons instead of in the fact that their names were "written in heaven." Their focus was on their desire for supernatural power rather than on the life-saving message of the gospel. David Guzik puts it this way:

> Some people get emotionally intoxicated after a successful service or the display of spiritual power. After God uses them in some way, they are arrogantly impressed with all *they did* for God. God wants us to always see that what He did for us always is far greater than what we could ever do for Him. It's good for us to be moderate in the joy we have over our *talents*, our *gifts*, and our *success*.[17]

We tend to bring God down to a level that we can better understand. We make a caricature out of God that, without realizing it, creates a god that is all about *us*. We all want to feel close to God and experience his comfort. But what if we do not get that? Would we still believe? In his book *The Story of Reality*, author Greg Koukl succinctly makes a point about this: "The saying goes, 'God has a wonderful plan for your life.' From what I understand now that perspective is in the wrong order. The Story is not so much about

17. Guzik, "Study Guide," B.1.e.ii.

God's plan for your life as it is about your life for God's plan. Let that sink in. God's purposes are central, not yours."[18]

Anyone can be "twitterpated." Anyone can feel the intensity and excitement of seeing their new love. Anyone can raise their hands in tears and passion, feeling what they believe to be the presence of God. But real love is what happens when that feeling goes away. God works supernaturally and performs signs, wonders, and miracles. But he does it in his sovereignty and timing. For those who are struggling with this, know that he does not love you less if you do not feel him all the time. This is why Jesus says he is the Bread of Life and the Living Water. His sustenance and love are not based on your performance or on how many experiences you have had that week. If God gave us nothing but salvation and a promise that he would never leave us or forsake us, would that be enough? If you had only Jesus without one single supernatural experience—no healing or miracles—maybe not even the ability to feel many emotions, would it still be enough reason to believe what you do? The question we all face is simple: Is Jesus *alone* enough? I wholeheartedly say, yes, he is enough. And he is worth it.

Bibliography

Doctrine and Covenants Student Manual. Salt Lake City: The Church of Jesus Christ of Latter-day Saints, 2018.

Franklin, Judy, and Ellyn Davis. *The Physics of Heaven*. Shippensburg, PA: Destiny Image, 2016.

Guzik, David. "Study Guide for Luke 10." Blue Letter Bible, n.d. https://www.blueletterbible.org/comm/guzik_david/study-guide/luke/luke-10.cfm.

Heiser, Michael. *Supernatural: What the Bible Teaches about the Unseen World and Why It Matters*. Bellingham, WA: Lexham, 2015.

Irenaeus. *Against Heresies*. Christian Classics Ethereal Library, 1885. From *Ante-Nicene Fathers*, translated by Phillip Schaff. https://ccel.org/ccel/irenaeus/against_heresies_i/anf01.ix.ii.html.

Johnson, Bill. *The Supernatural Power of a Transformed Mind: Access to a Life of Miracles*. Shippensburg, PA: Destiny Image, 2016.

Koukl, Gregory. *The Story of Reality: How the World Began, How It Ends, and Everything Important That Happens in Between*. Grand Rapids: Zondervan, 2017.

Mills, Joshua. "Encountering the Angels in Heaven—Part 1 (Activation)." YouTube, Sept. 3, 2019. https://youtu.be/S_SHChFDyfo.

Moreland, J. P. *A Simple Guide to Experience Miracles: Instruction and Inspiration for Living Supernaturally in Christ*. Grand Rapids: Zondervan, 2021.

Pivec, Holly, and R. Douglas Geivett. *Counterfeit Kingdom: The Dangers of the New Revelation, New Prophets, and New Age Practices in the Church*. Nashville: B&H, 2022.

18. Koukl, *Story of Reality*, 44.

Wallace, J. Warner. *Forensic Faith: A Homicide Detective Makes the Case for a More Reasonable, Evidential Christian Faith*. Colorado Springs: Cook, 2017.

Raising Kids with Confident Faith in a Secular Culture

Natasha Crain[1]

In 2011, I was a young mom with three kids under three years old. It is a stage of life in which many moms feel the isolation and loneliness of what can be a monotonous daily routine of diapers and sippy cups and little opportunity to connect with other adults. I was no different—I felt that deeply. Blogging became a go-to outlet for numerous moms in such a position at that time. With very little effort, a person could buy a website domain, download blogging tools, and start writing about the ins and outs of life in a way that generated instant community with readers. It sounded fun and rewarding, so I joined the "mommy blogger" world by creating my website that November.[2]

When I began blogging, I simply wrote about the very small things my husband and I were doing to raise our young children to know and love the Lord. For example, I talked about devotionals. I shared about cute hand motions to songs. I discussed serving others. I lamented the challenges of

1. I've had the opportunity to get to know Frank over the last several years, through initially being a student at CrossExamined Instructor Academy, then becoming an instructor, and eventually speaking with him at conferences. I have always been so appreciative of the way he generously shares his own platform to promote the work of up-and-coming apologists—including me. Over the last few years, he has been a wonderful encourager and supporter of my work, and he particularly has been an important example to me of an apologist who isn't afraid to step into the so-called "political" realm (which, of course, is just an application of worldview and apologetics). Frank genuinely cares about reaching skeptics, equipping believers, and developing new apologists to reach the world for Christ. It's an honor to be a small part of this volume dedicated to his work.

2. Today, my writing and podcasts can be found at www.natashacrain.com.

disciplining. To my surprise, my blog grew in readership, and people started regularly sharing my posts on social media. A much bigger surprise came when a sizeable number of skeptics started arriving at my site. They did not care about my writings on cute hand motions for songs, but they did care to let me know that I was doing irreversible damage to my kids by "indoctrinating" them with so-called religion. Over time, I was also informed by my newly found skeptical friends that there was no evidence for God's existence, the Bible is filled with errors and contradictions, evolution has put God out of a job, the Gospels are forgeries, Jesus probably did not exist, and the resurrection is an idea copied from pagan myths—among many other claims.

Needless to say, handling objections to the truth of Christianity was not exactly what I had in mind when I started a blog with a name as unprovoking as *Christian Mom Thoughts*. I had been raised in a Christian home, spent hundreds of hours in church growing up, and had never walked away from my faith; nevertheless I was totally unprepared to answer the challenges posed by online commenters. I knew I did not believe what they were saying, but to save my life, I could not have provided a well-informed response regarding evidence to the contrary. Before long I realized that my kids were growing up in a very different world than the one in which I grew up. They needed a level of spiritual training that I had never received—and I set out to learn how to give them just that.

Over the next three years, I poured myself into reading more than two hundred books on Christian apologetics and worldview. The more I read, the more passionate I became about the subject. I found it hard to believe that a lifelong Christian like me could have spent so much time in church and yet have been so utterly unequipped to respond to common challenges to the Christian faith. I wanted to change that, so I decided to convert my blog into a place where I would teach other Christian parents what their kids needed to know about apologetics in our increasingly secular culture. That resonated with a lot of readers, and my blog exploded in growth from that point on.

Fast-forward to today: I have written four books (three of which are apologetics books for parents), host two podcasts, and regularly speak at churches and conferences. God had some interesting plans for that little *Christian Mom Thoughts* blog.

A MOUNT EVEREST OF FAITH CHALLENGES

Because of the challenges skeptics posed on my blog, I saw the need for understanding apologetics firsthand, and that was very motivating to me. I assumed I could motivate others by simply sharing my story. However, in my experience speaking with parents over the last several years, unless the parents have *personally* encountered the need to answer difficult questions, they typically feel that teaching children apologetics is, at best, optional or, at worst, a distraction from what they believe to be more "spiritual" discipleship. There is a pervasive attitude that we all just need to do our best and leave the rest in God's hands—whatever a person's "best" might be.

With this in mind, I began opening my parenting talks by asking audiences to imagine the following:

> One day, you are walking out to your mailbox and run into your neighbor, Bob. The inevitable and miserable small talk ensues. You casually ask how things are going. To your great surprise, Bob tells you he has got something big in mind for the next few months: He is going to climb Mount Everest. You have never seen Bob do anything more physical than walk to his mailbox, so you are intrigued. You say, "Wow! That is amazing. So, what are you doing to get ready for that?"
>
> Bob replies, "Well, I know I am not one for exercise, but I have given this a lot of consideration, and I have a great plan. First, I know I am going to need some significant leg flexibility to get up the mountain, so you will probably see me in the front yard a lot doing leg stretches. Second, it sure seems like a mountain climber needs strong arms, so I bought some two-pound weights yesterday to build arm strength. And yes, I know what you are thinking . . . this will take some mental strength as well. So, I have signed up for a yoga class to learn meditation. As you can see, I am really doing my best to get up that mountain!"

At this point, I ask the audience, "If your neighbor said these things to you, what would you think?" The response is universal: "He is crazy!" or "He is going to *die* on that mountain!" Indeed, Bob would die climbing Mount Everest if he merely relied on his own ideas of what made sense for training. The reality is that there are specific challenges involved in climbing a mountain of that size, and specific challenges require specific preparation. Even if Bob was doing what he personally thought was best for training, if that was not what was necessary for training, he would be in for a dangerous, even life-threatening, surprise.

In the same way, many Christian parents are sending their children to "climb" a mountain of faith challenges today with little more preparation than a few jumping jacks of devotionals, occasional prayer, and—often irregular—church attendance. Yet, if a parent discovered their child had a deadly peanut allergy, they would conduct intensive research to determine precisely what was needed to protect their child from having a fatal reaction. They would not simply "wing it," hoping that they did their "best" to avoid peanut allergens. How do we then, as the body of Christ, convince parents to take their kids' discipleship as seriously as they would a deadly allergy? More specifically, how do we influence parents to recognize the integral importance of teaching apologetics and worldview as part of that endeavor?

While much could be said, I will focus the rest of this chapter on two key aspects of the answer to those questions. First, parents must strive to comprehend more fully how hostile today's secular culture has become toward Christians and Christianity. Understanding this drives a sense of urgency. Second, parents must be equipped with practical know-how to equip their children accordingly. Understanding this drives execution. In other words, parents need to (1) know the mountainous landscape and (2) know how to build a corresponding training plan to navigate it.

UNDERSTANDING THE (HOSTILE) LANDSCAPE

An important starting point for developing a grasp of the unknown or underappreciated challenges of today's culture is learning about the statistical landscape in America. According to the Pew Research Center, 65 percent of Americans identify as Christian.[3] At face value, it might seem that the cultural landscape is not, therefore, very hostile—it sounds as though the majority of those around us are Christians too. However, it is critical to understand that this kind of research only quantifies how many people self-identify as a given religious label. That kind of research provides no further information on what people *mean* by that identification. For example, by "Christian," a survey respondent could mean any of the following:

- They were raised in a Christian home, although they no longer have an active faith in Jesus.
- They generally agree with Christian values but reject core doctrinal tenets of Christianity like the resurrection.
- They reject the authority of the Bible but consider themself a "Jesus follower."

3. Smith et al., "In U.S., Decline," para. 1.

- They consider themself a Christian but also hold various beliefs that are in significant conflict with what the Bible teaches (such as reincarnation).
- They hold to the tenets of the historic Christian faith and are an active follower of Jesus.

A person would see the world very differently depending on which of the above meanings they assigned to their self-identification of "Christian." Thus, self-identification alone tells us very little about how people function culturally and in their personal lives precisely because it tells us nothing about what they actually believe.

Fortunately, researchers at Arizona Christian University's Cultural Research Center have provided the missing data link to help us understand what people *do* believe today. Their annual American Worldview Inventory uses over fifty questions derived from eight categories to classify respondents' worldviews. In other words, rather than ask people how they label themselves, researchers directly ask questions about people's beliefs and behaviors, and then the *researchers* identify which respondents have a biblical worldview.[4] In 2023, that number was just 4 percent, down from 6 percent in 2020.[5] Read that again:

> *Whereas 65 percent of Americans identify as Christian, only about 4 percent have beliefs and behaviors that correspond with what the Bible teaches.*

Christians with a biblical worldview are in a small, and shrinking, worldview minority. This has numerous implications for kids growing up in today's world, but when I share this data, people often respond by asking if this is anything new. After all, America has been de-Christianizing in some sense for more than one century. Are things really that different from when this generation of parents was growing up—so different that we need to disciple our kids in ways that we weren't discipled? Simply put, yes.

As I detail in my book *Faithfully Different: Regaining Biblical Clarity in a Secular Culture*, the picture has changed in four major ways.[6] First, researchers estimate that the percentage of American adults with a biblical worldview has declined by *half* over the last twenty-five years.[7] Historically, there has always been a gap in religiosity between younger and older

4. I interviewed the director of this research, Dr. George Barna, on my podcast, where he explained the research methodology in detail. Crain, "What Is Biblical Worldview?"

5. T. F. Munsil, "Biblical Worldview," para. 1.

6. Crain, *Faithfully Different*, 27.

7. Barna, "Dangerously Few Americans," 3.

generations, but researchers say that millennials and their predecessors differ more now than they have during the last seven decades.[8] Second, the percentage of Americans who identify themselves as Christian has dropped with particular rapidity in the last decade, and a drop has occurred in almost every Christian denomination.[9] It is clear that the mainstream cultural view of Christianity has become so negative of late that many are choosing to distance themselves from even the label. Third, those who no longer identify as Christian are overwhelmingly now identifying as atheist, agnostic, or "nothing in particular." These are worldviews that inherently share very little in common with biblical Christianity. If former Christians were converting to other theistic religions that share some fundamental worldview characteristics, those deconversions would likely have a less striking impact on culture than what we are seeing with the growth of atheism, agnosticism, and "nothing in particular." Finally, many of those abandoning Christian doctrine are now also abandoning Christian values—a simultaneous rejection that has not always been the case. Though Americans have long been in the historical process of discarding doctrinal specifics, the societal result has not always been as obvious as it is today, because people generally continued to hold values *consistent* with Christianity. Now secular culture is discarding the long hangover of Christian *values* as well.

Francis Schaeffer eloquently described this societal transition in his book *The Great Evangelical Disaster*:

> Christianity is no longer providing the consensus for our society. And Christianity is no longer providing the consensus upon which our law is based. That is not to say that the United States ever was a "Christian nation" in the sense that all or most of our citizens were Christians, nor in the sense that the nation, its laws, and social life were ever a full and complete expression of Christian truth. There is no golden age in the past which we can idealize—whether it is early America, the Reformation, or the early church. But until recent decades something did exist which can rightly be called a Christian consensus or ethos which gave a distinctive shape to Western society and to the United States in a definite way. Now that consensus is all but gone, and the freedoms that it brought are being destroyed before our eyes. We are at a time when humanism is coming to its natural conclusion in morals, in values, and in law. All that

8. R. Munsil, "CRC Study Finds Millennials," para. 5.

9. Cooperman et al., "America's Changing Religious Landscape," para. 1.

> society has today are relativistic values based upon statistical averages, or the arbitrary decisions of those who hold legal and political power.[10]

You might be surprised to learn that Schaeffer penned these words in 1984. As you may recall, the percentage of those with a biblical worldview in America has decreased by half since that time! It was bad then, but it is worse now.

It should be clear from this brief overview of the statistical landscape that our children are facing a cultural mountain overwhelmingly populated by people who either (1) identify as Christian yet have only a partially biblical worldview (to varying degrees by person), or (2) identify as atheist, agnostic, or "nothing in particular" and have a worldview consciously and explicitly at odds with a biblical one. That alone should significantly open our eyes to the implied difficulty of the surrounding landscape. But lest anyone wonder if a culture predominantly filled with people not holding a biblical worldview is really *that* challenging, a final critical point is in order.

When people reject a biblical worldview to any degree, they are effectively rejecting the authority of God. For if the Bible is God's word and reveals the nature of reality, holding any beliefs to the contrary of what it teaches is replacing the external authority of God with the internal authority of the self. Every human becomes their own arbiter of truth. Whether someone is an atheist, an agnostic, "spiritual not religious," a New Age adherent, a Christian who holds beliefs in conflict with biblical teachings, or one of any number of other spiritual identities, if they do not look to God as their authority on reality, they are looking to themselves. In other words, the tie that functionally binds the worldviews of millions of people with otherwise disparate beliefs is the authority of the self rather than the authority of God and his revealed word.

Why is this so significant for understanding just how hostile secular culture is? Because there can be no culture more fundamentally at odds with biblical Christianity than one bent on rejecting the very authority of God. Paul says in Eph 2:1–3 that all of us want to go our own way, and because of that, we are by nature deserving of wrath:

> And you were dead in the trespasses and sins, in which you once walked, following the course of this world, following the prince of the power of the air, the spirit that is now at work in the sons of disobedience—among whom we all once lived in the passions of our flesh, carrying out the desires of the body and the mind, and were by nature children of wrath, like the rest of mankind.

10. Schaeffer, *Great Evangelical Disaster*, 47.

A culture that has overwhelmingly turned to the authority of the self is not just minimally opposed to biblical Christianity. It is inherently opposed to God at the most fundamental level. Furthermore, the Bible makes clear in passages like this that *all* people find the "authority of the self" compelling. We *all* want to gratify the cravings of our flesh and follow its desires and thoughts.[11] Do not miss the significance of this implication: not only are we surrounded by a worldview profoundly at odds with what the Bible teaches, but we, by human nature, are also *drawn* to that worldview. Even Christians can struggle with self-authority. This is a rugged terrain in which to raise children, and we need a training plan to match the significance and nature of that challenge.

CREATING A TRAINING PLAN

Before I offer this plan, a caveat is in order. Nothing that follows should be taken as a spiritual guarantee. Discipleship is not a direct input/output system in which inputting *x*, *y*, and *z*, will be certain to result in *a*, *b*, and *c* in the life of your child. Such thinking is a "purchase mentality." With a purchase mentality, parents believe that they are effectively purchasing their kids' faith with the currency of their own efforts. The Bible neither claims nor suggests such a relationship between input and output. Proverbs 22:6 does say that if you "train up a child in the way he should go; even when he is old he will not depart from it," but proverbs are not promises—they are merely general principles.

Even though we are not called to be purchasers *of* faith, we are called to be investors *in* faith. Investors make contributions knowing that there is a risk of that investment not resulting in the desired outcome. The Bible has surprisingly little direct instruction on parenting, but Moses's words to the Israelites in Deut 6:6–9 provide a good picture of what that investment would look like:

> And these words that I command you today shall be on your heart. You shall teach them diligently to your children, and shall talk of them when you sit in your house, and when you walk by the way, and when you lie down, and when you rise. You shall bind them as a sign on your hand, and they shall be as frontlets between your eyes. You shall write them on the doorposts of your house and on your gates.

11. Crain, *Faithfully Different*, 133–92.

Investment is not for the fainthearted. It requires dedication to teaching our children God's truth at all times and in all places. The question I hope the following plan will answer is "What is the *content* of the teaching that children need in order to have a confident faith in the midst of today's hostile, secular culture?" I believe that content is comprised of four major knowledge areas: (1) what the Bible teaches; (2) why believe it; (3) what others believe; and (4) how to answer challenges.

What the Bible Teaches

The first part of this training plan sounds incredibly obvious. In fact, virtually every Christian parent immediately believes that they are doing this well. Additionally, parents think that since their children learn about the Bible at church, this step is well covered. However, when I say that parents need to ensure their kids understand what the Bible teaches, I am not speaking primarily of what generally constitutes revisiting Sunday School curricula. If a child grows up going to church even somewhat regularly, they will almost certainly know enough about major biblical stories to win a basic Bible trivia game—Noah built the ark; Joseph had a multicolored coat; Moses parted the Red Sea; Jonah was swallowed by a large fish; Daniel was thrown in a lion's den; and Jesus was crucified, buried, and raised from the dead. And while I am not flippantly suggesting that knowledge of these accounts is unimportant—the resurrection of Jesus is the truth test for all of Christianity—knowing about individual biblical stories is not the same as understanding the theologically rich narrative of salvation history that stretches across the Scriptures. And this matters because it is often a misunderstanding or mischaracterization of this broader Christian theology that skeptics abuse in order to mock, challenge, and deconstruct someone from the Christian faith.

A viral social media image I saw recently serves as an effective illustration of the point. The picture featured a sweet, smiling, preschool-aged girl holding a sign. On the left, it said, "According to religion I am broken, flawed, sinful, dumb, weak, and nothing." On the right, it said, "According to science I am full of wonder, smart, a great learner, beautiful, [and have] potential for greatness! Which do you think is damaging?" The image had been liked and shared more than 140,000 times online, and presumably, all those likes and shares reflected a popular belief that the sign was both accurate and compelling. However, consider the claim that religion says this girl is "broken, flawed, sinful, dumb, weak, and nothing" (in the context of the poster's comments, it was clear she specifically had the Bible in mind and not merely religion in general). Is that accurate? Well, the Bible *does* teach that humans are broken, flawed, sinful, and (spiritually) weak, but the creator of this image inferred from that fact that we are therefore "dumb nothings"! This is, of course, far from the biblical truth. The Bible says that we are made in the image of God himself (Gen 1:27), which instills in us an inherent value. Ironically, if humankind is the product of blind evolutionary processes, only then are we "nothings" with no inherent worth. Furthermore, if it is true that we are broken, flawed, and sinful, it is not damaging to know that—it is crucial information. It is only in light of this truth that we can understand our need for a Savior and value what God did through Jesus on the cross. Something does not become damaging simply because it is difficult to hear.

It is sufficient to say, for our current purpose, that merely teaching individual biblical accounts over time does not necessarily mean a child is internalizing the deeper theme of Scripture. We must be intentional in putting those pieces together with them, so that they do not fall prey to misleading rhetoric—as over 140,000 people did with this image. Some particularly helpful keys in developing a beyond-the-basics understanding of the Bible are as follows:

Emphasize family Bible study over devotionals.

Devotionals can be helpful, particularly with the youngest kids, but they should not be used as a substitute for Bible reading. Reading the Bible itself enables children to mature into independent Bible readers who understand how to approach and study the text because they have already witnessed it. You do not need a curriculum. You do not need games. You do not need to be a Bible scholar. You only need to set aside time each week, pick a book of the Bible, and work your way through it as a family, reading and discussing.

Equip your child to ask good questions during Bible study.

Today's culture is a self-centered culture, and unfortunately, it often affects how we read the Bible. We often begin by asking what a Bible passage mean for us, but better questions to teach children to ask are what the passage says about who God is, who they are, how they should relate to God, and what implications it may have on their lives. Learning to think in this way challenges kids to see a bigger theological picture beyond the more immediately apparent details of a given passage.

Teach your child how to personally search the Bible to find answers to questions.

The phrases "The Bible says" and "Jesus says" get thrown around with reckless abandon today. Unfortunately, given that so few people actually have a biblical worldview, those phrases often end with falsehoods. Anyone can claim to pass on a biblical teaching, but there are times when people intentionally mischaracterize what the Bible says and other times where there can be a genuine misunderstanding. Work to continually ensure your child understands the importance of studying the Bible personally and not just accepting what another person tells them—including you! When they ask a biblical question, you can emphasize this skill by working with them to find the answer in God's word rather than merely giving the answer to them.

Provide your child with examples that demonstrate common misunderstandings of what the Bible teaches.

Whenever you spot a social media post, meme, article, or anything else that mischaracterizes the Bible, use it as a teaching tool. Proactively bring it to your child for discussion. Show them what it *claims* the Bible says and then show them what the Bible *actually* says. Again, involve them in the process of finding the answer so that they learn to be independent Bible investigators. Having exposure to common counterfeit versions of Scripture greatly helps kids develop an awareness of how culture distorts God's truth.

Why Believe It

When I was relatively new to apologetics, I became curious as to whether apologists for non-Christian religions existed. I searched online for Muslim apologists, and I will never forget the first video I found. It featured a Muslim apologist answering one challenge after another from a nonbeliever. He deftly handled them all, and even sounded quite convincing. It took me by surprise, because in my newly found passion for apologetics, I wrongly assumed that only Christians could defend their faith well since only Christianity was true. That, however, is not the case. Anyone can learn to handle objections to what they believe to some degree. But it is far more difficult to make a positive case for the truth of a worldview if the worldview is false. Teaching your child how to make a case for the truth of Christianity is the "why believe it" part of the training plan.

Skeptics understand that many, if not most, Christians are unprepared to provide evidence for what they believe, and they often wield the tool of shame accordingly. For example, famous atheist and best-selling author Richard Dawkins says, "The Virgin Birth, the Resurrection, the raising of Lazarus, even the Old Testament miracles, all are freely used for religious propaganda, and they are very effective with an audience of unsophisticates and children."[12] Obviously, the goal of such statements is to make Christians feel ludicrous by pointing out the extraordinary nature of something like miracles. In this case, the unequipped child will feel foolish if they do not know why there is good reason to believe miracles are possible, that miracles happen, and that Christianity more broadly is true.

It is easy to feel that you are wrong in your beliefs if the majority of people around you believe something different. When you are in a small worldview minority (as Christian kids today are), it naturally raises the question, "Why should I believe I am right and most of those around me are wrong?" In fact, this is a great question to proactively pose to your children. Challenge them to consider that they should want to learn the evidence for Christianity, given that so many people believe different things. Point out that following Jesus requires us to deny ourselves and give our entire lives to him. Not only that, but people will hate us for what we believe, as we are increasingly seeing in culture. If living as a disciple of Jesus is this all-encompassing, we should want to be very convicted of the truth of Christianity.

So how do we teach kids to become "case makers"? It begins with recognizing that it requires more than a one-time teaching event. We must begin with small pieces of evidence when kids are young and progressively add to their understanding over time. This allows the evidence to become part of the worldview-shaping process rather than a disconnected cherry that eventually gets placed on top. To guide this process, it can be helpful to use the following four-question framework.[13] Broadly speaking, the answers to these questions build a case for the truth of Christianity, and even the youngest of children can begin to learn pieces of evidence for each one. Parents can cycle through the framework to teach age-appropriate answers

12. Dawkins, *Devil's Chaplain*, 150.

13. It is outside the scope of this chapter to provide answers to these questions, but my three apologetics books for parents provide answers as well as conversation guides. They are: *Keeping Your Kids on God's Side: 40 Conversations to Help Them Build a Lasting Faith*; *Talking with Your Kids about God: 30 Conversations Every Christian Parent Must Have*; and *Talking with Your Kids about Jesus: 30 Conversations Every Christian Parent Must Have*. More can be read about these titles and their tables of contents at www.natashacrain.com.

on a regular basis, each time adding more knowledge and examples relative to the time before.

What evidence is there for God's existence?

Answering this question involves considering the objective evidence for God's existence outside the Bible. Popular arguments toward this end include the cosmological argument, the design argument, and the moral argument. Despite their academic-sounding labels, each of them is accessible at an introductory level to even preschool-aged children using everyday examples (I demonstrate how to do this in chapters 1–6 of *Talking with Your Kids about God*).

Can multiple religions be true?

This is a rather simple, but necessary, logical point that connects the first and third questions. If there is sufficient reason to believe that God exists—as in question 1—then is it possible that he has revealed himself in a way that makes multiple religions true? The quick answer is no. Religions make logically contradictory claims about the nature of reality and therefore *cannot* simultaneously be true. It is possible that God exists and *no* religion is true—especially in the case that he never revealed himself—and it is possible that God exists and *one* religion is true—in the case that he did reveal himself. But it is not logically possible that multiple religions are true.

What evidence is there for the resurrection of Jesus?

After answering the first two questions, we are ready to ask if Christianity could be the one true religion. First Corinthians 15:14 tells us how to know if Christianity is indeed that: "And if Christ has not been raised, then our preaching is in vain and your faith is in vain." In other words, the resurrection specifically is the truth test for Christianity. We should emphasize this point with our kids, particularly because people today so often leave the faith for very different reasons than not believing the resurrection happened. And we should teach them about the historical evidence for the resurrection accordingly.

What evidence is there for the reliability of the Bible?

It is not enough to teach kids what is *in* the Bible; they must learn *about* the Bible as well. This includes answering questions about how the books of the Bible were selected, why some books were left out of the Bible, how we can trust the Bible's authors, and how we know the Bible we have today says what the authors originally wrote.[14]

What Others Believe

When my twins were two, I began to teach them how to read letters of the alphabet. Truth be told, I was a little bored with "nonproductive" play time and wanted to do something even marginally goal oriented with them. I had a magnetic board and taught them by putting up a letter and having them memorize what it was. By the time they were two and a half, they both knew all their letters well. One day, I bought an alphabet workbook to continue their learning. It had pages with letters mixed together and the instructions asked the child to circle all the instances of a specific one. I handed my son the first page, which had *c*'s and *o*'s. Despite having known his individual letters for almost a year, he was thoroughly confused by what was in front of him. He knew his *c*'s and *o*'s perfectly well in isolation, but when mixed together for the first time, they were no longer distinguishable in his mind. It was then that I realized context makes a significant difference in a person's understanding of a subject.

In the same way, we give children a much richer knowledge of the Christian worldview when we help them understand it in the context of non-Christian worldviews rather than teaching it in isolation. However, in the years that I have been speaking, there is nothing on which I have received more pushback from parents than the advice to spend a significant amount of time teaching kids what others believe. Parents often do not want to take time away from teaching their kids the truth, and the idea of taking that time to teach them lies is offensive. Appeals are often made to the much-repeated idea that federal agents do not learn to spot counterfeit money by studying the counterfeits; they study genuine bills until they have mastered the real thing. The idea being proposed is that once you know truth, you will automatically be adept at spotting falsehood—if you've got your *c*'s down, you'll automatically spot imposter *o*'s.

14. I cover each of these questions in chapters of *Keeping Your Kids on God's Side*. Additionally, I highly recommend J. Warner and Susie Wallace's book *Cold Case Christianity* for help discussing this subject with kids ages eight to twelve.

While this sounds good, it is a poor analogy. There is a major difference between studying a small, concrete bill and studying something as large and complex as a worldview. There are very few kids, if any, who know the Bible so deeply that they immediately know every falsehood when they see it. This is not to say that kids will not recognize *any* falsehoods based on the truth you have taught them—after all, some falsehoods are obvious. For example, if an atheist challenges a child by saying, "There is no evidence for God's existence!," it is abundantly clear that the claim conflicts with what the Bible teaches. But many of the lies prevalent in today's culture are far more covert. They are cloaked in sound bites like: "follow your heart"; "you be you"; "be your authentic self"; "happiness is the ultimate goal"; "judging people is bad"; and "love is all that matters." Many adult Christians are fooled by falsehoods like these precisely because they do not recognize how they conflict with biblical teaching. It is, therefore, highly idealistic to think that a child would not be fooled in the same way as long as you just taught them the truth. Teaching kids what others believe (for example, Buddhists, Muslims, Mormons, atheists, etc.) should include looking at both the beliefs themselves as well as the implications for how a person views all of reality.[15]

How to Answer Challenges

Before deconstruction became a major trend, a popular Christian rapper made news several years ago when he released a statement renouncing his faith. When I read that statement at the time, I remember being struck by the utter predictability of every claim he made against Christianity. His deconversion statement read like a play-by-play from the *2015 Internet Guide to Why Christianity Isn't True*. I must admit that, after I read it, my jaded side initially reacted with a mental shoulder shrug: "Nothing new here. Same tired set of claims." But then I realized that this was the same mental shoulder shrug I had begun making about 95 percent of the blog comments I was currently receiving from skeptics. It was not because I thought I was somehow better than those commenters or because those commenters were not raising important questions that should be answered. It was simply because I had spent the last several years making myself aware of the challenges to Christianity, reading what both Christians and skeptics said about those challenges, and concluding repeatedly that the case for the truth of Christianity remained powerfully strong. That is exactly the position we should want our kids to be in—where the challenges they hear from the world are nothing new, nothing shocking, nothing they have not heard

15. Crain, "How to Teach."

some version of before, and nothing they have not had the opportunity to investigate with you.

This is not as difficult to accomplish as you might think. The fact that these claims are so predictable means our job is both well defined and achievable. Think of it as helping your child study for an exam. You might not be able to anticipate every conceivable question they will get, but you can make sure they know what major subject areas they will encounter and how to think through the most important questions. They are not venturing out into a completely unknown environment. This test can be studied for.

This means proactively putting challenges in front of your child—not simply being prepared to answer questions they may bring to you. We do not wait around to see if our children will ask about US history to teach them US history; we know they need to learn US history, and we act on that knowledge. It is no different with proactively addressing faith challenges we know they will encounter. For example, even if your child never asks if the Bible condones slavery, you should still be the one to initiate a discussion on the subject, knowing that it is a common challenge posed to Christians. When we know what they are going to encounter on the mountain, we must put it in the training plan.

One easy way to teach your children about answering faith challenges is to simply pick one question each week to discuss as a family—at the dinner table, before bed, on the drive to or from school, or any other time that works in your home. You can easily pick questions from any book focused on apologetics. (There are one hundred questions covered in my three apologetics books for parents alone—and many more that are covered in other books!)

C. S. Lewis famously said, "I believe in Christianity as I believe that the sun has risen, not only because I see it but because by it, I see everything else."[16] In many ways, the hostile cultural mountain can block our kids' view of reality. It vies for their attention. But when we match our discipleship to the challenges of that mountain, we equip our children to keep their eyes on the Lord and develop a deep biblical worldview through which they "see everything else."

Bibliography

Barna, George. "Dangerously Few Americans Possess a Biblical Worldview, Inaugural CRC Study Finds." Arizona Christian University, Mar. 24, 2020. https://www.

16. Lewis, *Weight of Glory*, 141.

arizonachristian.edu/wp-content/uploads/2020/03/CRC_AWVI2020_Report.pdf.

Cooperman, Alan, et al. "America's Changing Religious Landscape." Pew Research Center, May 12, 2015. https://www.pewresearch.org/religion/2015/05/12/americas-changing-religious-landscape/.

Crain, Natasha. *Faithfully Different: Regaining Biblical Clarity in a Secular Culture.* Eugene, OR: Harvest, 2022.

———. "How to Teach Your Kids about Non-Christian Worldviews." Natasha Crain, Jan. 28, 2021. Podcast 2. https://natashacrain.com/how-to-teach-your-kids-about-non-christian-worldviews-podcast-2/.

———. "What Is a Biblical Worldview? With George Barna." Natasha Crain, Sept. 12, 2022. https://natashacrain.com/what-is-a-biblical-worldview-with-george-barna/.

Dawkins, Richard. *A Devil's Chaplain: Reflections on Hope, Lies, Science, and Love.* Boston: Mariner, 2004.

Lewis, C. S. *The Weight of Glory.* New York: HarperOne, 2001.

Schaeffer, Francis A. *The Great Evangelical Disaster.* Wheaton, IL: Crossway, 1984.

Smith, Gregory A., et al. "In U.S., Decline of Christianity Continues at a Rapid Pace." Pew Research Center, Oct. 17, 2019. https://www.pewresearch.org/religion/2019/10/17/in-u-s-decline-of-christianity-continues-at-rapid-pace/.

Munsil, Tracy. "CRC Study Finds Millennials Have Radically Different Beliefs about Respect, Faith, America." Arizona Christian University, Sept. 22, 2020. https://www.arizonachristian.edu/2020/09/22/crc-study-finds-millennials-have-radically-different-beliefs-about-respect-faith-america/.

Munsil, Tracy F. "Biblical Worldview among U.S. Adults Drops 33% Since Start of COVID-19 Pandemic." Arizona Christian University, Feb. 28, 2023. https://www.arizonachristian.edu/2023/02/28/biblical-worldview-among-u-s-adults-drops-33-since-start-of-covid-19-pandemic/.

Wallace, J. Warner and Susie. *Cold Case Christianity for Kids: Investigate Jesus with a Real Detective.* Colorado Springs: Cook, 2016.

Subject Index